The Fast Future Blur

The Fast Future Blur

Discover Transformative Interconnections Shaping the Future

The Faculty From the Fast Future Executive

WILEY

Registered Office(s)
John Wiley & Sons, Inc., 111 River Street, Hoboken, NJ 07030, USA
John Wiley & Sons Ltd, The Atrium, Southern Gate, Chichester, West Sussex, PO19 8SQ, UK

Editorial Office
The Atrium, Southern Gate, Chichester, West Sussex, PO19 8SQ, UK

For details of our global editorial offices, customer services, and more information about Wiley products visit us at www.wiley.com.

Library of Congress Cataloging-in-Publication Data is Available:

ISBN 9781394220403 (Cloth)
ISBN 9781394220410 (ePDF)
ISBN 9781394220427(ePub)

Cover Design: Wiley
Cover Image: © The Preparation Company

SKY10072368_041124

Contents

Foreword: Ambiguous, Adroit and Around Corners: The Era of Future Blur Leadership

Nitin Rakesh, CEO Mphasis

In history, we use 'once in a generation' to refer to tectonic shifts in our world, be it geopolitics, technology, business models or societal changes. We have seen the word 'great' attached to these events, the great recession or as in recent times, the great resignation. But what if 'once in a generation' is now experienced every 3 years instead of 50 or 100? Exponentiality, speed and specializations are all coming together to create challenges that have never been experienced before.

Anticipation is no longer just a desired but an essential skill among leaders. Anticipation is a capability that organizations need to master, where strategy is an exercise in fluidity and execution is an exercise in adaptability.

Societies around the world grapple with shifts in technology, climate, labour migration, a push towards localization, the imbalance of talent availability and finally a global currency order that is being challenged by the emerging world. These make it incredibly harder for leaders and companies to lead their businesses while driving an innovation, growth and customer agenda of their future.

We know that there will be multiple transformative 'once-in-a-generation' events over the course of the next decade. The only way to navigate these successfully is to master thinking at the intersections of multiple industries, disciplines, technologies and cultures. It needs leaders to reimagine the nature of disruption itself.

Reimagining Exponentiality

Exponentiality has always been indicative of change or impact that overhauls all known or normal assumptions. The era of blurs, when there are so many influences on a business, is seeing an impact beyond normal understanding of exponential. How can you reimagine exponential?

Take the example of climate change. Over the past few years, we have had multiple exponential events that are on scale that most cities or public administrations were not geared up for. Humans like to anchor to places, to locations associated with their heritage. When this becomes impermanent, the assumptions of lifelong stability change. Due to these changes, we have also seen changes by insurance companies in how they manage their business. We now have locations where insurance is no longer an option for protecting a business or a house.

Reimagining exponentiality is understanding that tectonic changes are real. Covid was an event that most people of the new generations never imagined as possible. But it did happen, and it did change human habits at a 'full human scale' of 8 billion people.

A similar event is in progress with AI. Changes that seem distant are now suddenly real and mainstream. We are already living in a world where millions of people use products or services that are AI driven, even without realizing it. But the aspect that this has a multidimensional impact makes it exponential reimagined. This is not just a graduation from a calculator to spreadsheets. The impact on daily lives is so immense that it cuts across so many aspects of life on our planet. The pervasiveness of this technology, while still in the early adoption curve, is an example of exponential reimagined.

Reimagining Speed

The fastest humans can travel today is possibly on a space rocket. An earlier case was the Concorde aeroplanes, which flew for 27 years at Mach 2.04 before they were retired. Modern fighter jet pilots achieve high speeds. For most normal people, even watching a Formula 1 car race at about 250 km per hour is scary.

For many years, speed has been spoken about, but most businesses never put that as a central principle of business. Organizations are built to last. Frameworks applied are meant to create a predictable outcome through repeatability, efficiencies and retention of knowledge. Organizations' approaches and habits reflect this efficiency or repeatability mindset. The planning to strategy cycle, budgeting processes, talent planning to hiring cycles are all built around predictability. Investors don't like surprises and at the same time, leaders don't like to shift quickly as it results in internal chaos.

Very few companies have understood and used speed as a competitive advantage. However, speed is not an input, or a factor of time as used in project management. These companies and their leaders think at the intersections of multiple disciplines and apply those learnings to their business context. While companies continue to build their domain dominance, many of their innovative approaches often are learnings from other sectors. This enables leaders to be on an 'always learn' mental model that helps them adapt their companies in real time, often building capabilities ahead of time.

Reimagining Interconnectedness

We have educated, trained and rewarded leaders over the past 50 years to lead and run predictably. The assumptions of a generation continue to be made irrelevant and redundant at a speed never experienced before. Technologies that seemed distant become mainstream and change the habits of people. Businesses that viewed capabilities as belonging to another industry get disrupted by the very same capabilities.

In any industry, the ability to see around the corners is dependent upon how leaders connect dots that are seemingly unrelated. The ability to understand the interconnections between multiple disciplines is critical to shape strategy in ambiguous and fluid environments.

The ability to interconnect multiple disciplines is counter intuitive to how leaders and professional have been trained. Our education system categorizes you into specializations. Careers are built in domains where expertise is built over years. As a result, we find it difficult to understand the need to develop the interconnected view both within and outside an industry. Some of the best disruptions have come from ideas that exist outside an industry. Fintech and Technology sectors are two examples of this.

But how does one practise interconnected learning? Professionals and leaders who demonstrate this curiosity and comprehension are best placed to shape strategy in fluidity.

Being a Fast Future Blur Leader

A Fast Future Blur Leader (Figure 0.1) is one with a speed bias, to learn, understand, connect and apply seemingly disparate ideas of the future; today.

This is a perfect summary of all three areas that are being reimagined in a world where lines blur to create both; new opportunities and unknown challenges. The best way to learn for the new world

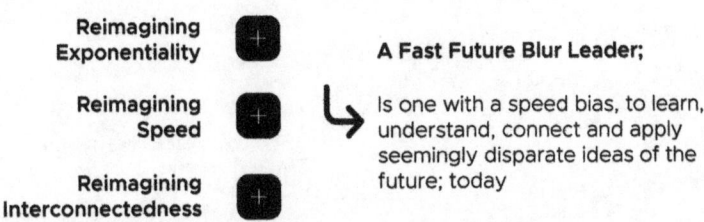

Figure 0.1   A fast future blur leader.

is to reimagine how you learn and apply ideas. Learning broadly and interconnectedly builds a comprehensive knowledge and skills base that gives you the agility. So, when change comes suddenly, you are ready.

Acknowledgements

Our heartfelt gratitude to the multitude of well-wishers of The Fast Future Executive and founding team member, Divya Kapoor.

Chapter 1

The Fast Future Arsenal: Unbundling, Rebundling and Innovating at the Intersections

Sangeet Paul Choudary

My daughter loves her Lego sets. Over the years, she's acquired a range of Lego sets – ranging from cityscapes to complex motor vehicles – and built them block-by-block as per the instructions. But once built, she promptly pulls them apart – block-by-block – and throws them in with the pile of all the Lego blocks across all the Lego sets she's ever acquired. Lego's prescribed recipe holds her interest for exactly one iteration.

Once disassembled, that growing pile of Lego blocks is where the magic lies. A wheel from a dumpster truck ends up as a roller skate for a 'Lego alien' she's been creating. A triangular wing off an airplane set ends up as a skirt pleat on a large Lego doll she's been working on. She returns to that pile every day to create assemblies limited only by her imagination.

Over the past couple of decades and more, every new generation of digital technologies has had one repeated effect on the landscape of enterprise value creation – reduction in transaction costs that emerge in inter-firm coordination.

These falling transaction costs transform the landscape of value creation into a pile of Lego blocks – building blocks of value that can be recombined into new business models. All business model innovation today follows a cycle of unbundling and rebundling, much like throwing Lego blocks into a pile and reassembling them in innovative new ways. Traditional boundaries of business model innovation no longer hold sway. Value is increasingly created at the intersection of previously unconnected domains, where you find fundamentally new ways to recombine – or 'rebundle' – these building blocks to solve problems for customers.

Business Legos – the Economics of Unbundling

Transaction costs [1,2] determine the manner in which firms organize themselves and interact with other players. To minimize transaction costs, most industrial-era firms engaged in vertical integration.[3] Integration offered greater control and minimized transaction costs by absorbing all value-chain activities inside the firm.

But with the rise of digital technologies, three specific changes play out[4]:

First, global connectivity – powered by smartphone penetration and social technologies – have driven the creation of a global network of connected producers and consumers of value, allowing businesses to specialize in certain activities and coordinate with other firms for other activities across the value chain.[5]

Second, the adoption of the cloud enables interoperability across value chain activities.[6,7] Firms increasingly specialize in a few activities and attract partnerships for complementary value creation. 'Do what you do best, partner for the rest'.

Finally, the growth in data generation and aggregation,[8] largely driven by global adoption of social technologies and sensors, coupled with improvements in machine learning and artificial intelligence (AI), enables firms to coordinate across many more partners and interfaces at scale, leveraging data to manage coordination at these interfaces. Firms can also exercise control over resources and actors without requiring explicit ownership or traditional employment relationships.[9,10]

As a result of these three factors, business capabilities are increasingly getting unbundled from the vertically integrated structures that dominated the industrial era. Using application programming interfaces (APIs), firms can effectively open up digital capabilities and services to external stakeholders, and plug-and-play with each other.[11] Today's business operates more like a huge pile of Lego blocks. Business capabilities are modular and can plug-and-play across each other.

Consequently, this vertically integrated value chain starts to unbundle[12] and new specialized firms emerge. With lower transaction costs, these firms increasingly plug-and-play across a growing landscape of unbundled specialized firms.

This also enables firms to more easily co-create value with creators of complements.[13] For example, mobile applications act as complements to a smartphone's operating system, increasing the scope of the phone's functionality. Similarly, cloud-hosted software programs like Slack, the enterprise chat software, and Zoom, the video communication tool, interoperate with a wide variety of applications using APIs, thereby enabling a large scope of functionalities for consumers.

In this new landscape of value creation, unbundled firms increasingly specialize in key activities and invest in ensuring their interfaces (comprising technology, process and people) are designed towards smooth plug-and-play value creation with partners.

The Cycle of Unbundling and Rebundling

Unbundling disrupts the status quo.

Fintechs specializing in one activity unbundle the financial services value chain, healthtech firms specializing in one aspect unbundle healthcare and specialized energy startups unbundle (and, indeed, reimagine) activities of traditional utilities.

However, unbundling leads to higher coordination costs.[14] Moreover, while digitization reduces many forms of transaction costs, certain transaction costs – particularly those related to ensuring safety, managing quality and enforcing property rights – increase.[15]

These costs are resolved through rebundling.[16] Rebundling involves bundling multiple unbundled capabilities into a cohesive customer-centric offering. This is where value is recombined towards solving a customer problem.

Industrial-era firms operated within prescribed industry boundaries determined by the boundaries of the production process. Rebundling operates not around production processes but around customer value propositions. Consider the financial services industry, for instance. The industry boundaries are structured around traditional financial products. But in a connected world, an integrated customer value proposition may have to be bundled using components across multiple industry boundaries – housing, automotive, local commerce and others.

Much like the specific configuration of Lego blocks prescribed in a Lego instruction booklet, industrial-era firms embodied business models that were inelastic and unresponsive to consumer needs.

True innovation – as my daughter discovered – lies in unbundling these blocks, throwing them back into the pile, and 'rebundling' them to create entirely new creations, many of them having been created for the first time in the history of mankind (Figure 1.1).

Rebundling also enables sustainable value capture.

In the news media industry, the traditional newspaper bundle was unbundled by digital distribution on the web. Eventually, Facebook rebundled it as a news feed and arguably Google did the same through its search engine. Both 'rebundlers' then centralized advertising power and moved it away from the old bundles.

Similarly, in the music industry, file-sharing services like Kazaa and Napster unbundled the music album (the original bundle) but Spotify's playlists rebundled them and successfully captured value.

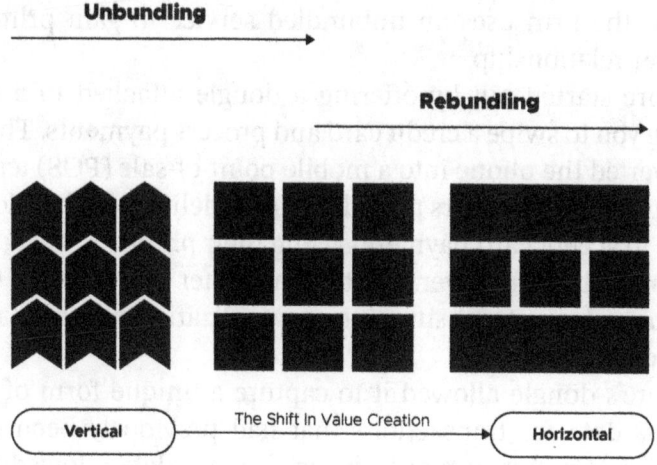

Figure 1.1   Illustrative diagram of the shift from vertical to horizontal value creation through unbundling and rebundling.

In both these examples, unbundling served to unseat incumbents but it was only through rebundling that value successfully accrued to new players.

Rethinking Value with Rebundling

As new digital technologies increasingly unbundle value chains, rebundling holds the key for the Fast Future Executive. Unbundled services won't sustain unless they serve as beachheads to attract customer engagement and then leverage that customer chokepoint to rebundle services around key consumer needs.

Consider Square, which started with a smartphone-based point-of-sale terminal for merchants on the move. Using this beachhead, it has expanded to an end-to-end financial services bundle centred around the merchant, spanning financing, payroll, payments and more.

Typically, rebundling follows three key steps centred on consumer needs.

First, the firm uses an unbundled service to gain primacy of consumer relationship.

Square started out by offering a dongle attached to a phone, allowing you to swipe a credit card and process payments. This dongle converted the phone into a mobile point-of-sale (POS) terminal, allowing service providers providing home delivery and off-location services to accept card payments using their phone.

Second, the firm leverages this customer relationship to capture data and construct superior personalization and user reputation models.

Square's dongle allowed it to capture a unique form of data – payments data for transactions that had previously been carried out in cash. Capturing money-in, money-out data allowed Square to start building credit scores for this group of merchants, thus far underserved by traditional banking.

Finally, using these superior data models and leveraging its primacy of customer relationship, the firm rebundles other services around the consumer.

Today, Square rebundles a host of merchant services around its payments suite. The Square Card – a debit card that allows merchants to access money in their Square account – allows Square to act as the de facto bank account for merchants in the cash economy. Square Capital lends money to merchants using credit scores built on actual sales data from their POS terminal. Square Cash – typically a consumer-focused solution – also serves as a light payroll application, allowing merchants to directly pay their employees through the application. Square also manages the merchant's customer directory and provides integrated analytics across the merchant's activities.

Platforms and Standards – the Purveyors of Rebundling

In a connected landscape of value creation, rebundling is best achieved[17] through two mechanisms: promoting open standards and setting up proprietary platforms.[18]

Firms may create the basis for rebundling by agreeing and aligning on open standards. Standards enable rebundling as multiple firms build towards an agreed standard, ensuring greater interoperability across their products and services. In general, standards are specifications that determine the compatibility of different technological components. Standards increase the ability of firms building these components to coordinate their activities towards solving a customer problem.[19]

Consider, for example, the USB standard popularized by Intel which simplified and standardized connections of computer peripherals to the personal computer, allowing device functionality to be unbundled from the personal computer and rebundled based on the user's needs. For instance, a user could now supplement external memory, performance and interface needs by merely plugging in relevant devices to their PC.

The adoption of a common standard by all market participants increases the availability of solutions that serve as complements to that standard[20] – as with the explosion of peripherals in the PC market example above, with the adoption of the USB standard. This creates a network effect where greater usage of the standard is strengthened by the availability of more complements, driving further adoption of the standard. This eventually leads to 'winner-take-all' outcomes where a single standard may dominate.

Beyond standards, platforms are today a far more dominant agent for rebundling.

A platform[21] is a business based on enabling value-creating interactions between external producers and consumers. A platform provides an open, participative infrastructure for these interactions and sets governance conditions for them. Platforms generate value by reducing transaction costs and coordinating diverse external actors. They also benefit from network effects, particularly indirect network effects, where greater participation by producers of complements increases the platform's value for consumers and vice versa.

Platform firms own key control points[22] or competitive bottlenecks which other partner firms need to access. The ownership of these control points provides strategic leverage to the platform firm. For instance, platforms like Google and Facebook control user relationships and data which provides them leverage over other ecosystem firms looking to target these users.

We are increasingly seeing the rise of platform-mediated rebundling of value chain activities across a whole range of industries,[23] including financial services, logistics, manufacturing, and healthcare.[24,25,26]

Healthcare Legos: Unbundling with APIs, Rebundling with AI

Armed with the tools of unbundling and rebundling, let's look at an industry where two key shifts – increasing deregulation driving the adoption of APIs, and improving technological benefits of AI – are working together to create a new landscape for value creation.

Care delivery is increasingly becoming modular, as it gets unbundled from traditional care facilities.[27] The proliferation of sensor-enabled wearables[28] has driven the rise of self-assessment by consumers and remote monitoring of patients by providers, unbundling care from traditional facilities. Urgent care clinics,[29] retail medicine[30,31] and telehealth,[32] have also created new models of care delivery.

Away from the consumer, producers – healthcare providers, pharmaceutical manufacturers and healthcare device manufacturers – are increasingly adopting cloud-hosted infrastructure[33] to manage their business processes.

The unbundling of healthcare delivery from traditional institutions and the shift of healthcare production to cloud-hosted infrastructure are driving greater modularity across the healthcare value chain, transforming it into a pile of Legos that can be increasingly recombined into new business models.

While unbundling healthcare delivery increases consumer choice, the lack of data interoperability, for example Electronic Health Records (EHRs) interoperability,[34] creates a fragmented patient journey, as patients cannot easily port their data from one provider to another, or integrate data from wearables with their

EHR data. Despite greater consumer choice, the coordination costs to drive end-to-end patient care increase.

However, two key shifts – *increasing data interoperability* and *improvements in AI and machine learning* – are driving down coordination costs, leading to new value creation through rebundling.

First, increasing data interoperability, driven through the adoption of FHIRs (Faster Healthcare Interoperability Resources), enables the *creation of standards*[35] for data exchange, allowing developers to build APIs to access datasets across different systems. FHIRs allow sharing of specific pieces of information[36] without passing along entire documents, which also further increases modularity.

The second shift, improvements in artificial intelligence (AI) and machine learning (ML), change the economics of healthcare production and delivery, allowing platforms to establish a key control point for rebundling, to coordinate activities across the healthcare value chain.

AI and ML play two key roles in healthcare.[37] First, ML models that analyse structured data – imaging, genetic, EMR data and so on – may be employed to study patient populations or perform diagnosis for specific patients.[38] Second, natural language processing (NLP) techniques[39] process unstructured data – clinical notes, voice recordings and so on – to create machine-readable, structured data. This structured data can then be analysed using ML.[40]

Advances in AI and ML commoditize prediction.[41] With growing data interoperability and accessibility, predictions become more accurate as well as more applicable across a wider scope of diseases.[42] This reduces the cost of medical diagnosis, which can now be increasingly performed by machines. This, in turn, makes it feasible to perform diagnosis more frequently and easily, and also unbundles diagnosis from traditional care providers.

At the consumer end, this enables an increasing number of diagnoses to be performed as ongoing self-assessments, aiding disease management outside the care facility. Back at the healthcare provider, doctors and radiologists can now spend less time diagnosing, and make more granular judgements on the appropriate intervention on the basis of these diagnoses.

Next, the ability to extract data from unstructured notes and voice records reduces operational overhead for doctors, while a home-based voice assistant can better capture patient data without requiring the patient to visit a care facility.

By commoditising data capture, assessment and diagnosis, the frequency of these activities may be increased, while also unbundling them from in-facility patient interactions.

Effectively, improvements in AI and machine learning, coupled with increasing data interoperability, drive unbundling across the healthcare value chain and set the stage for rebundling.

Consider Google's healthcare strategy rebundling healthcare operations, diagnostics, drug R&D, surgery, and claims management, around the adoption of Google Cloud. The HIPAA-compliant[43] Google Cloud, combined with the Google Healthcare API,[44] acts as the initial beachhead enabling healthcare providers to store and aggregate data across multiple sources. Further, Google's DeepMind enables access to diverse, siloed data in a standardized format, enabling a wider scope of data elements to be analysed for clinical decision making.

Closer to the consumer, Apple is rebundling a range of healthcare services using the Apple Health Record[45] as a key control point. Apple's Health Record aims to be the central health record for users, combining data from acute care – currently stored in EHRs – with data from a variety of wellness and disease management devices and services, using FHIR-based integration. Apple's partnerships with health systems and EHR vendors[46,47] enable it to integrate EHR data with the Health Record. Apple also partners with Health Gorilla, a clinical data API exchange, to integrate diagnostic data.[48]

Apple's Health Record acts as a key control point rebundling across five diverse communities of producers looking to access these consumers – developers, device manufacturers, healthcare providers, pharma companies and medical researchers.

First, Apple provides access to its health record API to third parties through a software development kit called HealthKit.[49] Every app connecting to HealthKit may access data from the Personal Health Record. Prominent device manufacturers, like Nike and Jawbone, use the HealthKit API to integrate their devices as complements to the Personal Health Record.[50]

Next, Apple's CareKit[51] enables care providers to develop apps that monitor patients across the care pathway, particularly to manage chronic diseases.

Finally, Apple's ResearchKit[52] enables medical researchers and pharma companies to conduct studies leveraging the iPhone's user base. Apple makes it easier to identify, target and recruit eligible candidates for a research study, based on their health-record data.

Apple, Google, Microsoft and Amazon are also bundling connected devices and services around their respective consumer touchpoints.[53] The Apple Watch Series 6[54] includes an electrocardiogram and a blood oxygen monitor. Medical device complements may include diagnostic tools that physically connect to the iPhone[55] or integrate with the Apple Watch.[56] Google's research experiments with the Study Watch[57] indicate that it is likely to use connected wearables to assess, diagnose and manage diseases. Amazon's wearable Halo captures a variety of healthcare indicators using 3D body scans and voice tone analysis.[58]

In addition to building proprietary platforms for rebundling, BigTech firms also engage in open standards development. Open standards development may help change the competitive dynamics in an industry by commoditizing incumbent advantages.[59] While traditional firms, particularly EHR vendors, resist interoperability in healthcare, the BigTech firms are working together to promote open standards. Google and Amazon have joined efforts to support FHIRs through Project Blue Button, which aims to make it easier for patients to view and download their health records.[60,61] They are also implementing the standard in their cloud infrastructure and consumer-facing applications. Google's "Cloud Healthcare API" provides a solution for storing and accessing healthcare data in FHIR format,[62,63] while Apple has implemented FHIRs in its consumer-facing Health Records.[64]

Through a combination of open standards and proprietary platforms, these firms work on rebundling value around key user journeys – both for consumers and for producers, while also setting up control points that make other value-chain actors dependent on them.

Innovation at the Intersection

Firms engaging in rebundling actively try to shape the boundaries of their partner ecosystems, not just their own role within it. Much like Lego recombinations defy the instruction booklet, and indeed the boundary of a specific Lego kit, the new ecosystems that emerge from such innovation no longer adhere to traditional industry boundaries nor is such innovation restricted to domain expertise within that industry.

Effective rebundling requires innovation at the intersection.

In the industrial era, competitive advantage was built around managing scarce supply-side resources (e.g. oil, minerals, etc.). The production processes that converted these resources to usable products defined industry boundaries.

In the digital era, competitive advantage is built around managing scarce demand-side resources (e.g. consumer engagement and data). Accordingly, traditional industry boundaries and domain definitions are no longer relevant. Managing the scarce resource of consumer engagement requires firms to become customer-centric and rebundle all capabilities required to deliver a customer-centric offering.

To effectively rebundle towards solving a customer problem end-to-end, the Fast Future Executive needs to work across domains and across industries, no longer bound by their production boundaries, but focused solely on whatever it takes to deliver the end-to-end customer journey.

The Fast Future Arsenal

Understanding unbundling and rebundling is key to understanding new value creation in the digital economy. Unbundling dissolves boundaries of value creation, rebundling redefines new shapes in which value is created.

Understanding the mechanics of unbundling and rebundling is critical to answering (1) how we maximize value creation while preventing wealth concentration, (2) what we regulate and what we do not regulate, and (3) where we cooperate and where we compete.

The tools of unbundling and rebundling in the Fast Future arsenal also present a fundamentally new approach to innovation. In this landscape, value lies in staying laser-focused on customer needs and innovating at the intersection of diverse, even unconnected domains, to create a cohesive bundled solution that solves the customer problem. This book is your guide to identifying those powerful intersections and spotting opportunities for new value creation.

Chapter 2

Regenerative Innovation: Exploring the Potential of Digital Platforms for Ecosystem Health

How businesses can harness platform models for network effects, coordination and localization in service of societal and planetary health

Jessica Groopman

What Is Innovation in a Changing World?

The last two decades of business innovation have been characterized by the digital revolution: a period in which data and digital technologies permeated every industry, transformed business models and recalibrated global market dynamics.

Each technology trend and business opportunity outlined in this book relies upon a liveable planet and functional society. Yet, technologies, industry and economics broadly have become detached from their ecological and social foundations. Orienting business around short-term profits has detached innovation from the health of the whole

Looking forward, a new revolution in business innovation is taking shape. The role of innovation in the twenty-first century is to realign our technologies, organizations and markets in service of social and planetary well-being. This is, after all, critical for long-term resilience.

By reimagining the application of one of our most powerful tools, digital platforms, businesses can shift away from extractive, polarizing, waste-producing models. Instead, we can leverage platforms as tools to help regenerate life, borrowing design inspiration from billions of years of evolution to harness platform models for ecosystem health.

This chapter explores three ways digital platform models can support regenerative innovation:

- Network Effects and Scale
- Coordination and Collaboration
- Access and Localization.

Businesses of Tomorrow Will Be Anything but Business as Usual

Modern organizations face a world of constant change. Recent years have confronted businesses of every size and sector with digital, geopolitical, environmental, economic and workforce disruptions. Not only are disruptions coming from multiple vectors, but it is also clearer now than ever that companies and their stakeholders exist within a complex fabric of interconnected systems – systems that are dynamic, influence one another and require adaptation and resilience.

They are forcing organizations to reckon with an uncomfortable fact: *business as usual is not adaptive for the twenty-first century* (Figure 2.1).

The trends underlying these disruptions and the reckoning to adapt to this 'new normal' have far deeper roots. Assumptions of stability, predictability and endless profits for a few at the expense of endless extraction of the whole, have dominated business models and markets for decades.

Starting with the first industrial revolution, the world's natural resources have fuelled tremendous economic growth for the past 200 years. The last 50 years have seen an exponential surge in the extraction of non-renewable resources, with no outlook of diminishing global demand.[1] The structures of conventional business haven't just become disconnected from living systems, many are synonymous with brutal exploitation of people and planetary resources.

Systemic effects, such as a factory emitting pollutants that harm local communities and people's health, are not reflected in the market price of goods and services. So-called 'externalities' are, quite literally, viewed outside business value, accounted for only in terms of calculating risk.

The way we conduct business has us on a path of accelerating this model of degeneration. We are now facing multiple planetary

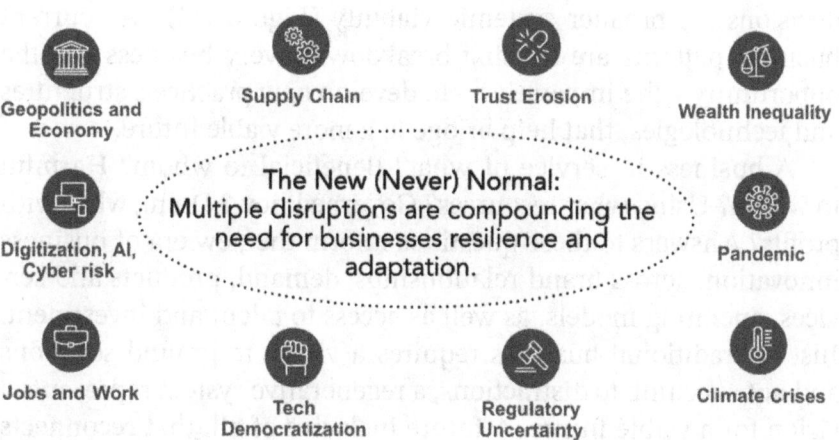

Figure 2.1 The new (never) normal.

and social crises, including biodiversity loss, climate breakdown and runaway pollution, as well as profound social and economic inequities. The model is not just unsustainable, it's unfit to support a growing population and coming generations to thrive.

The transformation we're calling for is not about feel-good PR, altruism or 'greenwashing'. It is not merely a reframing of 'sustainability' or ESG, that now fraught but ever inadequate acronym for environmental, social and corporate governance reporting. It is about leaders confronting the practical reality that the fate of any organization wishing to thrive for the long-term is directly tied to the fate of the planet and functional society.

We must learn how to meet and work within our existing systems that are breaking down, while simultaneously nurturing the conditions and innovations that will enable emergence of a more viable, a more *regenerative* system.

> *We are not living in an era of change. We are living in a change of era. We need to ground the current chaos within the shifts we have every 500 to 1000 years. We are now living through such a shift.*
>
> (John Fullerton, Founder of the Capital Institute)

Innovation leaders will be familiar with the Three Horizons framework, which we present here as a model to apply business decisions for broader systemic viability (Figure 2.2).[2] As current business patterns are causing breakdown, every business has the opportunity – the imperative – to develop new practices, structures and technologies, that help bridge to a more viable future.

A business in service of what? Beneficial to whom? Harmful to whom? Using what resources? Governed how? Doing what with profits? Answers to these questions inform the new era of business innovation: across brand relationships, demand, products and services, operating models, as well as access to talent and investment. Just as traditional business requires a vision to ground solutions and not succumb to distractions, a regenerative system represents a vision for a viable future. A future inclusive of all, that reconnects

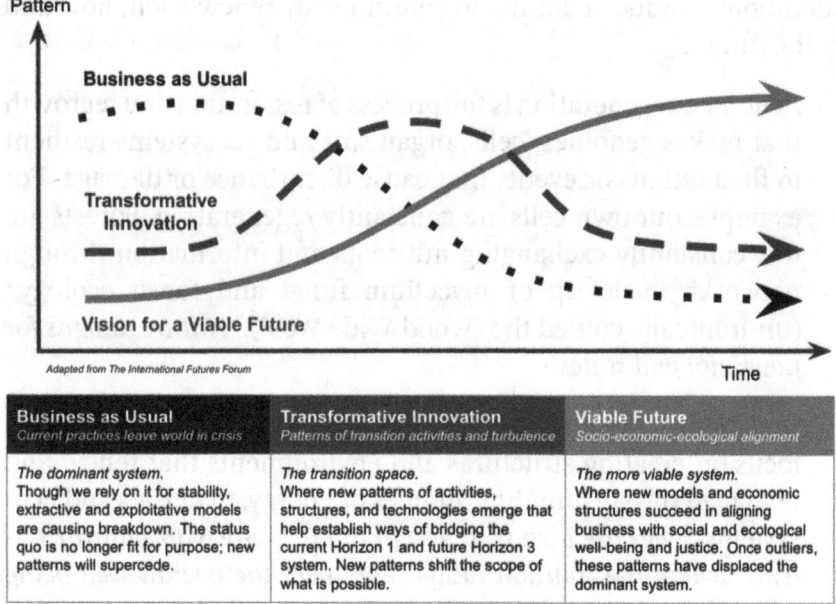

Figure 2.2   Three Horizons framework, business innovation towards a viable future.

business with societal and planetary health, and harnesses technologies to do so.

A Reorientation of Business Innovation: Regeneration

As organizations across every industry awaken to this imperative for transformation the orientation of innovation shifts. How can we design our organization, products, services, partnerships and supply chains in service to life and systemic health? While these questions may sound daunting, the good news is we have four billion years of experience to learn from – that of the Earth itself, and the process of regeneration.[3]

What does 'regeneration' mean? Life-giving: the word 'regenerative' means 'to produce new' or 'to bring forth again', creating the conditions conducive for life to continuously renew itself, now and in the future.

- *In nature*: regeneration is the process of restoration and regrowth that makes genomes, cells, organisms and ecosystems resilient to fluctuations or events that cause disturbance or damage. For example, our own cells are constantly regenerating. Forests are too, constantly exchanging nutrients and information through networks made up of mycelium fungi and forest ecology,[4] (un-ironically coined the 'Wood Wide Web').[5] *Nature designs for flows, not end states.*

- *In design*: 'regenerative' describes principles and processes that focus on creating structures and environments that renew and revitalize the surrounding sources of energy, materials and eco-systems. *The core idea is to design in harmony with natural systems, where the solution design enhances the overall well-being of both people and the planet.* Regenerative design is emerging across a wide field of disciplines. For example, architects and urban planners are designing materials and buildings that generate more energy than they consume, improve air quality, sequester carbon, incorporate natural light for heating and cooling, and even share surplus energy locally. *Nature never does one thing at a time.*

- *In innovation*: regenerative innovation puts life at the centre of value creation. It refers to the development and implementation of new ideas, products or processes that aim to restore, renew or revitalize ecosystems, organizations, communities and economies. Regenerative innovation is not only about reducing negative effects, but actively contributing to systemic health, and the resilience of natural resources, social systems and economic structures (Figure 2.3). *Nature is a set of interconnected relationships.*

It is not the strongest of the species that survive, nor the most intelligent, but the one most responsive to change.

(Charles Darwin)

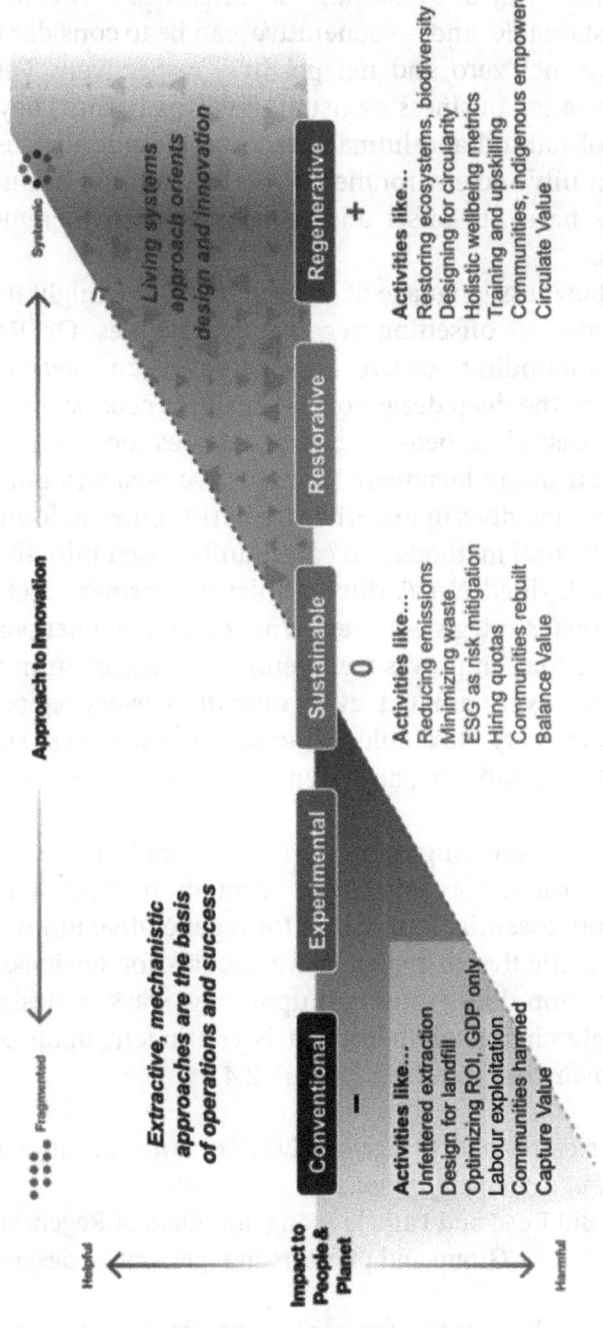

Figure 2.3 Regenerative innovation: a living-systems approach to value creation.

One simplified way of evaluating the difference between 'Conventional', 'Sustainable' and 'Regenerative' can be to consider them as net negative, net zero and net positive, respectively. For net negative businesses, 'business as usual' involves harm. They rely on extraction of natural and human resources despite the costs to human, community and environmental health. Net zero businesses aim to do less harm, to offset and to counter with incremental improvements.

Using the business language of 'externalities', one might understand 'Sustainable' as offsetting negative externalities. Or 'Regenerative' as compounding positive externalities, even *internalizing* externalities into the deep design of the business ecosystem. What co-benefits, or cascading benefits can businesses incorporate as a function of their doing business? Regenerative business practices often emphasize activities in material circularity, renewable energy, healthier agricultural methods and community-based initiatives.

In their book titled *Net Positive*, Unilever's former CEO Paul Polman and global strategist Andrew Winston define a net positive company as one that 'improves well-being for everyone it impacts and at all scales – every product, every operation, every region and country, and for every stakeholder, including employees, suppliers, communities, customers, and even future generations and the planet itself'.[6]

However, understanding regeneration by simply framing it as 'negative-zero-positive' or defining it through specific activities overlooks a more essential foundation for regenerative innovation. Shifting from extractive to regenerative models for business and systemic innovation doesn't *just* call upon new ways of designing products, supply chains, or metrics, it is contingent upon something far upstream: our mindsets (Figure 2.4).

> *The first step on the path to regenerative work is not a change of techniques but a change of mind.*
> (Bill Reed and Pamela Mang, founders of Regenesis
> Group and pioneers in regenerative design)

Today, the 'machine' is the predominant metaphor in our way of thinking and approaching just about everything. Mechanistic ways

from **SEPARATE PARTS**	to **INTERCONNECTED WHOLES**
from **MECHANISTIC**	to **HOLISTIC, SYSTEMIC**
from **SHORT-TERM**	to **LONG-TERM**
from **LINEAR**	to **CIRCULAR**
from **CONTROL**	to **STEWARDSHIP**
from **COMPETITIVE**	to **COLLABORATIVE**
from **SCALING UP**	to **SCALING OUT**
from **GLOBAL FRAGILITY**	to **LOCAL ABUNDANCE**
from **SHAREHOLDER WEALTH**	to **STAKEHOLDER WELLBEING**
from **PROBLEMS**	to **POTENTIAL**

Figure 2.4 Regenerative transformation requires shifting mindsets.

of thinking and designing rely on reductionism and linear causality, viewing any 'thing' as made up of discrete parts with predictable interactions that can be controlled. This approach seeks to understand and manipulate individual components, often overlooking or ignoring the complex, emergent properties that arise from interactions within the system.

This lens informs how we separate our industries into classifications, our businesses into functional silos, problems into parts, 'success' into singular metrics, and more. Indeed, business is full of mechanistic metaphors, from referring to employees as 'cogs in the machine' to 'chains of command' in leadership, to 'optimizing input and output efficiency'. As we all know (and have witnessed in recent years), even the most 'well-oiled machine' businesses are vulnerable to systemic disruptions – economic, supply chain, ecological, societal. . .

While the reductionist approach has been instrumental to countless scientific and technological discoveries from the atom to the aeroplane, it is at odds with how living systems work. It is not inherently bad or even wrong, it is just incomplete. It is inadequate for dealing with and adapting to the complex realities of life. And critically, *we live in a time that calls on us to re-member and re-align ourselves, and our technologies, businesses and economies with the living world.*

In contrast, a regenerative approach embraces the inherent interconnectedness and dynamic nature of systems, and life on the planet. Instead of viewing problems and opportunities as isolated parts that can be controlled, we look for potential in the patterns and relationships and seek to enable them by embracing as systemically whole a lens as possible. Instead of ignoring uncertainties or the non-empirical, we must incorporate more holistic ways of knowing and asking, such as cultural, indigenous, intuitive and tacit knowledge.

Shifting our focus from short-term gains for the few, to multigenerational outcomes encourages us to consider the responsibility and consequentiality of decision making. Moving from linear to circular/cyclical thinking transforms how we understand cause and effect and the role of feedback loops, allowing us to consider flows, the use of waste and energy optimization, and see more broadly the impacts of our actions. Regeneration is not a destination, but a process.

Embracing greater collaboration over pure zero-sum competition acknowledges that working together often leads to more valuable results, less risk, and greater abundance. Finally, regeneration, and life itself, happens in *place*, i.e. in local bioregional context. Thus, there is no single model to be transmitted and imposed, but many models that allow for the conditions for life based on the local social and environmental dynamics.

> *The kind of attention we pay to the world changes the world we pay attention to.*
>
> (Ian McGilchrist)

Principles for regenerative innovation

Incorporating both modern scientific consensus and a range of indigenous wisdom traditions, the Capital Institute proposes the following principles as a guide for regenerative design for economic systems (Figure 2.5).[7] We propose extending these principles for business and technological innovation because both are, after all, embedded in our economic systems.

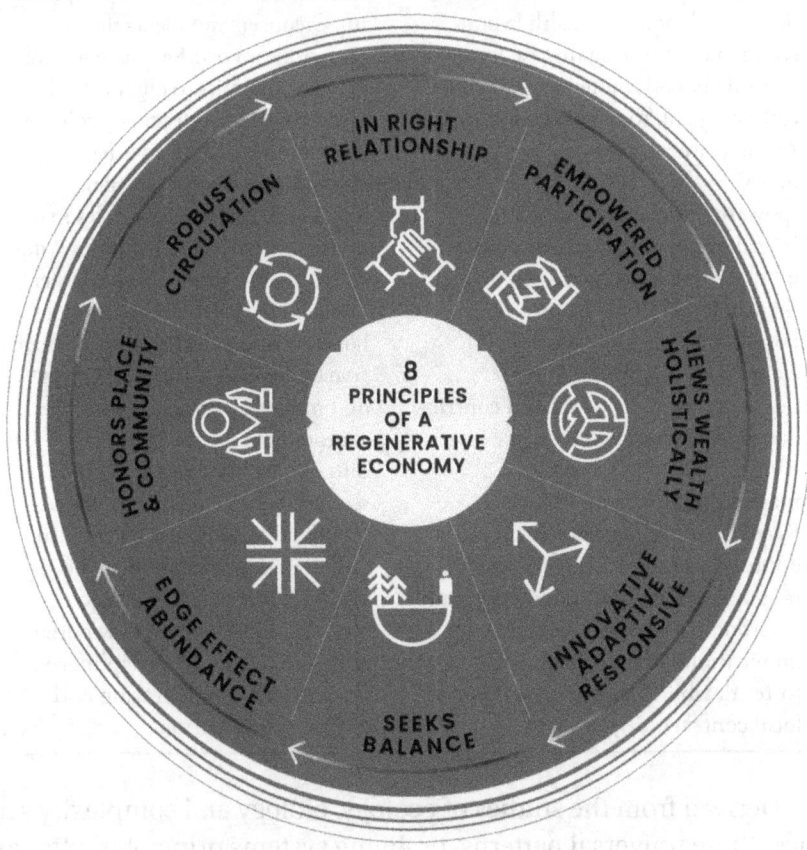

Figure 2.5 The principles of a regenerative economy.

In Right Relationship: Recognizing interconnectedness with all life, develop systems that foster reciprocity and mutualism, and recognize impact in relation to the other systems and contexts in which we are embedded.

Views Wealth Holistically: Healthy ecosystems have sufficient resources for all species to survive and thrive. Construct value frameworks that define and manage wealth expansively, incorporating diverse forms of capital beyond financial, material, technological, to recognize natural, social, cultural, experiential and more.

Empowered Participation: Interdependent systems empower unique contributions of the parts to the whole's systemic health. Formulate structures where every element is empowered to both negotiate for their needs and contribute to the overall health of the larger whole.

Honour Community and Place: Regeneration starts locally. Craft approaches that honour the uniqueness of each community, history and environment, ensuring designs and applications – however global – foster flexibility and are rooted in local contexts.

Robust Circulatory Flow: Mirroring biological systems' circulatory and metabolic dynamics, regenerative design aims to ensure healthy flows of energy, materials, money and information, in which 'waste' is recirculated into value-enhancing flow.

Innovative, Adaptive, Responsive: Systems are in a state of constant flux, for which 'fitness' is about adaptability. Create environments that encourage innovation and entrepreneurial dynamics to align with the evolving needs of systemic health over short-term individual desires.

Seeks Balance: Healthy systems harmonize multiple variables in a unified whole instead of optimizing single ones at the expense of others. Pursue dynamic balance through harmonizing paradoxes, i.e. competition and collaboration, efficiency and resilience, diversity and coherence, masculine and feminine, different ways of knowing, all in service to the health of the whole.

Edge Effect Abundance: Creativity and abundance flourish at the 'edges' of systems. Encourage cross-fertilization and new potentiality through multi-disciplinary interactions, collaboration and diverse participation.

Derived from the studies of ecology, biology and complexity science, these universal patterns, or 'living systems principles' offer an important framework for designing in ways that mimic and align more closely with the resilience and efficiency observed in natural ecosystems.

While these concepts may feel foreign to business and economic orthodoxies of the twentieth century, regeneration is nothing new. The interconnectedness of life and ecological knowledge are central to many indigenous and spiritual traditions, and to our survival story as a species. Nowadays, modern ecological and biological sciences are demonstrating how life supports itself, reiterating our knowledge of resilience across species. Meanwhile, as 'sustainability' falls short, the regenerative imperative is gaining traction in the business community.

> *This is not about making the businesses of the twentieth century less bad; it is about inventing the businesses of the twenty-first century.*
> (Erinch Sahan, Business & Enterprise Lead Business & Enterprise Lead Doughnut Economics Action Lab [DEAL])

As Regenerative Business Rises, Leaders Look to Technology

The concept of regenerative business is on the rise globally, as businesses increasingly recognize the inadequacy of conventional models and the need for change. In the face of rising systemic risks facing all businesses,[8] and a chorus of alarm from scientists, and increasingly economists,[9] cost–benefit models are shifting. Corporations are facing growing pressures from investors, policymakers, consumers, employees, advocacy groups and even business leaders themselves.

Asset managers representing trillions in assets have increased pressure on clients, to 'internalize externalities' both for risk mitigation[10] and value creation.[11] The $400 billion earmarked for clean energy from the United States' Inflation Reduction Act is also starting to flow, among countless other examples of more environmentally and socially supportive policies globally. Some 140 countries and hundreds of enterprises have made commitments to decarbonize.[12] Thousands of more ambitious organizations are striving to become regenerative (Table 2.1).

OUR PURPOSE

The regeneration of the planet is at the heart of our business model. Every time you purchase Guayakí Yerba Mate, you're creating a positive global impact. We call it **Market Driven Regeneration™**, and it's the driving force behind everything we do.

Figure 2.6 Guayakí, global yerba mate tea brand, centres regeneration into its business model and market strategy. The company's agroforestry practices are designed to replenish ecosystems and uplift communities in the South American Atlantic rainforest, where the yerba mate is sourced.

In sectors such as agriculture, food and textiles, regenerative principles are being put into practice in ways that compound stakeholder benefits simultaneously: restoring soil fertility, sequestering carbon, reducing emissions, promoting animal welfare, empowering farmers and improving nutritional integrity and customer experiences, *all while unlocking radical new value models*. The number of companies adopting regenerative agriculture practices has grown by nearly 130%, from at least 239 in 2019 to at least 549 in 2022, according to a 2023 Regenerative Industry Landscape Report.[13]

Pragmatic organizations recognize that the 'new' (i.e. never) normal requires a shift in mindset and approach but are struggling to understand the critical role of technologies and data. To date, there has been relatively little analysis into the role of digital and emerging technologies to advance regeneration.

We live in a time that is awash with digital technologies, from AI to blockchain, from wearables to robots, biotech to 3D printing.

Table 2.1 Regenerative business on the rise.

Corporate Activities	Investment and Start-up Activity	Cross-industry Applications	Business Ecosystem	Cultural and Consumer Trends
Many of the world's largest corporations have announced regenerative objectives and activities. While talk is cheap, these companies have enormous influence on markets, policymakers and their ecosystems.	Hundreds of millions of venture capital, institutional, and development funds are pouring into regenerative projects across other 'tech' sectors	The regenerative design paradigm is gaining traction across industries reconnecting business to place.	A broader movement of regeneration-focused constituents across business value chains and networks.	Countless studies show consumers, citizens' and employees' expectations are shifting, demanding organizations act more socially and environmentally responsibly.
• Patagonia	• Agtech	• Agriculture	• Business communities	• Brand purpose
• Unilever	• Foodtech	• Architecture	• Consortia	• Fair trade
• Nestlé	• Fintech	• Finance/Textiles	• Consultancies	• Fair pay/Labour
• Interface	• Climatetech	• Fashion	• Design firms	• Recycling
• Walmart	• Naturetech	• Hospitality	• Events/Conferences	• Animal welfare
• Danone	• Circularitytech	• Retail	• Books	• Organic
• IKEA	• Energytech	• Real Estate	• Course curricula	• Transparency
• The North Face	• Govtech	• Tourism	• Think tanks	• Product sourcing
• General Mills	• Biotech	• Manufacturing		
• Guayakí	• Welltech	• Bioregional Development		

While no technology is a silver bullet, humanity's ever-expanding toolkit can help us drive positive change. This chapter will explore the regenerative potential of *digital platforms* – a foundational tool for enabling network effects, coordination and localized access.

How can we apply digital platforms for regenerative innovation?

Re-applying Our Digital Platforms

In the past couple of decades, the world has seen an explosion of digital platforms. The platform economy is estimated around $6–7 trillion in economic activity,[14] across different industries like e-commerce, social media, cloud computing, financial services, energy and more. The world's largest tech companies – Apple, Alphabet (Google), Microsoft, Amazon, Alibaba, Meta (Facebook), IBM, Tencent among others – are all companies with platform-based business models. While these companies have amassed trillions in economic value, their monetization models and designs have often been applied in ways that have degenerated health, and brought about harm to individuals, communities, societies and to the planet.

- *E-commerce platforms have accelerated the linear economy*, as ever-accumulating packaging, single-use, low durability goods end up in landfill.
- *Social media platforms have accelerated political division and polarization*, and amplified loneliness, unhealthy social comparison, and mental health issues for youth.
- *Cloud platforms have accelerated power asymmetries in critical areas*, from natural resource extraction to behavioural data surveillance, from worker rights to disadvantaging small businesses.
- *Many platforms have prioritized proprietary gains over broader ecosystem benefits*, deprioritizing areas like interoperability, openness and information integrity.

'What's good for the platform has often been bad for the ecosystem,' says platform expert and author, Sangheet Choudhary.[15] 'We have to think about this when we try to build platforms in industries where the greater good is sometimes much more important than the profit model the company has. It is important to not just benefit from the business model but to figure out models of governance and finance that benefit the ecosystem.'

The point is not to condemn platforms as a technology, rather to re-envision how we harness and apply them in regenerative ways. The point is to detach platforms from linear, polarizing, extractive models, and repurpose their technological capabilities towards regenerating value, health and potential across ecosystems.

The Platform Opportunity for Regenerative Innovation

Digital platforms are software systems or applications that facilitate interactions and transactions between different groups of users. They play a significant role in the modern economy, fostering innovation, enabling entrepreneurship and connecting people in ways that were not possible before the digital age. Platforms can take various forms and serve diverse purposes, catering to many different industries and needs.

- *Social media and content sharing platforms* facilitate social interactions, content sharing and networking among people. (Examples: Facebook, Instagram, Twitter, LinkedIn; YouTube, Vimeo, SoundCloud)
- *Online marketplaces and e-commerce platforms* connect buyers with sellers to enable the transfer of goods and services and can include access for freelancers offering specific services or handmade/crafted products. (Examples: Amazon, eBay, Shopify, Alibaba)
- *Sharing economy platforms* facilitate peer-to-peer transactions, allowing individuals to share resources, services or skills directly with one another. (Examples: Airbnb, Uber, TaskRabbit)
- *Gig economy platforms* help connect gig workers (freelancers) with customers looking for specific services, such as transportation or food delivery. (Examples: Etsy, Upwork, Fiverr, Uber, Lyft, DoorDash)

- *Cloud computing platforms* provide on-demand computing resources and services over the Internet, including storage, databases, computing power, and increasingly advanced analytics and AI/ML. (Examples: Amazon Web Services (AWS), Microsoft Azure, Google Cloud Platform)
- *Educational platforms* offer online courses, tutorials and educational materials, making learning accessible to a global audience. (Examples: Coursera, edX, Khan Academy)
- *Communication platforms* facilitate real-time communication, messaging and collaboration among individuals or teams. (Examples: Square, Skype, Zoom, Slack)
- *Financial platforms* provide online financial services, including digital payments, lending and crowdfunding. (Examples: PayPal, Block, Funding Circle)

When designing for regenerative innovations, the question is less about the platform type and more about the economic and behavioural incentives the platform and its technologies help support. *Of what purpose is the platform in service?*

Platform-based business models, or platform businesses, are those that utilize an online platform to create value by facilitating interactions, transactions and exchanges between two or more groups of users. Users can be buyers and sellers, service providers and customers, civilians and political representatives, or any other stakeholders in a market. Modern digital platforms and platform-based business models have brought about a wide range of benefits and risks for businesses and individuals alike (Table 2.2).

Remember, individual and business benefits and risks are not the same as ecosystem benefits and risks, often seen as 'externalities'. We invite readers to consider the many ways platforms have enabled both beneficial feedback loops, like 'democratizing access', as well as negative feedback loops, like increasing power asymmetries, across the ecosystems in which they operate.

Many readers will be familiar with platforms across these areas. All will have experienced, whether directly or indirectly, some of these upsides and downsides. But to what extent are today's platform businesses designed to enable broader 'net positive' value for society and the environment?

Table 2.2   Benefits and risks of platform-based business models.

Benefits	Risks
Increased reach and access: Platforms provide a gateway to access wider audiences. Businesses can more easily expand their customer base, users can reach one another. Both gain access to resources and expertise, often across borders.	**Dependency on third-party platforms:** Relying on external platforms defers power to them. Reach and user experience (UX) can be impacted by sudden changes in policies, algorithms, partnerships or other whims.
Network effects: As more users and stakeholders join the platform, the value of the platform increases, creating a feedback loop or 'flywheel' of attracting more users and expanding potential value.	**Monopoly concerns:** Dominant platforms can wield their enormous influence to crush competition, saturate markets, harm users and impose unfair and abusive practices on others.
Cost-efficiencies: Operating on existing platforms can reduce setup, marketing, legal and transaction costs, improving accessibility for small businesses.	**Platform fees:** Additional platforms fees or commissions can cut into profits making the business model unsustainable for SMBs. Free platforms can also compromise user data privacy.
Scalability and resource utilization: Digitization and cloud platforms enable operations to scale up or down based on demand, offering infrastructure that can enable more efficient liquidity via resource utilization, in many areas from cloud computing to car-sharing to circularity.	**Overlooks local needs:** Technological dependencies and one-size-fits-all service models can be at odds with local dynamics, cultures and resources, and impose undue burdens on communities and SMBs.
Big data and analytics: Platforms wield big data sets and analytics, which can help businesses and users alike make more informed decisions.	**Diverse data privacy and security concerns:** Sensitive customer data on platforms raises diverse security and privacy concerns, from increased threats of cyber-attacks to harmful targeting-based business models.
Incentivizes innovation: Platforms encourage product redesigns and continuous optimization by providing both analytics and development environments for stakeholders to co-create better products and services.	**Unintended consequences:** Dangerous incidents, negative reviews, or otherwise injurious repercussions on platforms can harm reputations, communities and societal trust.

(Continued)

Table 2.2   (Continued)

Benefits	Risks
Governance, verification and compliance: Platforms often act as an intermediary between parties and can offer services that ensure verification of authenticity, identity, certifications and compliance, that help improve trust in digital marketplaces.	**Regulatory and legal challenges:** Platform businesses often face complex regulations, tax issues and legal challenges in different regions and countries.
Encourages discovery and diversification: Platforms enable users to more easily search and discover community connections, information, goods, resources and services than they could otherwise. Businesses can diversify their offerings by collaborating with other businesses within the platform's ecosystem.	**Filter bubbles or loss of serendipity:** As discovery algorithms tend to show users what they want to see based on past behaviour and preferences, they may be less likely to encounter unexpected, contrasting or more diverse recommendations.
Brand equity: Platforms can boost positive user interactions and brand equity by facilitating better business practices, streamlining safety and compliance, hosting ratings and reviews, and utilizing data-driven insights to drive improvements.	**Loss of user trust:** Platforms present many risks to trust, from poor design decisions to security breaches to unauthorized use of data for monetization.

If value lies in the facilitation of interactions, transactions and exchanges, how can platforms be designed to regenerate relationships between users, to facilitate transactions and exchanges that compound benefits for more stakeholders?

Regenerative Potential for Platform Models

Platforms today can help address a range of social, environmental and other systemic problems. But to date, most successful platform implementations have been financed through Venture Capital (VC), which has led to platforms optimizing for the narrow metric of return on investment (ROI). The VC imperative of maximizing investor returns is often the context in which platform businesses deprioritize other metrics and externalities.

Designing platform business models for regenerative potential thus begins with assessing their financing and governance mechanisms, to ensure platforms can displace singular profit metrics with diverse metrics of well-being. Only then can platform business models reframe 'externalities' and ecosystem risks – social, ecological, health, financial, cyber – and internalize them as business opportunities for ecosystem collaboration and innovation.

How can platforms centre justice and equity, orienting metrics around helping those most in need of resources connect with the resources they need? How can platforms centre the well-being of communities, regions and the planet itself in financing and governance models? This reframe is foundational for ensuring digital platforms – and the digital economy broadly – are used to address the world's systemic problems.

Innovation is about reorganizing existing elements in new ways. The opportunity we have now is to harness the proven capabilities of digital platforms in regenerative ways.

Our analysis of the benefits of digital platforms, regenerative business potential and alternative financing and governance models finds three main ways digital platforms can foster more regenerative innovation:

1. *Network effects and scale* to address societal challenges and systemic change by scaling the conditions for ecosystem adaptation and innovation.
2. *Coordination and collaboration* to facilitate healthy relationships (i.e. interactions, transactions and exchanges) across diverse and disparate stakeholders.
3. *Access and localization* to centre inclusive participation, cultural, and bioregional contexts in the development of the digital economy.

The following sections will explore how digital platform models can support more regenerative outcomes. Each analyses the types of network effects, coordination and localization that platforms can enable, various finance and governance models, and what design considerations can help compound ecosystem health and value. Each section also profiles real-world examples across different platform models. Because platforms tend to use (and evolve alongside) various other technologies, we also list the key emerging technologies on the horizon for each of the three areas.

Network effects and scale

Digital platforms and their business models excel at achieving network effects and scaling due to their ability to connect many users, facilitate interactions seamlessly, and serve as substrate for an evolving set of use cases and exchanges. Take ride-sharing giant Uber: the more drivers and riders, the more useful the platform; the more useful the platform, the more transferable the platform is into other markets; the more transferable, the more efficient and cost-effective, and thus Uber has not only branched into other areas of transportation and services, but inspired other platform models to serve other markets, such as in B2B. This self-reinforcing cycle, also called a network effect or flywheel, is what drives scalability of platforms.

However, scale (as measured only by business growth for growth's sake) can have detrimental consequences. As alluded to in Table 2.2, some of the world's largest platforms have had crushing consequences on small businesses, local economies and environments. Network effects that enable platform scale come in multiple forms and can have cascading positive or negative impacts (Figure 2.7). The question for regenerative innovators is how to 'stack' positive network effects that improve the health of the ecosystem.

We can harness digital platforms to support network effects to *scale ecosystem health*. The key is focusing on enabling network effects across multiple organizations, not just the organization running the digital platform. It is not about scaling single metrics or

Direct Network Effects	Indirect Network Effects	Multi-sided Network Effects	Supplier/Compatibility Network Effects
When the value of a platform increases for existing users as many additional users join. E.g. more friends on a social network site enhance experience users.	When the value increases for one user group as more users from another group join. E.g. more app developers join a platform because of its user base; users are then attracted to more available applications.	When the value increases as multiple distinct user groups interact, each group benefits. E.g. a marketplace platform, where payment processors, sellers, and buyers benefit.	When the value increases as more suppliers or third-party services join and integrate into the platform, expanding options for user groups across the ecosystem.
Local Network Effects	Data Network Effects	Same Group Network Effects	Incentive Network Effects
When the value increases for users within a specific geographical area. E.g. ride-sharing services, where more drivers and riders enhance utility locally.	When the value increases as more exchanges provide more data, which can improve algorithms. AI, UX, personalization, platform services.	When value increases for a specific demographic as similar users join, it benefits that community. E.g. a professional networking for those within a specific industry or field join.	When value of an incentive or tokenized asset increases as more users participate, a micro-economy emerges. E.g. tokens, credits, rewards, governance stake, etc.

Figure 2.7 Types of network effects.

growth, but about scaling the conditions for an ecosystem to be able to adapt and innovate, and better circulate value. Ecosystem-based business models can also distribute risk and foster novel financing and governance models.

In the following examples, we will see how a new generation of businesses is applying digital platform models to create network effects that help bring together relevant ecosystem stakeholders to scale systemic change. First, in plastics, then in the food system, and finally in material science. These examples all harness platforms for big data orchestration and analysis, for productization, and combine open-source and proprietary assets to create multi-stakeholder business models with multiple kinds of network effects.

Digital Platforms Exemplifying Regenerative Potential through Network Effects

EXAMPLE 1: Empower, HowGood, Materiom
Empower offers a global marketplace platform for plastic waste, using technology for transparent recording and rewarding of plastic deposits. By giving plastic a marketplace value, the platform incentivizes stakeholders to contribute, fund, account for, source from and monetize plastic circularity. The platform helps create an economic foundation for scaling the network effects needed to enable plastic circularity and ecosystem restoration.

The challenge: The production of plastics has skyrocketed (Figure 2.8), with over 50% of all plastics produced after the year 2000.[16] Single-use, toxic and non-biodegradable plastics result in severe consequences, contaminating soil and marine ecosystems, harming wildlife and endangering human health. Microplastics, which are microscopic pieces that break down from single-use plastics, have been found *everywhere* – not just landfills – from the air to waterways, our foods, even within our bloodstreams and breastmilk.[17] Worse, many plastic products use combinations of different plastic types which make separating and re-using them difficult. Plastics can be contaminated and require significant infrastructure

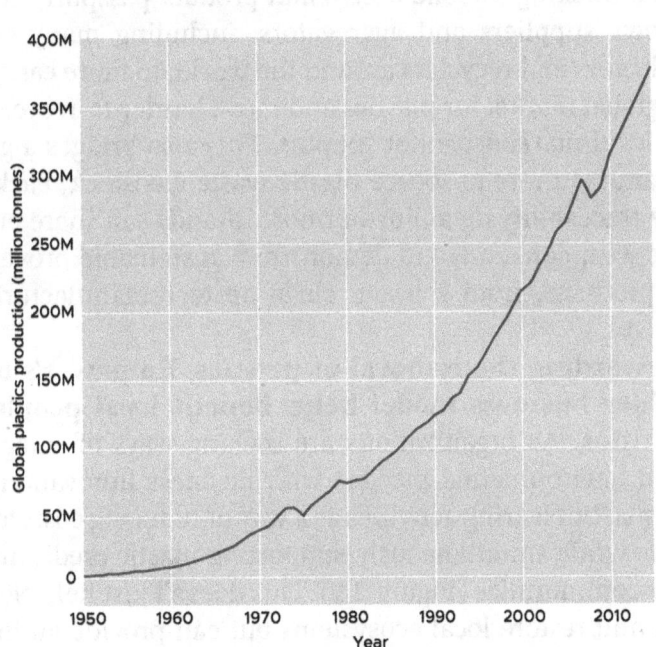

Annual production of virgin plastic

More than 50% of all plastics were produced after the year 2000

Figure 2.8   Annual production of virgin plastic.

and resources to repurpose, which undermines the economic viability of 'closing the loop' – particularly when 'virgin' production costs are lower. Local recyclers often cannot reach global manufacturers, despite their demands for waste plastic feedstocks. In addition to radical reduction in plastic-based materials, what is needed is a way of pricing in and incentivizing global plastic supply chains networks to connect and shift from linear to circular.

Empower's platform enables tracking across the entire plastics value chain. Operating across more than 40 countries, it uses blockchain to enable traceability by certifying product passports as immutable records, and tokenizes plastic credits to incentivize people to contribute. By easily tracking plastic from clean-up to processing, manufacturers and brands are more easily able to comply with regulations and certification requirements, such as in Europe.

Simple tracking, mobile access and product passport transparency allows suppliers and aggregators, including many smaller scale collectors and recyclers around the world, to more easily plug into the global market for plastics and move harder-to-recycle plastics that local markets cannot support. This also bridges a gap for larger manufacturers to source plastic waste feedstock, backed by verifiable traceability data. Furthermore, brands can share product passports with consumers to demonstrate sustainable provenance of their products, from a beach clean-up to remanufacturing to store shelves.

By rewarding the removal of plastics, Empower's multistakeholder business model helps benefit local people and communities. As organizations are seeking ways of integrating social and environmental pledges with business innovation, they can fund plastic clearing activities as a way of reducing costs to their feedstocks while simultaneously supporting plastic credit monetization for communities (Figure 2.9). This doesn't just help clean up pollution and restore local ecosystems but can provide an income stream for marginalized communities. At the time of writing, the company claims to have helped more than 18,000 waste workers in marginalized communities generate wages through plastics, having removed and recertified over 35,000 tons of plastics.

Empower is one of several organizations working towards this critical effort. In fact, others, such as Plastic Bank, Rebound and CleanHub are enabling plastic processing marketplace tools and plugging into plastic credit networks.[18] By rewarding the removal of plastic waste for local communities and collection organizations, platforms can help scale network effects across a wide range of constituents, *and* redirect leakage of plastic out of the environment back into the economy.

- **Brands** improve on sustainability targets, traceability, brand lift
- **Consumers** benefit from more sustainable products, less single-use plastics
- **Manufacturers** improve efficiencies and cost savings, greater supply chain predictability

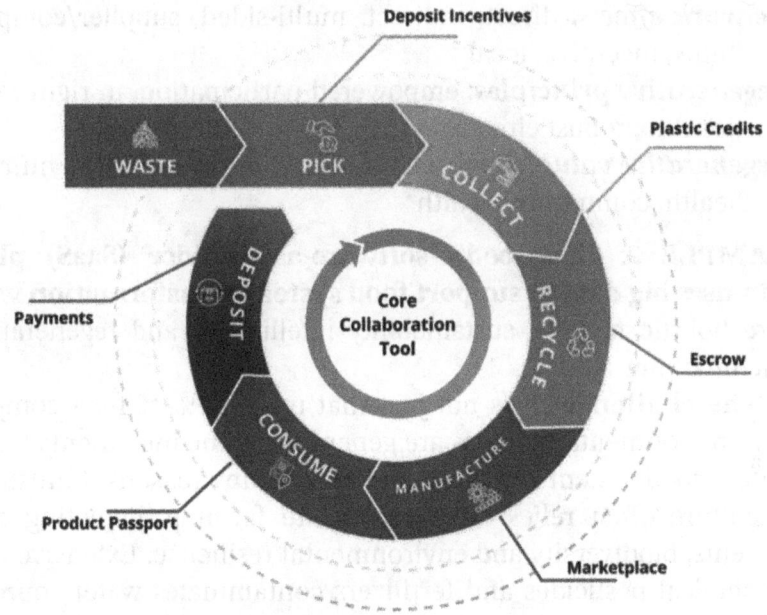

Figure 2.9 How Empower's platform supports the circular economy.

- **Suppliers** gain as recycling industry grows, plastics processing scales, new revenue streams for other post-consumer plastics feedstocks
- **Collectors** gain revenue streams for local recyclers, plug into global marketplace
- **Marginalized communities** gain wages and employment opportunities
- **Environmental ecosystems** endure less plastic!
- **Data** across environments, plastics, organizations

Industries: plastics, consumer packaged goods
Parties: business-to-business; nonprofit org-to-business; civilian-to-business
Platform benefits: discovery, reach, governance/verification, innovation

Network effects: direct, indirect, multi-sided, supplier/compatibility, incentive, local

Regenerative principles: empowered participation, in right relationship, robust circulation

Regenerative value: supply chain health, business health, human health, community health

EXAMPLE 2: HowGood's software-as-a-service (SaaS) platform uses big data to support food system transformation with more holistic metrics, sustainability intelligence and regenerative benchmarking.

The challenge: It is not just that up to 87% of food companies' environmental impacts are generated by the ingredients,[19] the modern food system is unsustainable for many reasons. Industrial agriculture often relies on monoculture farming, depleting soil nutrients, biodiversity and environmental resilience. Extensive use of chemical pesticides and fertilizers contaminates water sources and harms ecosystems. Industrialized farming often subjects animals to overcrowded, stressful conditions, routine use of antibiotics, and limited access to the outside, resulting in increased disease prevalence, and ethical concerns around animal welfare. It also entrenches inequities by favouring large-scale, corporate farms with significant financial resources, advanced technologies, and access to global markets, while marginalizing small-scale farmers and agricultural communities with limited resources. The global food supply chain, with its long transportation routes, contributes to significant carbon emissions, exacerbating climate change.

A Trucost analysis found industrialized farming costs the environment the equivalent of about $3 trillion every year in externalized costs.[20] On top of all of this, the market has struggled with transparency and understanding around how to take action for sustainable impact, including, but far beyond, carbon emissions. The system is in dire need of new incentives to turn around farming practices, localize the economic value created from farming in communities, and to support healthy food access for all.

HowGood's platform offers a data-driven and automated way of improving accountability across food supply chains substantiated on hard social and environmental impact data. Hosting a database of over 33,000 materials, chemicals and ingredients from 600 vetted data sources, it analyses some 250 sustainability attributes to define 'health' across eight core metrics (Figure 2.10).

HowGood brings together large food brands, retailers, ingredient suppliers and restaurants *around these metrics,* to measure, manage and innovate around the environmental and social impacts of their food supply chains. Organizations use the platform to assess and verify impact data of their ingredients, grounding information across the eight metrics to drive strategic decision making around sourcing, manufacturing, merchandising and marketing of sustainable products. Companies can compare and identify ingredient alternatives, track progress against their goals and against industry benchmarks and key competitors.

Its '*Impact Spectrum*' helps companies across the food industry gain a more holistic perspective on their impacts, supporting decision making towards more regenerative outcomes. On the negative end of the spectrum are damaging, extractive, oppressive and/or abusive practices. The mid-point represents a 'net-zero' perspective, that doesn't cause harm but also doesn't benefit. The positive end of the spectrum doesn't just avoid harm, but it also improves and develops positive social and environmental impacts of the product's production.

HowGood's approach is focused on accelerating network effects across the entire food system. Facilitating the following for one business increases the value of this information for others.

- **Agreeing on common metrics** to support regenerative agriculture is a foundational step for shifting the incentives and economics underpinning our food system. Common metrics help guide education and build farmers' incomes by providing 'ecosystem services' (aligned with metrics).[21]

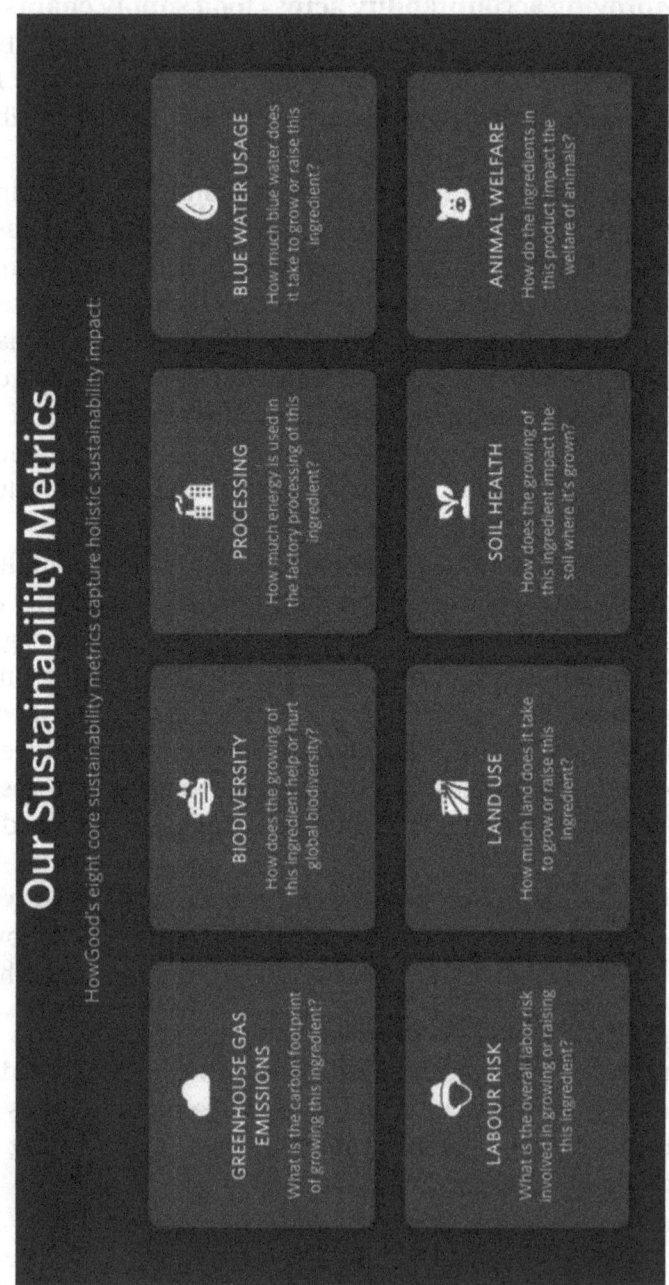

Figure 2.10   HowGood's core metrics.

- **Marketplace incentives.** Credits representing these services attract buyers across the value chain, from corporates, governments, investors and philanthropists, which creates mechanisms to share the cost of farmers' transitioning to regenerative agricultural practices.
- **Verifiability and trust.** Metrics alignment is also key for traceability and clear policy to ensure stakeholders can audit and validate claims, and to ensure farmers are rewarded for their practices.
- **Multi-sided/multi-stakeholder benefit.** Collectively this provides a way for suppliers and brand adopters alike to align food production with healthy outcomes from the land, farmers, customers and the bottom line. HowGood also focuses across the supply chain, from suppliers to retailers.
- **Platform accessibility.** The company prices its year-long contracts based on company size and needs, which makes the platform accessible for small businesses and emerging brands, not only large conglomerates.
- **B2B2C enablement.** In addition to the brand equity and marketing opportunities these metrics help substantiate, HowGood also offers a free app for consumers, also called HowGood, where they can scan product barcodes to access information about product sustainability. Such transparency helps empower consumers and drive more informed decision making while shopping, amidst an already booming increase in demands for sustainable products.[22]
- **Data and analytics.** HowGood's big data platform continues to grow and develop over time, improving both algorithms and incorporating the latest science, new data for category expansion and to incorporate geographic standards, and learnings to improve metrics and applicability in localized contexts.

Consider the network effects on the broader food system if the world's leading food/ag brands, such as Danone, Mondelez, PepsiCo and Bayer centred these metrics in their value chains and supported their supply chains to achieve them (Figure 2.11). They

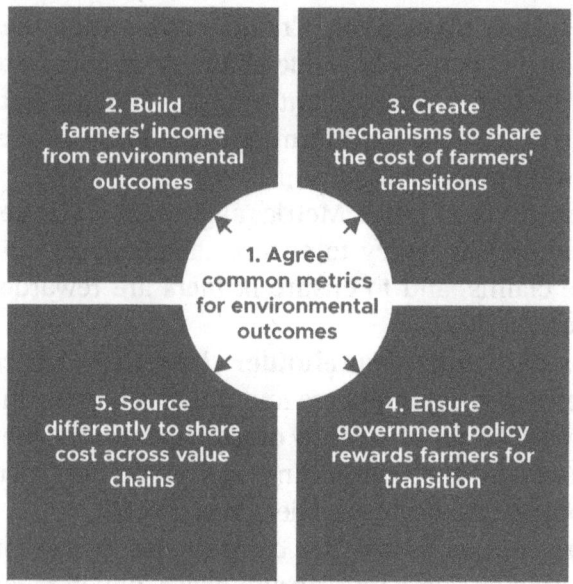

Figure 2.11 Network effects on the food system.

are all working alongside HowGood in the Sustainable Markets Agribusiness Taskforce. At the time of writing, HowGood counts 5 of the top 10 global consumer product companies as customers. It also plans to expand this model into apparel, cleaning supplies, and beauty, claiming a total addressable market of over $16 billion.[23]

Industries: agriculture, food/beverages, hospitality, chemicals
Parties: business-to-business
Platform benefits: brand equity, big data and analytics, standards/verification, innovation
Network effects: data, indirect, multi-sided, incentive, same group
Regenerative principles: views wealth holistically, in right relationship, seeks balance
Regenerative value: soil health, animal health, human health, farmer health, business health

EXAMPLE 3: Materiom's biotech platform analyses nature's building blocks to accelerate commercialization of bio-based materials. With open data and AI, Materiom empowers scientists, material developers and brands to accelerate R&D in the shift from petrochemical-based products to bio-based products.

The challenge: Fossil-derived materials and petrochemical-based products are fundamentally undermining our health, our ecosystems, and humanity's ability to sustain ourselves and our economy on earth. Yet these plastics and chemicals are pervasive across industries worldwide, from packaging and electronics to healthcare, construction, paints, fertilizers, adhesives and far beyond, accounting for millions of tons in annual production. The need is not only to recycle them, but to limit their production in the first place, and replace highly extractive materials with renewably sourced materials that don't compromise on performance and safety.

> *For billions of years, plants and animals have evolved to make materials with a particular set of ingredients that other organisms know how to source, use, breakdown, and use again. It's time we took notes.*

(Materiom)

The platform gathers and analyses big data on renewable feedstocks and abundant sources of natural biomass, like mycelium, seaweed or agricultural byproducts. Using 'green chemistry' (i.e. life-friendly) principles, Materiom screens materials to assess biodegradability, nutrient value, and sustainable sourcing practices based on their ingredients and processing. Its AI-powered service helps material-science researchers accelerate experimentation and modelling to more rapidly source and optimize biopolymers to create bio-based 'recipes' for specific material performance needs. The platform also helps designers tailor materials towards specific product niches, customer requirements, circularity and localization.

Materiom enables global access through its open data commons, further accelerating R&D. By open-sourcing the

latest peer-reviewed data, recipes and knowledge across its collaborative community of over 5,000 members, Materiom also helps
accelerate materials development and go-to-market, while lowering
barriers to entry in materials markets around the world. Its commitment extends to the use of FAIR data principles – making data
findable, accessible, interoperable and reusable – to ensure everyone, everywhere, can make use of open data to build a regenerative
materials economy.

**The platform also ensures regional contexts and com-
munities are not harmed by new recipes.** Materiom uses
sourcing analytics to ensure that recipes are designed to prevent
over-extraction in any specific locality. It works with companies,
cities and communities to support the development of local bioma-
terial supply chains that nourish local ecologies and economies.

**The platform's potential for network effects is signifi-
cant given that plastics are used across dozens of industries.**
Breakthroughs in one industry could rapidly accelerate biomate-
rial innovations in another. Electronics packaging could inspire
another in automotive interiors, a recipe for extreme temperature
stability in aerospace, may translate well into construction. Materiom could help accelerate this through its marketplace, which
already matches material developers and consumer goods' companies based on performance and procurement requirements.
Industry consortia or supply chain partners could partner to
accelerate R&D in plastic alternatives and develop shared equity
models like in the pharmaceutical space, only in this case, incen-
tivized *towards renewable materials*.

Industries: material science, chemicals, manufacturing, plastics
Parties: business-to-business, research/developer-to-business
Platform benefits: discovery, big data and analytics, standards/
    verification, innovation
Network effects: direct, indirect, data, multi-sided, same group
Regenerative principles: in right relationship, seeks balance,
    empowered participation, honours place and community
Regenerative value: supply chain health, human health, business
    health, data health

Key Emerging Technologies for Network Effects

- **AI** across numerous applications to support data analysis, greater 'ESG' and health accountability, optimizing processes and relationships; 'regenerative AI' as an orientation for training models.
- **Digital wallets** for enabling easier access to digital marketplaces and cross-jurisdiction transactions and interactions.
- **Online learning tools and assistants** to foster awareness, skill development, ease onboarding.

Coordination and collaboration

Digital platform business models enable coordination and collaboration among stakeholders by providing a centralized medium for interaction and shared governance. Platforms like Slack, for instance, help businesses collaborate internally and across other businesses. Additionally, marketplace platforms support coordination by hosting governance regimes such as identity and transaction verifications, certifications and ratings, supply chain transparency and regulatory compliance. Through these mechanisms, platforms play an integral role in fostering trust across disparate stakeholders, breaking down traditional geographic, transparency or access barriers, and allowing otherwise untrusting parties to collaborate, exchange and collectively drive innovation.

Types of Coordination & Collaboration

1. Across buyers – sellers – suppliers – other stakeholders
2. Identity verifications

(continued)

(continued)
   3. Transaction verifications
   4. Product/service certifications
   5. Supply chain transparency (provenance, labour, sourcing)
   6. Shared storage and security
   7. Regulatory compliance
   8. Communications and meetings
   9. Project management and co-creation
   10. Shared governance

Though many successful platform business models offer these capabilities today, consolidation of platforms has come at the cost of asymmetries in power, influence, access and data. For example, when a few decision makers running a large, centralized platform decide on a policy or product change or overlook a security risk, millions of people and businesses are impacted, sometimes to ruinous effect. A global reaction has emerged against this fundamental imbalance and hyper centralization of BigTech (and other industries) in the form of the blockchain-based 'Web3' movement. This movement harbours an ethos of decentralization, seeking to use distributed ledger technologies to decentralize data, compute, decision-making (i.e. power), while enabling new models for cooperation and coordination. Of course, *tools are only part of the coordination and collaboration story – coordinating humans' intentions and aligning incentives is the fertile ground for regenerative innovation.*

We can harness digital platforms to drive coordination and collaboration in *service of healthy relationships*. How can we design platform business models *to help steward* 'right relationships' and among stakeholders, communities and environments in which they operate? To drive collaboration and interconnections across disciplines, sectors, cultures and contexts? To value holistic forms of wealth by valuing what is not priced in?

In the following examples, we will analyse both blockchain-based and other digital platform businesses that are facilitating coordination of new models of governance and accountability, asset sharing and even capital. These examples all harness platform marketplace models for improving the circulation of ideas, materials and energy, coordinating stakeholders in ways that align economic with societal benefit.

Digital Platforms Exemplifying Regenerative Potential through Coordination & Collaboration

EXAMPLE 1: BackMarket, Gitcoin, Savvy Cooperative
BackMarket's digital marketplace for refurbished electronics helps coordinate stakeholders to close the loop on e-waste and open up access to reliable tech for all. The platform connects buyers and sellers of smartphones, laptops, TVs, wearables, gaming, e-mobility and countless other devices from all the leading manufacturers.

The challenge: Technology manufacturers have long prioritized planned and perceived obsolescence as part of their business models, contributing to the 54 million metric tons of e-waste generated annually.[24] When this waste is burned or dumped in landfill, it has toxic impacts on the human and environmental health of these communities, often in West Africa or Asia. The cycle of investing in new, or settling for lower quality or no access, has also exacerbated the digital divide between technology have and have-nots.

BackMarket is using its digital platform to coordinate stakeholders around a solution that is both sustainable and cost effective, converting this massive global challenge into an opportunity. Promising '*better than new*', it partners with certified refurbishers to repair electronics for resale, at a ~70% lower price than new.

- **Coordinates the marketplace,** enabling discovery, connecting buyers and sellers from different regions, and managing partners to refurbish products.
- **Coordinates trustworthy re-sell**, working with certified refurbishers to conduct stringent 25+ point verification of

authenticity, functionality, security, data erasure, battery, testing, cleaning, and more; resold with a 12-month warranty protection, ratings and reviews, and responsive customer support.
- **Coordinates secure payment and logistics**, ensuring that transactions are conducted safely, transparent tracking, protecting both buyers and sellers from fraud.
- **Coordinates with manufacturers** to provide a marketplace for branded shopping experiences of their pre-owned devices.

As a result the platform enables compounding benefits across stakeholders (Figure 2.12).

- **Consumers benefit** from lower prices without sacrificing device performance, discovery beyond their local market, and enjoy warranty, customer service, and cash for trade-in. Additional discounts for students and military.
- **Environment benefits.** Refurbishing electronics contributes to the reduction of electronic waste, lowers carbon emissions associated with manufacturing new devices, and conserves valuable natural resources. It claims to have averted 1 million tons of CO_2 emissions.[25]
- **Societal benefits** of increasing accessibility to quality devices, reducing health consequences of communities impacted by mining and landfill.
- **Manufacturers benefit** by extending product lifespan, contributing to the circular economy, reduced Scope 3 emissions, and improved brand equity.

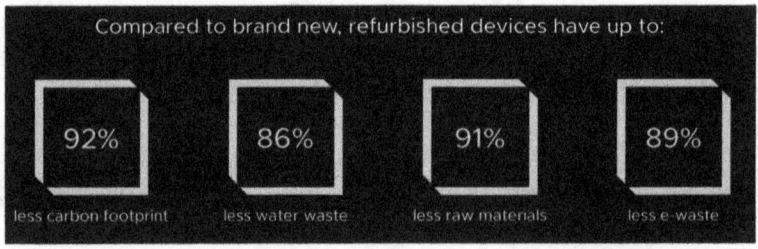

Figure 2.12   Refurbished devices' benefits.

- **Refurbishing partners benefit** through increased demand for refurbished devices, growth in circular economy.
- **BackMarket benefits,** taking a 10% share off the refurbished sale price, and hosts direct brand partnerships. The company reached a valuation of $5.7 billion in 2022 after raising $510 million in a Series E funding round. It is operating in 17 countries at the time of writing.[26]

In BackMarket's own journey to become a B-Corp, it has instituted itself as a purpose-driven organization, forming a steering committee to ensure it fulfils its purpose: 'to empower people to make machines last through circularity and repair'.

Industries: electronics, technology, mobility
Parties: business-to-business, peer-to-peer, business-to-consumer
Platform benefits: discovery, standards/verification, cost efficiencies, brand equity, innovation
Coordination: across disparate stakeholders, transaction verification, product certification, compliance
Regenerative principles: robust circulation, empowered participation, in right relationship
Regenerative value: supply chain health, human health, business health, environmental health

EXAMPLE 2: Gitcoin is a crowdfunding and collaboration platform that coordinates stakeholders to fund and innovate open source and digital public goods. Through blockchain-enabled infrastructure, it empowers communities and entrepreneurs to fund digital tooling for the commons, without having to rely solely on big donors.

The challenge: Open-source projects and public goods generally, while critical for accessibility, community and collaborative innovation, are often underfunded. Though some businesses have built highly successful businesses off open source, most businesses instinctually select proprietary product models. This results in a model in which talented developers – employed during the day – tend to volunteer their hours to open source unpaid, and during off-hours.

Gitcoin's platform coordinates stakeholders across the ecosystem to submit ideas, vote on ideas, contribute funds, tokenize capital, collaborate on projects and allocate those funds digitally. It uses blockchain, smart contracts and application programming interfaces (APIs) to anchor traceability of funds, to manage permissions, privacy and identity and reputation management, and to help secure projects from bots and bad actors. The platform also enables quadratic funding,[27] a fancy term for using a unique mathematical formula that rewards funds based on the number of people who have donated, not only donation size. In effect, this prioritizes projects with a broad appeal from many funding parties over those with similar liquidity but reliant on fewer larger donors.

It aligns the needs and incentives of developers, donors and those wishing to support the development of digital public goods. Developers have an incentive to work on more than just the most-well-funded projects and earn cryptocurrency rewards for their contributions to open-source, while small donors can support the projects they regard as most worthwhile. Additionally, Gitcoin is a community owned and governed platform – a Decentralized Autonomous Organization (DAO, in Web3 parlance) – in which token holders select platform stewards and delegates to guide the direction of the platform. The community also offers educational resources and technologies focused on the development of digital public infrastructure.

Enabling both coordination and collaboration, Gitcoin is helping fund open source and scale broader decentralized web innovations by providing a platform for a community of donors and developers, and attracting other organizations to join. Since its founding in 2016, Gitcoin's grants programme has distributed over $50 million through 3.8 million unique donations to early-stage builders championing 3,700+ projects across open source software, decentralized finance, climate, community engagement and other digital public goods. It has also partnered with organizations like the World Health Organization, the Internet Archive, and the Electronic Frontier Foundation to support open source innovations for digital public goods infrastructure.

Industries: technology, finance, international development
Parties: peer-to-peer, entrepreneur-to-organization
Platform benefits: discovery, standards/verification, cost efficien-
cies, resource utilization, innovation
Coordination: across disparate stakeholders, identity, transaction
verification, transparency, compliance, shared governance
Regenerative principles: robust circulation, empowered partici-
pation, views wealth holistically
Regenerative value: innovation health, entrepreneurial health,
business health, digital ecosystem health

**EXAMPLE 3: Savvy Cooperative is a digital marketplace con-
necting patients with healthcare providers, to collaborate on
and be compensated for innovating patient-first solutions.**
Patients and their loved ones can share their experiences and inputs
directly with healthcare professionals conducting research, testing
prototypes, creating campaigns and more.

The challenge: Healthcare experiences are not always pleas-
ant, to put it mildly. Healthcare providers have also overlooked,
undervalued or struggled to reach patient populations to improve
and innovate. On top of financial and access issues – not to mention chronic illness suffering – this creates yet more challenges for
patients and further taxes the patient–provider relationship.

'The Match.com **of patient insights',** Savvy connects patients
to a wide range of professionals across clinical research, digital
health, hospital systems, insurance companies, pharmaceuticals,
medical devices and nonprofits. They facilitate several interactions
across patients and companies:

- The platform posts an ongoing feed of 'gigs', to which patients
  can apply.
- Coordinates candidates with companies for selection and
  introduction
- Platform-hosted workshops
- Manages direct and referral compensations, in multiple countries
- Maintains data compliance
- Fosters collaboration around both common and rare diseases,
  sourcing people from diverse backgrounds

Savvy is also a cooperative, meaning patients can become co-op members, and share partial ownership of the organization. They also have a vote in Savvy's decisions and direction, and share in its annual profits. This doesn't just provide a source of income, but also a sense of purpose, co-innovating solutions from which others can benefit.

Industries: healthcare, pharmaceuticals, insurance
Parties: business-to-business, business-to-consumer
Platform benefits: discovery, standards/verification, cost efficien-
   cies, brand equity, innovation
Coordination: collaboration, across disparate stakeholders,
   transaction verification, product certification, transparency,
   compliance
Regenerative principles: robust circulation, empowered partici-
   pation, in right relationship
Regenerative value: human health, business health

Key Emerging Technologies for Coordination and Collaboration

- **Blockchain** for encoding transaction intermediation, decentralized methods of funding, traceability, and computation, distributed autonomous organizations (DAOs).
- **Tokenization** for developing new assets and incentives, to create market value and coordinate stakeholders to restore undervalued resources.
- **Digital twins and digital passports** for replicating real-world entities or identities, to streamline collaboration in design, traceability, multi-party monetization models, product innovation.
- **AI and computer vision** for more easily processing physical goods in a marketplace, such as waste-sorting, or using augmented reality for real-world identification.

Access and localization

Digital platforms are a critical tool for promoting access and localization by breaking down geographical barriers and adapting their offerings to meet the specific needs and preferences of local communities. For instance, educational platforms like Coursera offer courses from universities worldwide, granting learners access to quality education from renowned institutions regardless of their location. Platforms like Alibaba, eBay or Etsy enable local artisans and businesses to reach global markets. But technology platforms have tended to apply technical approaches to localization, such as language translation or payment methods, rather than enabling local communities to *localize the value of digital services* to their own contexts.

Types of access and localization

1. Offering digital resources or infrastructure to be locally designed and applied
2. Enabling cultural expression, recognizing cultural significance
3. Offering local resources, service matching
4. Calibrating to suit connectivity or computational variations
5. Ensuring tools are accessible for disabled or demographic-specific participation
6. Empower personal agency around data, privacy and digital safety
7. Facilitating environmental restoration and bioregional needs
8. Enhancing well-being of individuals and communities
9. Stimulating local economic health
10. Acknowledging and bridging socioeconomic disparities

While platforms can foster accessibility to resources, services and markets, many large platforms have deprioritized localization in their quest for scale, enabling access but failing to tailor services, governance or value models to local markets and bioregions. Furthermore, access to reliable enough internet for people to take advantage of digital services is still unavailable for some 40% of the world's population, according to a 2022 study by the Alliance for Affordable Internet.[28] Thus, by focusing on scale over local enablement, platform businesses risk further alienating the digitally disenfranchised, and exacerbating inequities.

We can harness digital platforms to improve access and to centre bioregional and cultural contexts in the development of the digital economy. How can we design platform business models to empower participation, to honour community and place, and seek balance between local and global dynamics? In the following examples, we will analyse how the scalability, access and technological enablement that platforms provide can empower local economies and accelerate innovation *in the local context*. These examples all harness platforms to empower local populations with greater agency, participation and share in the value exchanges the platform enables.

Digital Platforms Exemplifying Regenerative Potential of Localization

EXAMPLE 1: Regen Network is a global marketplace and contracting platform for local communities working together to incentivize ecosystem regeneration. It provides tools and infrastructure to create, track and trade digital ecological assets called ecocredits, which represent verified ecological benefits, such as carbon sequestration, biodiversity restoration, and water quality improvement.

The challenge: In the face of climate change, biodiversity loss and land degradation, our economies have not 'priced in' or agreed upon asset classes that reflect or can incentivize ecological restoration.

As a result, current economic models incentivize land degradation and fuel climate change. While many organizations are willing to invest in carbon credits or other types of restoration to support their sustainability commitments, a broader market for 'ecological benefits' remains nascent. As in the carbon market, issues remain around the difficulties of measuring, tracking and standardizing ecological impacts, as well as the transparency and traceability of them. This market is essential for incentivizing ecological restoration and using market forces to incentivize it.

By verifying positive changes and providing rewards for ecological regeneration, Regen Network enables contracting and agreement on the valuation of regenerating natural assets, such as forests, biodiversity, waterways and grasslands. Because different bioregions have different ecological needs and challenges, Regen Network is designed to support localization in a number of ways:

- **Provides a modular platform** that can be customized to meet the specific needs of different bioregions. For example, a bioregion may want to develop its own set of ecological standards or create a different approach to issuing ecocredits.
- **Works closely with local communities, land stewards and organizations** to develop and implement ecocredit projects. This helps to ensure that the benefits and monetization of ecological regeneration are shared equitably and that the projects are aligned with the needs of the local community.
- **Develops tools and resources to help local communities localize the Regen Network platform.** For example, it is developing a library of localized ecological standards and a toolkit for developing and implementing ecocredit projects.
- **Develops educational resources and training programmes** to help local and scientific research communities learn about and use the Regen Network platform and advance scientifically rigorous methodologies and credit standards for ecological regeneration.

- **Translates the Regen Network platform into multiple languages** to make it more accessible to people around the world.
- **Promotes community governance** of the blockchain protocol.

Regen Network has the potential to play a major role in promoting localization and ecological regeneration around the world (Figure 2.13). The platform anchors ecological data on the Regen Ledger blockchain, ensuring transparency and accountability and the proper issuance, transfer and retirement of credits. It has worked on projects covering over 15 million hectares of land and has more than 40 methodologies under development, with a marketplace that connects 'retail' investors and corporate buyers and brands.

Industries: agriculture, food, finance
Parties: business-to-business, nonprofit-to-business, organization-to-markets

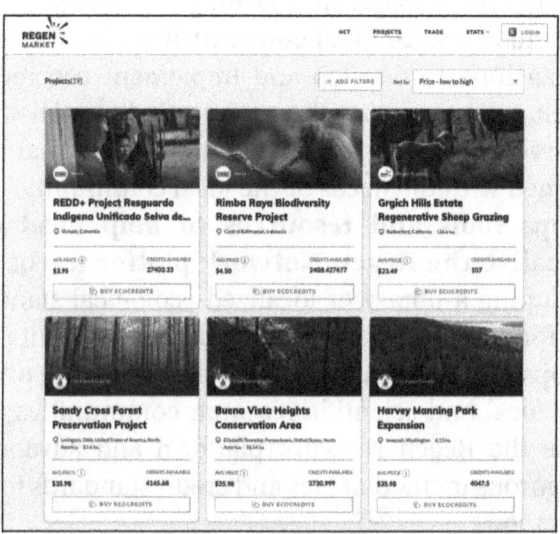

Figure 2.13 Regen Network projects and ecocredits.

Platform benefits: discovery, standards/verification, network effects, brand equity, innovation

Localization: stimulating local economies, bioregional restoration, bridging disparities, local resources, digital infrastructure, language translation

Regenerative principles: views wealth holistically, empowered participation, in right relationship, honours place and community, edge effect abundance

Regenerative value: environmental health, community health, human health, business health

EXAMPLE 2: Fairbnb is a short-term rental marketplace and cooperative that recirculates value within the communities it serves. Like Airbnb, Fairbnb's sharing economy platform enables digital search, discovery, booking, host verification and liability oversight for tourists, and has simple user interfaces and comparable pricing. Where Fairbnb diverges is in the design of its business, operating and platform model, to ensure positive impact on the communities it serves by recirculating economic resources locally, promoting and funding local projects and initiatives *with every booking*.

The challenge: The sharing economy platform aims to correct the extractive practices and asymmetries that have harmed many communities with the explosive growth of Airbnb. The Silicon Valley giant has enabled unsustainable levels of tourism at the expense (literally) of local communities, while skirting local taxes and requests to share data with local councils. Its promotion of large commercial 'super users' and landlords has resulted in their domination of local markets, driving up premium prices for short-term tenants year-round. This hasn't just sped up gentrification but created even greater barriers for affordable housing for locals and long-term tenants, fragmented communities and closed local businesses. In effect, local economies have not reaped the benefit of local tourism.

Fairbnb's model takes 50% of all platform fees and reinvests them back into local social and environmental or community projects or not-for-profit organizations, which are chosen by each city's respective hosts, travellers and locals. As a cooperative, collective ownership of the Fairbnb platform means it is owned by those who use it and are impacted by its use, such as hosts, guests, local business owners and neighbours. It is governed by citizens and works with 'Local Nodes' to define rules to protect each neighbourhood and keep profits within communities (Figure 2.14). Democratic governance makes Fairbnb a space where community members can work together and collectively decide how the platform will be run in their neighbourhood. This approach also invites local projects, B-Corps, Associations, and others onto the platform, which hosts a social network that connects experts, change makers and key partners to find new business opportunities.

Transparency and accountability are essential for Fairbnb to sustain its differentiation at scale. They are committed to open data and compliance with local and regional legislation balanced with the privacy and security needs of platform members, and work with local governments to promote regulations that encourage sustainable tourism. The platform is operational across all of Europe, the United Kingdom and is expanding into Canada.

Industries: travel, hospitality

Parties: business-to-business, peer-to-peer, nonprofit-to-business

Platform benefits: discovery, standards/verification, network effects, brand equity, innovation

Localization: stimulating local economies, bridging disparities, local resources, digital infrastructure, language translation, service-matching

Regenerative principles: empowered participation, honours place and community, robust circulation

Regenerative value: community health, business health, nonprofit health

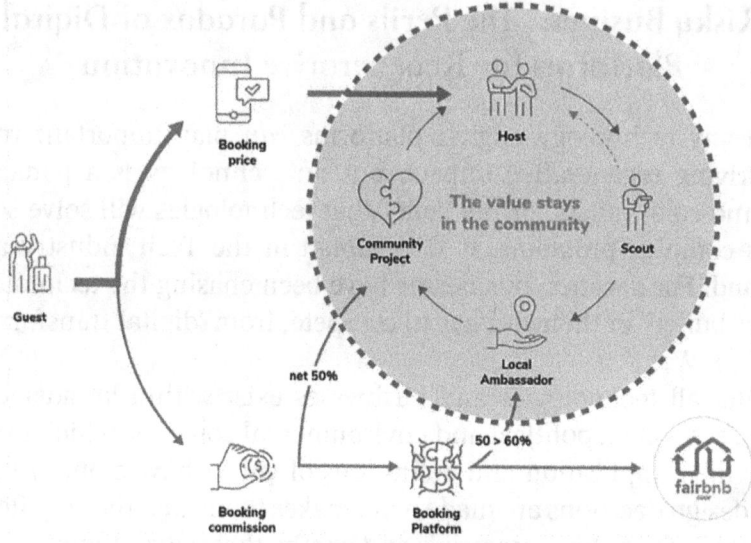

Figure 2.14   Fairbnb ensures value stays in the community.

Key emerging technologies for access and localization

- **Internet of Things sensors, devices or microgrids** to enable more local compute power and local networks in areas with unreliable network bandwidth or transmission.
- **AI for language translation and assistive tech** to enable more demographics to access and engage with digital platforms and services, i.e. speech recognition, text-to-speech, closed captioning, low-power devices.
- **Satellite imagery and analysis** for supporting regional opportunities, such as in land restoration.

Risky Business: The Perils and Paradox of Digital Platforms for Regenerative Innovation

Like any technology, digital platforms *can* play important roles in driving regenerative impact, but no technology is a panacea. Techno-solutionism, or the belief that technologies will solve society's complex problems, is widespread in the Tech industry and beyond. For decades, businesses have been chasing the technology silver bullets in their hunger to compete, from 'digital transformation' to 'Web3'.

But all technologies and businesses exist within broader cultural, economic, political and environmental contexts, which influence their application and definitions of value, how monetization and design decisions are made, who makes them, and the very flows of data, information, materials and energy that power them.

The peril is in seeing digital platforms as the ticket to regenerative innovation, rather than an element in a broader ecology of what is needed to bring about systemic change. As outlined earlier, the mindset of people – investors, business leaders, builders and designers, and users – is the more transformative element than the tools, as it guides how we adopt and apply them.

Even the best intentions can have unintended consequences. Two examples we can learn from as we apply digital platforms for regeneration include scale and Jevon's paradox. Scalability, or the objective to increase growth has been a core goal of many digital platform businesses to date. So-called 'blitz-scaling' is a term referring to the recommended start-up tactic to dominate markets by prioritizing speed over all else, risk-taking in the face of uncertainties, and 'acquiring' users over monetization. In other words, *growth at all costs*. But optimizing for unbridled scale over all other objectives also carries second and third order negative effects. Examples include:

- *Ethical breaches*, where rapid growth can compromise on ethics, compliance or safety standards, such as around privacy, security, worker exploitation or public health;

- *Financial instability*, where overlooking a sustainable monetization model can lead to bankruptcy, negatively impacting investors, employees and communities;
- *Power asymmetry*, where monopolization stifles healthy competition, limits choice, impacts prices and thwarts innovation;
- *Community disruption*, undermining local economies, such as in infrastructure, housing, displacement or community engagement; or in cultural traditions where large corporations impose homogenized products or one-size-fits-all services.

Scaling is critical to the transformations needed to align our economies with a liveable planet and healthy society, from the circular economy to electrification. But here is where striking the balance between scaling *up* versus scaling *out* is essential, i.e. harnessing the 'global' efficiencies and transferability of digital platforms, with 'local' context-specific flexibility and binding mechanisms.

Another complexity underlying digital platforms is Jevon's paradox, the phenomenon where technological improvements in resource efficiency lead to increased consumption – not conservation – of that resource. Oil refineries, cars, appliances, and industrial processes have all exemplified Jevon's paradox, whereby efficiency gains achieved through these innovations did not reduce demand for energy, rather reduced costs encouraged higher usage, stimulating greater economic activity and resource utilization. In the context of environmental sustainability and community impacts, digital platforms and their underlying orbit of hardware, software, storage and AI spell significant computation, heat, emissions, water, electronic waste and land use. The IEA and MIT predict that by 2030, data centres could devour up to 21% of the world's total electricity supply, up from 1–1.5% currently.[29] And this energy consumption is not to mention whatever product or service activities platforms themselves help scale.

Inevitably, new consequences and implications will continue to emerge with the next generation of digital platforms, just as they have with the previous generation. Already, a whole new class of digital rights and regulations, ethical considerations, economic models and technological innovations have materialized as responses to the downsides of the first generation of digital platforms.

From Flywheel to Adaptive Cycle: A Framework for Regenerative Innovation with Platforms

We know digital platforms can be powerful catalysts for change, because they have already had enormous material and cultural impacts on how we connect, shop, consume media, engage politically and more. But the advent of digital platforms has also had significant downsides and extractive harms on individuals, communities, businesses and the planet.

The fundamental question this chapter seeks to pose is *how we can (re)harness these technologies to realign our economics with the planet and a healthy society?* How can positive network effects, coordination and collaboration across stakeholders, and empowered localization and access help:

- increase citizen/consumer awareness and influence to drive social innovation;
- inspire and accelerate business transformation, investor interest, and political will; and
- create new incentives and reframe competitive dynamics, metrics and asset classes?

The fundamental shift regeneration invites from businesses is shifting from focusing narrowly on the businesses' own success to *focusing on the relationships* the business creates and on whose health it is reliant. Relationships – with diverse stakeholders both inside and outside organizations – are what enable adaptability and resilience.

To apply the platform opportunity to regenerative innovation, we propose a rethinking of the infamous 'Platform Flywheel' to instead embrace the ecological patterns of the Adaptive Cycle (Figure 2.15). The Adaptive Cycle represents dynamic stages of change in complex systems. Just as organisms and systems adapt and evolve, platforms can as well. Systems experience four phases:

1. Growth and development
2. Conservation and stability
3. Release and disruption
4. Reorganization and the emergence of new structures

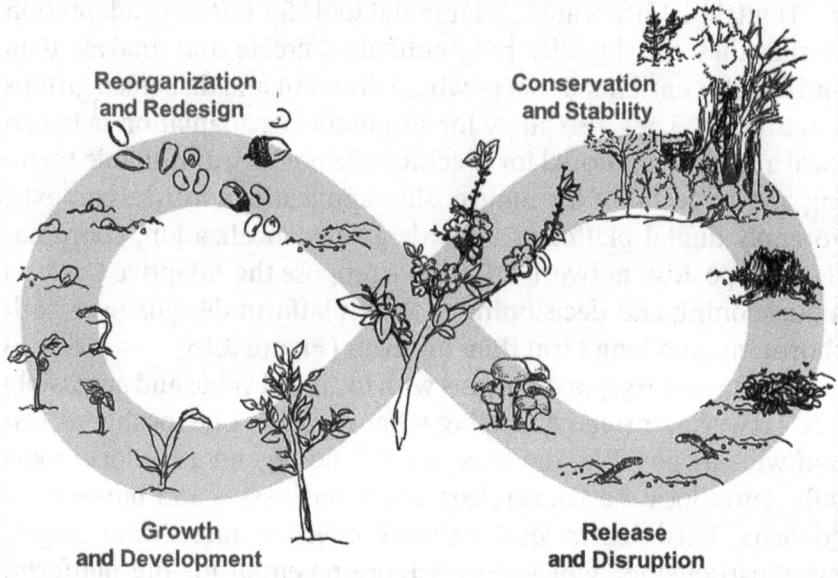

Figure 2.15 The Adaptive Cycle.

The adaptive cycle represents relationships by highlighting the *feedback loops* and *interconnectivity* between an organism (or organization), the elements that influence it, and its response and subsequent development. As the system evolves, *existing relationships transform* and *new ones emerge*, playing a pivotal role in determining the system's resilience, adaptability and capacity to innovate.

This forms a continuous cycle or infinite loop of adaptation and evolution – of growth and stability, stability and change, breakdown and reorganization, innovation and growth.

This cycle exists across multiple scales – small/local, regional and large/global – as well as different cycle speeds, slow and fast. Events at one scale can have cascading effects on other scales. For example, a local environmental disturbance can impact regional ecosystems, which in turn affect the global climate.

Digital platforms are fundamental tools for business adaptation in that they are digitally programmable, create and analyse data and enable centralized spaces where different and dispersed groups can interact. They also allow for simultaneous adaptation between local and global, tailored for specific stakeholders, and enable tracking and traceability for repurposing applications in like contexts. To apply digital platforms towards greater localization, coordination and positive network effects, we propose the Adaptive Cycle as a questioning and decisioning tool for platform designs over both short-term and long-term time intervals (Figure 2.16).

Platform *development* begins with localized value and accessible UX. However, instead of scaling what works in one locality as fast and wide as possible, the most viable and regenerative local tools will centre local needs, services, small businesses and bioregional contexts. This creates local network effects – more value begets more participants, which begets more potential for the platform. This drives development and growth of the platform, and greater facility to extend those network effects for other localities.

More participants, use cases and localities also create more need for platform-level coordination and collaboration, to be able to sustain the *stability* of the system, and drive greater network effects across multiple communities and organizations. This is where regenerative platforms can *cultivate the conditions to enable ecosystem innovation*. In other words, how can the platform facilitate multiple disparate parties to more effectively coordinate and collaborate to drive regenerative benefit?

Of course, platforms don't exist in a vacuum, but are constantly influenced by the infinite potential for change and *disruption*. In the near-term sense, platforms must constantly respond to user needs or pains. But these can also be significant disruptions like a new regulation, conflict or catastrophe on the ground in a locality. There can also be even greater existential destruction the platform must contend with, such as the urgent need for a new business model or a cybersecurity breach.

Regenerative Innovation 69

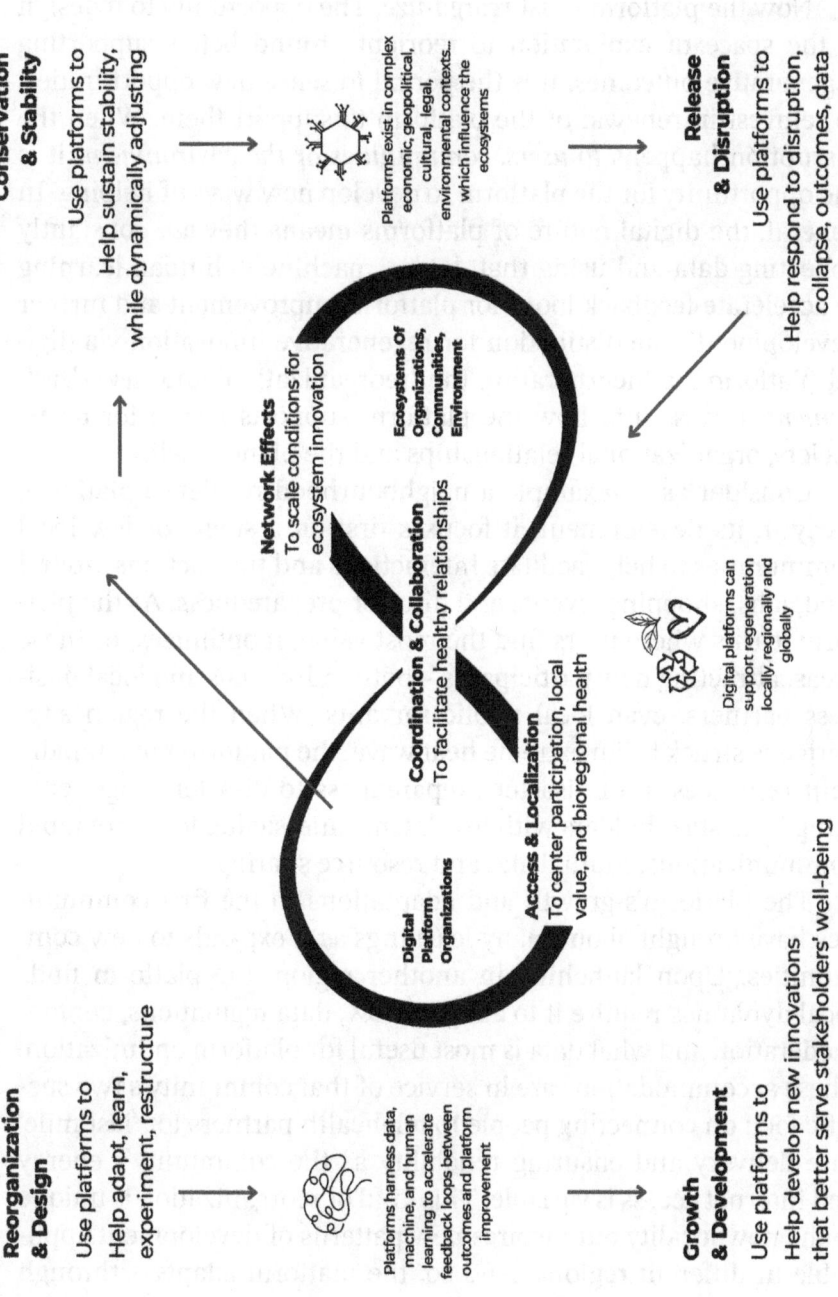

Figure 2.16 Tools for adaptation: how digital platforms enable localization, coordination and network effects.

Now the platform must *reorganize*. The opportunity to redesign is the space of exploration to reorient around better supporting regenerative outcomes. It is the period to sense new opportunities, to reinvest in renewal of the platform to support them. When the disruption happens *to users, communities or the environment,* it is the opportunity for the platform to develop new ways of helping. In general, the digital nature of platforms means they are constantly collecting data and using that data + machine + human learning to accelerate feedback loops for platform improvement and further development. The distinction for regenerative innovation via digital platforms is incorporating the 'reorganization' and *new development* process into how the platform supports health for users, society, organizational relationships and the planet itself.

Consider as an example a neighbourhood resilience platform. Early in its development, it focuses first on a single or few local communities to help facilitate interactions and transactions around food, jobs, shopping, events and disaster preparedness. As the platform learns where users find the most value, it optimizes for those areas, attracting new participants – both individuals and local business partners, even local public servants. When the region supported is struck by an extreme heat wave, the platform must rapidly shift resources from disaster preparedness to disaster triage, enabling local stakeholders with low latency messaging for more rapid communications, mutual aid, and resource sharing.

The platform's growth and adaptations in the first communities have brought about many learnings as it expands to new communities. Upon launching in another region, the platform finds local dynamics require it to adapt its UX, data regulations, content moderation and what data is most useful for platform optimization. These accommodations are in service of that community's two specific foci: on connecting people to telehealth partners for 'last mile' care delivery and ensuring reliability as the community's energy and internet access is variable. This kind of reorganization is unique to the new locality but inspires new patterns of development applicable in different regions. And so, the platform adapts – through data, machine and human learning – to accelerate feedback loops between needs, outcomes and platform improvement.

Platform practitioners may question the difference between this framework and the oft-cited 'flywheel effect'. In a business context, a 'flywheel effect' is adapted from a mechanical flywheel's ability to store and release energy. It is a commonly cited framework for platform businesses to explain the momentum gained by persistent efforts to align all areas of the platform around core business goals, like delivering a better customer experience, expanding market share or optimizing revenues.

Whereas the flywheel represents a tool of momentum, the adaptive cycle represents a process of transformation and innovation.

Key Questions to Ask:

- How are our organization's strategic decisions incorporating regenerative principles into digital platform design, investment, partnership, supply chain?
- How is our digital platform enabling co-benefits or cascading benefits?
- What value is created for all stakeholders, e.g. customers, civilians, employees, communities, leadership, shareholders, partners, suppliers, government, land stewards, animals, nature and so on, as a function of this platform? And how do our key performance indicators reflect multiple forms of capital (financial capital, natural/living capital, intellectual capital, social capital, and so on)?
- How is platform data (strategy, collection, circulation, governance, intelligence, ethics, compliance, monetization, and so on) supporting our capacity for adaptation and regenerative business practices?
- How are our product / service roadmaps designed for adaptation (when inevitably, things shift and disruptions require course-change)?

Conclusion

You never change things by fighting the existing reality. To change something, build a new model that makes the existing model obsolete.

(Buckminster Fuller)

A new model is in sight. The forces influencing businesses of the twenty-first century are an invitation to innovate, to realign business with social and planetary health and harness technologies to do so.

We have the tools. The transformative potential of digital platforms holds great promise for regenerative innovation: to support network effects that create the conditions for systemic change; to help coordination and collaboration across diverse stakeholders; and to centre localization and empowered participation in the development of the digital economy. Reimagining how we apply platform models, we can repurpose their technological capabilities away from accelerating extraction and exploitation, and towards regenerating value, justice and health across ecosystems.

What we need is the will. Regenerative transformation in business and technology starts with the minds and hearts of people. Investors, leaders, entrepreneurs, designers, builders, growers, policymakers and the rest of us: each has a role in creating new models for generations to come.

Chapter 3
Thinking Like an AI Native

A Roadmap for Leaders and Businesses to Understand and Shape AI-Driven Businesses

Hari Abburi and Efi Pylarinou

The Advent of Digital Natives and Customer Centricity

As the world transitioned from linear industrial to digital-native businesses, a key argument by CEOs and Boards for the billions invested in transformations has been the pursuit of customer obsessed, experience-centric brands. Almost 18 years since the start of the Web 2.0 phase that has seen Uber, Amazon and Airbnb become part of our daily lexicon, many traditional linear or industrial companies continue to struggle with their digital transformation.

The fundamental shift in the recent digital transformation era originates from the deployment at scale of real-time data and smart analytics, enabling agile pricing and frequently launching new products and services based on customer-feedback loops. It has also allowed for the successful integration of B2C and B2B worlds into hybrid ecosystems or into successful D2C business models.

The digital-native world has been predominantly marked with the birth of platform business models that stake a claim to fame on offering unparalleled customer choice at a fraction of the cost of a traditional business. We do certainly live in a world where every company needs to think and act like a technology, data and platform business. This has led to almost 90% of the assets in S&P 500 companies becoming intangible.[1]

However, it has been more of a challenge for B2B businesses to adopt platform thinking and become D2C models to reduce costs and drive greater efficiencies to their customers. Most companies struggle to balance out their digital transformation between three key impact areas: Impact to customers, impact to ecosystem and impact to operations. The ability to invest in digital comes with finite resources – capital, talent and time. Companies like JP Morgan Chase with deep pockets and a long-term strategic vision from the CEO, have allocated and created focused service groups to build digitally native fintech products and services while transforming their traditional banking model. Their approach to innovation and digital transformation is not incremental but part of the company's strategy. In 2018, they created the Digital & Platform Services group; in 2020, they increased their IT budget by 25% to $12 billion; and in 2023, to over $15 billion.[2]

However, we have also seen companies continue to struggle to focus their investments to achieve the right customer outcomes. Bed Bath & Beyond (BBB) filed for bankruptcy in early 2023 even though they had declared success in their growth through digital just two years earlier saying, 'sales last year were driven by strong digital growth of 86%.[3] BBB focused much on omni-channel customer acquisition with limited or no focus on value to ecosystem or operations. Their app replicated the merchandise in the store but failed to transition customers from products to experiences thus replicating a transaction-based model onto an online version.

Another foundational layer of digital business models has been the ability to drive usage-based revenue that offers a longer customer revenue lifecycle as compared to a 'buy and bye' transaction. This is driven by 'SaaS' models that have helped businesses be more agile as the product development or feature development was done faster and better by specialist services firms than the company trying to build a technology platform from scratch.

The shift to subscriber-based revenue models has shown that best-in-class SaaS businesses grow over 100% each year and the top tier SaaS businesses reach $1 million ARR within 9 months.[4]

A powerful digital disruptor at the intersection of platforms and SaaS, is fintech. Fintech innovations bringing to market digital D2C capabilities have filled gaps that traditional financial providers could not fulfil and have created new customer experiences by successfully embedding financial services where the customer is.

Klarna, the pioneer of the 'Buy Now Pay Later' (BNPL) offering, is such an example. Founded in 2005 with a transaction at a Swedish bookshop called Poketklubben, it is today valued at US$6.7 billion.[5] Klarna created an entirely new segment of embedding unsecured lending in D2C e-commerce businesses and delivering an innovation of instalment payments at the point of sale. As a result, the Buy Now Pay Later landscape has grown since beyond D2C and globally with offerings online and in store, for SMEs and large enterprises and in various sectors beyond retail (e.g. healthcare).

Embedding financial services in non-financial businesses has huge potential and will continue to evolve beyond the BNPL unsecured credit case. The 'magic' can happen when the data from the customer experience of embedding financial services can be leveraged to create differentiated marketplaces or platforms. Klarna is such an example, as it has grown into a shopping marketplace with its own app and its embedded BNPL services.

Two key questions standout in understanding the journey to digital:

- Did mere aggregation of supply and demand fill a services gap to create growth or scale, or did platform business models really deliver customer centricity?
- If digital transformations created faster businesses but did not deliver customer centricity, where did these companies go wrong?

It is true that platform businesses can better aggregate a choice of services to a customer and, because of the technology foundation, they are able to morph faster and better to serve the ever-changing customer needs. This is the one key reason for all companies to think like a platform. The idea to build product lifecycle in a platform business is typically one-quarter of the time as compared to a traditional company. This ability on speed delivers a surprise element to customers and hence filling not just a service gap but also an experience gap.

In the pursuit of digital, many companies forget that it is a reimagination of their value to customers and business model. The true agility in digital comes from understanding that for a business to be at the speed of the customer, it needs to apply lateral thinking that cuts across industry boundaries, builds different or unfamiliar capabilities, reinvents work methods to serve the customer and uses design as a key driver of economic value.[6]

Repeatedly, we have seen companies spend on digital with mixed results. In many cases, we see digital just replicate an existing process or experience. They miss the opportunity to redesign the experience to the customer. As a result, we do have companies that have invested time, effort and money into digital and yet continue to operate in a linear business model. This is when the boards start to question the spending and the digital agenda is back to the drawing board.

We now see companies in five stages of transformation:

- Companies still in the initial stages of adopting digital
- Companies that have successfully delivered a digital transformation
- Companies that were born digital
- Companies embedding AI as co-pilot
- Companies that will now be born AI and digital

As we lay out the five dimensions of an AI native business in this chapter, a good starting point will be to understand the distinction between traditional businesses, digital natives, blockchain natives and AI natives.

Four Distinct Business Archetypes

Businesses are continuously evolving at accelerating rates. What we think of as traditional businesses today, were probably innovative in the 1970s (e.g. discount broker Charles Schwab, digital office equipment and leasing provider Xerox) or in 2000 (e.g. online broker E-Trade, retailer JC Penney with its catalogue business). As computers and programming evolved, software became an enabler to automate business processes. The shift from the analogue world to the digital world happened with the dozens of innovations in electronic hardware and software – programmable logic controllers, computers, digital cellular phones, microprocessors and the Internet.

We are now officially in the second decade of the Fourth Industrial Revolution (4IR).[7] All businesses of all sizes use computers, the Internet, tablets and cell phones and continuously strive to digitize their processes. Nowadays, we typically characterize a business as traditional if it was born before 2000, is struggling to integrate new technologies to its existing operations and still lacks the necessary customer-feedback loops.

Traditional businesses are increasingly focused on transforming towards a genuinely digital business, as the threat from the innovators and from traditional competitors who are advancing their digital transformation is intensifying. These transformation journeys have proven often to be complex, time-consuming and costly. Undoubtedly, replacing legacy systems, especially business-critical ones, is not straightforward.

In some cases, traditional businesses increase their IT budgets with a focus on a major digital revamp but fail to realize the business benefits even though they often exceed their IT budgets. The initially successful launch of the consumer banking arm of Goldman Sachs, Marcus, in 2016 is such an example. Even though it attracted $100 billion in deposits and started growing a retail lending business, Goldman's consumer banking ambition was abruptly stopped on its track in late 2022. It was a combination of the lack of long-term commitment from leadership and mounting losses of approximately $3 billion.[8]

Time and human resources are the biggest obstacles rather than capital, especially for large and publicly traded companies. General Electric (GE) is an example of this, with its unsuccessful digital revamp that started in 2011. With a vision to become a 4IR software data player, GE built a large-scale Internet of Things (IoT) platform, adding sensors to products and transforming its business models for industrial products. In 2015, it launched GE Digital but despite investing billions, the lack of revenues pushed management to stop the transformation journey in its tracks.[9]

Traditional businesses are also burdened by a genuinely different mindset than that of digitally native businesses. Although both types of businesses may focus on efficiencies, their business design results in a strikingly different feedback loop with their customers. In traditional businesses there are so many silos that the feedback loop with their customers is fragmented and, in many cases, beyond repair.

Customer centricity in the current digitally native sense – real time feedback and ability to implement rapid adjustments to products or services based on data – is not a core business design of traditional businesses. For both consumer-facing (B2C) and Business-to-Business (B2B) digitally native businesses, efficiently running their business with this type of customer-centric mindset and a data-driven decision-making approach, are core to their design.

Traditional businesses are increasingly recognizing the need to adapt to the changing era of the 4IR to remain competitive. The journey to close the gap with the digitally native businesses is a moving target and truly a journey. While traditional businesses advance on their digitalization roadmap, digitally native businesses continue to refine their operations, increasingly broaden their business boundaries and innovate to stay competitive. A business that was a disruptor in the 1990s, the early web adoption decade, is not necessarily what we would consider today a digitally native company.

A great example of how disruptors change the rules of the game and change the shape and size of the gaps between traditional businesses and digitally native businesses, is Amazon in its early years. As many of you may recall, Amazon started out as a digital mail-order book seller in 1995. As a disruptor to established traditional book selling chains such as Borders and Barnes & Noble, its success was not a given as it remained unprofitable until the end of 2001.

Fast forward ten years later, and Borders went out of business in 2011, as it was late to embrace the web, e-commerce and the e-book reader revolution. Barnes & Noble with its e-book reader, Nook, survived but went through very challenging times. In 1995, Amazon was clearly a disruptor who leveraged two newly born 'offsprings' of the internet revolution – e-commerce and e-book readers. By today's standards I wouldn't call Amazon a digitally native company at launch although the company had a customer-centricity mindset at its core.

Amazon undoubtedly has earned today's digitally native characterization following the famous 2002 Jeff Bezos memo.[10] The memo, known as the 'API Mandate' was an internal memo sent to the entire company instructing IT to design application programming interfaces (APIs) so that all internal communications are strictly via these APIs. The mandate required all teams to expose their data and that all APIs be well-documented and maintained, and more importantly externalizable. This laid the foundation for data-driven decision making and seamlessly flowing customer feedback loops. It was also the foundation that enabled Amazon over the subsequent years to build one of the most complex Platform-based Ecosystems (PBEs) that exist with integrated businesses ranging from retail e-commerce, a sellers' marketplace, logistics, cloud, payments, streaming and so on.

The current standard of a digitally native business is one that operates first and foremost on a holistic view of the customer rather than a fragmented one. The kind of customer-centricity developed by digital-native businesses has given birth to the experience economy which continues to evolve as we speak. Just before the dawn of the twenty-first century, Joseph Pine and James Gilmore coined the term *Experience Economy*[11] and highlighted the emerging shift from a commodity-based economy focused on goods, to a service-based economy focused on services, to an experienced-based economy.

Digitally native businesses nowadays are fully native to the experience economy and focus on efficiencies that create memorable experiences. They go beyond the functional part of transactions and run their businesses with different key performance indicators (KPIs).

Customer engagement is tracked and measured based on more than a dozen metrics that traditional businesses can't measure and or don't include in their decision-making processes. For example, user experience online metrics like bounce rates, click-through rates, session duration, time-to-response to customer inquiry, churn rates and community engagement. Innovation in their products and services is data-driven and extracted based on analytics from their world view of customer-centricity which continues to evolve. This makes it even more difficult for traditional businesses to close the gap. Even if a traditional business transitions fully to the cloud and breaks data silos with internal and external APIs, unless the business culture changes, traditional businesses can't operate as a digital native.

To start closing the gap, a traditional business needs to realize that it will have to reconcile two strikingly different views of economic activity. The view of digital natives who have created the experience economy and is in alignment with Pine & Gilmore's metaphor 'Work is Theatre & Every Business a Stage'. And the view of a traditional business which is more aligned with 'Work is Transactions & Every Business is a Checkout Counter'.

A great example of a traditional business that embarked on a successful digital transformation journey is Ping An. The company was founded in 1988 in Shenzhen, China as a traditional insurance company and in the beginning of the twenty-first century it embarked on a customer-centric transformation journey. This included a full shift to cloud computing, data analytics and artificial intelligence (AI) for its processes, products and services. It created a customer-obsessed business culture which, combined with its technological capabilities, enabled it to grow into an ecosystem that includes offerings beyond insurance.

A traditional insurance business became a stage (business operations operating behind the scenes) on which the company choreographed scenes for customers so that routine transactions were delightful. Starting from its insurance offerings, it was able to scale digitally claim management with its ultra-speed on-site city inspection and its one-click arrangement services. In addition, Ping An blurred the lines between several traditionally siloed industries, insurance, banking and healthcare, and choreographed scenes for customers who are delighted to participate in a holistic journey that serves their needs. Ping An can personalize customer experiences with its use of data and AI analytics and continuously innovate like a theatre business with unique story-telling narratives for each participant.

Digital-native businesses are capable of broadening the initially laser-focused scope of their business while creating seamless digital connectivity between platforms, so the customer is served more holistically, and the company learns and innovates further from this holistic customer view. Examples of successful integration of loosely related services to create a digitally native ecosystem in the experience economy, range from Big Tech companies to smaller specialized companies.

Apple is a great example of a Big Tech hardware company founded in 1976, which continues to grow its digital finance business that includes Apple Pay launched in 2014, Apple Card (2019), Apple Tap to Pay (2022), and Apple Pay Later (2023). It took Apple Pay four years to start scaling significantly. In 2018, Apple Pay processed globally 1 billion transactions per month and by 2022, there were 507 million Apple Pay wallets in 76 countries, and Apple Pay generated $1.9 billion in revenue in 2022.[12] Although this is a small percentage of the $394.3 billion revenue of Apple in 2022, it is core to the customer-centric journeys of the Apple ecosystem – hardware, entertainment, services. It also shows the strategic commitment to their stage vision instead of the checkout-counter mindset that would dismiss Apple Pay since it only generates roughly 0.5% of total revenues after 8 years.

Blockchain-native businesses are a distinct breed of businesses propelling the evolution of the Web3 economy. Their principles are data-sovereignty, revenue sharing with users participating in the network, and decentralization at the organizational level of the business. In contrast, both traditional and digital-native businesses are based on a conventional centralized business model. Blockchain natives aim for as much as possible disintermediation and decentralization. Their businesses operate mostly on a consensus-driven decision-making framework. Their services aim to be on a peer-to-peer (P2P) basis with no need for authorized intermediaries behind the scenes.

P2P payments and lending were both born out of the experience economy. Now they are mainstream and offered by digital-native businesses or even by traditional businesses through partnerships with digital-native providers. Venmo in the United States, Revolut in Europe, PayTM in India and M-Pesa in Africa, are examples of P2P digital-native providers. However, the rails on which all these businesses operate behind the scenes are the traditional banking rails. They have built digitally native businesses on top of the legacy systems at the base layer, and they depend on several partnerships.

In contrast, blockchain-native businesses use various blockchain layers as the rails to move value from one wallet to another. These blockchains were born mostly in the past decade. Bitcoin was launched in 2009, Litecoin in 2011, Ripple in 2012, Ethereum in 2015, Polygon (ex- Matic) in 2017, Solana and Avalanche in 2020 and so on.

In the blockchain world, there is no need for a bank account or an authorized intermediary to authenticate, clear and settle a payment transaction from one entity to another. Clearing and settlement are simultaneous and processed through the consensus mechanism of the blockchain, and several functions are programmed and executed via smart contracts instead of intermediaries (e.g. Automated Market Makers on Decentralized Exchanges).

Wallets in blockchain-native businesses are non-custodial and provide access to the blockchain network, unlike the Apple, Klarna or Alibaba wallets which interface with authorized central money or banking providers (card networks, banks, e-money licensed service providers, and so on) to enable the user to deploy their assets which are held at an authorized entity. Non-custodial wallets (like MetaMask and Trust Wallet) in the blockchain world are more like a personal digital vault granting exclusive access to the owner to his/her digital assets which exist on a blockchain.

Web3 is redefining the governance of our digital world, aiming to enable privacy, redefine money, business processes and governance. Decentralized Autonomous Organizations (DAOs) are the north star of blockchain-native ecosystems. They are organizations that operate through a set of smart contracts and protocols rather than a centralized entity or human control.

Smart contracts are foundational elements of blockchain-native businesses. They shouldn't be confused with legal contracts or smart in the sense of making good decisions. They are programmable and self-executing as programmed, nothing more and nothing less. They enable human disintermediation when desirable. Uniswap is an example of a blockchain-native business. It is a Decentralized Exchange (DEX) built on the rails of the Ethereum blockchain. Users can exchange one cryptocurrency for another without the need of human market makers (centralized entities with people and algorithms that match supply and demand in traditional markets, like Citadel Securities). Uniswap has designed smart contracts (i.e. self-executable programs) that set the price of the exchange based on the supply and demand in the liquidity pool. This mechanism is called Automated Market Makers (AMMs) and is now used by other decentralized exchanges but also adopted in pilots of cross-border wholesale Central Banks Digital Currencies (CBDCs).[13]

Blockchain natives aim to build Web3, enable the creation of new digital assets through tokenization of existing assets, enhance transparency and liquidity, and change governance. Blockchain-native businesses are more in alignment with '*Work is value exchange & Every Business is a Decentralized Autonomous Organization (DAO)*'.

Change, evolution and innovation are unstoppable and the overlap between these three types of businesses is shyly emerging.

In some cases, traditional businesses are transforming successfully into digitally native ones. Traditional businesses are already offering innovative products launched by digital natives (copying them or in partnership with them), contributing to their mainstream adoption and in some cases managing to leapfrog them. Digital-native businesses evolve and continue to raise the bar of excellence in the experience economy.

Traditional and digital-native businesses are dipping their toes in the emerging Web3 economy. They are finding ways to shyly contribute towards the increased adoption of blockchain-native products and services mainly through partnerships with block-chain providers. Some are launching non-fungible tokens (NFTs) as an extension of their innovation efforts in customer experiences, like the Swoosh Nike platform with digital Nike wearables and the Starbucks loyalty program 'Odyssey journeys', which includes collectibles and exclusive coffee experiences. Others are launching separate divisions with open-source blockchain backbones. JP Morgan launched Onyx in 2020, with B2B infrastructure services for tokenization, a permissioned distributed ledger for coin transfers between financial providers. In 2021, Block's (ex-Square) TBD division was launched, born out of Jack Dorsey's vision to build an open-source platform for Bitcoin developers and for decentralized finance (DeFi). Currently, there is no business that has transformed from a traditional or a digital-native business into a blockchain business.

Digitally native businesses have been leading the adoption of AI in their businesses as their technology architecture allows them to analyse more data and in real time. In addition, their plug-and-play native architecture has resulted in increasing use of AI in various parts of their business operations. Typically, starting with customer-facing processes (AI in customer service), then using AI in fraud detection for their online and digital transactions, and then using AI in designing products and services.

Block is an example of a digitally native company that has been increasingly using AI. From fraud detection on their P2P payment app, CashApp; to reduce internal manual work; to advise sellers on their marketplace as to which Block ecosystem product is best for their business needs; all the way to using machine learning to originate loans to the sellers on Block's seller marketplace. Ping An has also been using AI in more than a dozen areas of its ecosystem. From credit-scoring decision making, to pricing insurance products, all the way to AI-powered medical diagnosis tools for its healthcare businesses.

Traditional, digital native, and even some blockchain-native businesses will become increasingly AI-powered as they integrate various advancements in AI – from the foundation models powering up the new Generative AI subsector of machine learning to more AI tools. However, that doesn't mean that these companies are AI-native businesses. This is, actually, a distinct emerging business category that will lead to further transformations of existing businesses and to the birth of completely new ones.

A business that is using AI is not necessarily an AI-native business, much like a traditional business using several digital tools isn't necessarily a digitally native business.

Foundation Models, the New Kid on the Block

Striving to close the gaps between digital natives and traditional businesses continues to be the modus operandum in all economic activities. Even at government and regional levels, this dynamic and elusive tug-of-war is at work. Deploying technical resources like cloud, efficient computing power, plug-and-play operational designs, agile innovation and technologies like AI, blockchain and IOT, to align with strategic objectives, is what everyone strives for.

The challenge is always found in the misalignments of tech implementation with business strategy. Digital natives are better at this because that is the only way they know how to operate. Their cloud-first modular approach enables them to grow from a business with one offering to a platform or a platform-based ecosystem. Speed, experimentation and reiterating is second nature to them. Using data analytics and AI to analyse their feedback loops with customers, is standard for them too.

The common and increasing use of AI by digital natives should be viewed as traditional AI deployment. AI processes are plugged into various modules of a digital-native business architecture. The obtained data analytics are interpreted and considered by the business, but the context of these analytics is left to humans and has been impossible to scale.

Bloomberg, one of the biggest financial data, news and market intelligence global providers, has have been offering its customers access to a broad range of AI-powered analytics tools for a while already. For example, it offers Nature Language Processing (NLP) powered sentiment analysis of any company based on their data sets (current and historical sentiment analysis of any company). However, Bloomberg can't answer customer follow-up questions like (a) Does the market sentiment of this company correlate with its customer satisfaction rankings, its stock price movements, and the company's cyber and supply chain risks? (b) How does the company's sentiment compare to its competitors' sentiment over time, and what insights can be gained from this comparison? (c) How effectively has the company managed negative sentiment spikes in the past?

This is the type of contextual service that the newly released BloombergGPT large language model, trained on a mix of Bloomberg proprietary data and public data, aims to offer to Bloomberg customers.[14]

However, even with these types of capabilities, AI isn't embedded into the Bloomberg terminal to locally process a customer's activity and make suggestions to the customer based on their activity on the terminal. Bloomberg, for now, doesn't have the ability to contextualize a customer's activity with its analytics and suggest additional relevant topics to research. This requires a totally different design of the Bloomberg terminal than the current one, which is linear and based on similar tags and keywords.

In plain words, AI isn't yet an embedded functional part of the business products or services or the enterprise. It is an add-on, a plug-in in a very small part of one of their customer-facing business offerings. It can't help the business innovate, build new products and services, make better strategic decisions, improve organizational capabilities and so on. It is not integrated in the business architecture, nor in any other part of the operational side of the business.

A digital-native lending business which already uses AI to assess the credit worthiness of a borrower relies on its own remote computing resources to perform this specific AI task in the cloud. The AI processes in assessing credit worthiness are some type of machine learning – supervised machine learning or unsupervised machine learning, or neural networks, etc. Although these machine learning processes may be continuously improved, a typical digital-native business relies on several separate such AI processes running independently for different business tasks. There is no feedback loop between these separate AI-powered processes.

Ironically, this plug-and-play AI deployment in different parts of a digital business resembles the lack of feedback loops that is characteristic of a traditional business. If a digitally native lender runs an AI process for credit scoring at origination of the loan, another one for fraud detection, another one for collection and delinquency management, and yet another for personalized offerings; then AI is not natively embedded in the business.

A retailer that uses Generative AI to exclusively handle the negotiation of supplier contracts, is another example of traditional AI deployment at the strategic level. Walmart launched such an AI pilot to negotiate all its supplier contracts, as early as 2021. The pilot was strictly focused on negotiating not-for-resale items, like shopping carts, fleet services and other equipment used by Walmart to serve end customers. The negotiations were complicated as they included price discount offers based on sales volumes or assortment of items, a variety of payment schedules combined with discounts for early payments, but also different extended payment terms, and the negotiation of different options of contract termination. These pilots resulted in three times the expected rate of successfully reaching an agreement, an average of 3% in cost savings, and an extension of payment terms to 35 days.[15]

Using Generative AI to negotiate supplier contracts for shopping carts, using another AI to manage the inventory of shopping carts, and another AI to learn from customer in-store use of shopping carts, means that AI is not actually embedded in the business.

A different example of a retailer using AI in several ways to empower customers and to grow its business offerings, is IKEA. IKEA's vision is to empower their customers and to be seen also as an Interior Design Consultancy. They have been deploying AI towards Do-It-Yourself (DIY) services and for personalized human interior design advice.

Since 2021, they have been reskilling their call centre staff to become remote interior design advisers as they delegate routine customer inquiries to their AI chatbot, Billie. In mid-2023, IKEA reported that their chatbot, Billie, effectively managed 47% of customer inquiries since launch and they have successfully reskilled 8,500 call centre workers to serve customers as interior design advisers.[16] In 2022, they also launched IKEA Kreativ which offers customers a way to design and visualize home and office spaces from their own computers or smartphones. IKEA Kreativ combines decades of IKEA expertise with the latest developments in spatial computing, machine learning and 3D mixed-reality technologies. An AI-native business would have integrated foundational models not only in specific areas of its business but into its entire value chain. This would provide contextual feedback loops along the entire value chain of the business, which includes the enterprise, its ecosystem and its customers.

Contextual services for customers, and enterprise and ecosystem capabilities that can be 'homogenized' are the north star of AI-native businesses and what differentiates them from digital natives. Building machine learning systems for a wide range of applications – this is homogenization – is standard when designing foundation models and is a core differentiator between an AI-native and digital-native business.

Foundation models must be integral part of an AI-native business. Contextualizing some customer services here and there, won't cut it. To reap the benefits of these emerging new technologies, businesses need to let go of their linear thinking and their plug-and-play approach with regards to AI integration. Foundation models are a game changer, as they will transform businesses from the strategy level to all aspects of the business.

The technology behind foundation models has evolved over time but it was only in 2021 that the Stanford Institute for Human-Centered Artificial Intelligence's (HAI)[17] coined the term. By now, we are all familiar with mass applications built on top of some of these foundation models, like ChatGPT or Dall-E.

'Foundation models' represent a paradigm shift in AI systems because they are a new approach to building AI models that are trained on vast amounts of unlabelled data and can be adapted to a wide range of business applications with fine-tuning. They are very different in nature compared to the backbone of traditional AI which has been and remains focused on task-specific AI training.

Foundation models aren't being explicitly programmed based on our linear thinking and our insights. As a result, these models generate outputs that aren`t necessarily anticipated, since we didn't program them.

And this is exactly where even digitally native thinkers may find it challenging to let go of their linear thinking which is often incompatible with these foundational models. Linear thinking wants to trust a credit worthiness model that includes data of variables like historical data of our payment history, our income history, our credit history and so on.

Once a foundation model suggests lending to someone who, by traditional creditworthiness metrics, is unqualified, we will reject its suggestion. *Linear thinking insists either* on the How *the model obtained the specific output, and/or* on the Why.

AI-native businesses will develop 'surrogates' for trusting foundation models and the applications built on them. Once we buy in to the emerging AI paradigm shift, new forms of trust will become standard. Various dynamic performance metrics of foundation models could become the standard for trusting these models instead of linear model thinking.

Foundation models are the new kid on the block, pushing the digital-natives' thinking to another level. The vast amount of data on which they are trained is mind blowing and continues to rise. Foundation models are not task-specific AI models; however, for now they are data-type-specific or specific to one modality to another.

We already have a whole new world of Large Language Models (LLMs) trained on massive amounts of text data with their output also being text. Another category is Variational Autoencoder foundation models (VAEs), which learn the underlying probability distribution of a data set and generate new samples. Examples are combining text and images like DALL·E 2, or text and music, like JukeBox. Generative Adversarial Networks (GANs) can be trained in any one type of modality (image, text, video, music, synthetic data) and generate synthetic data of that specific modality.

A great example to understand this fundamental differentiator – foundation models are not task-specific AI models – is Bloomberg's foundation model, BloombergGPT, which is being trained on huge amounts of Bloomberg financial data – market data, company filings, press releases, financial news, research reports and other financial documents from the Bloomberg Terminal and on general-purpose text.

Up until now, Bloomberg has been deploying several application-specific natural language processing (NLP) models. The approach has been a different NLP model for sentiment analysis, another one for news classification and yet another one for named-entity recognition. The new foundation BloombergGPT model is being trained to handle a wide range of applications with little fine-tuning.

The next evolution for foundation models will be multimodal models. This will be a major inflection point enabling the launch of AI-native businesses designed on these foundations. It will empower us to deal with levels of complexity that have been unimaginable up to now and, at the same time, challenge our linear frameworks. AI-native businesses will operate much like a non-linear ecosystem operates. The complexity and non-linearity of a galaxy is a good analogy for an AI-native business.

AI-native businesses will integrate foundational models in their entire galaxy, which includes the enterprise, its ecosystem and its customers.

The Five Dimensions of an AI-native Business

A classical approach to digital transformations has been to map the value of digital to the customer, operations and ecosystem. This model has helped leaders to get very clear and sharp about where to invest and to assess where exactly the impact of investments would be. This has also helped boards gain the confidence that the millions being spent on digital transformations had an identifiable, tangible and, importantly, an explainable impact to stakeholders. However, this also created a challenge as the three areas were often viewed in isolation, hence not fully understanding the interdependencies between the value to the customer, the value to the operations and the value to the ecosystem.

Fast forward to 2023, we are now faced with greater complexity given the transformative potential of the recent advancements in AI. The traditional value assessment of digital is inadequate to help leaders plan a business-wide AI transformation.

At the same time, the customer should remain at the centre of an AI-first business transformation. The adoption of AI, digital or blockchain are not destinations but means to serve changing customers' needs, expectations and experiences. Customers don't really care about industry boundaries, product segments, go-to-market models or technology platforms.

An AI Business-wide Transformation approach

The single most important success factor for an AI-led business-wide transformation is for leaders to be able to map their business onto dimensions that enable them to assess impact, anticipate issues, build capabilities and understand the required investments.

It is imperative for success that we look at AI as a core business-wide capability imperative rather than just a technology. To help leaders think like an AI-native business, we have developed a framework based on five dimensions that offer a holistic view starting with the customer.

The five dimensions are:

1. Discovery
2. Design
3. Decision
4. Dexterity
5. Deduction

To help leaders further refine their strategic intent, we explain these five dimensions of an AI-first business-wide transformation through the lens of the customer, the enterprise and the ecosystem (Figure 3.1).

Discovery

Thinking and acting like an AI native starts at the discovery level for customers, the enterprise and the ecosystem.

1. Context for the customer

Google turned 25 in 2023. In these 25 years, it has forced companies to redraw their customer journeys that start with Google or other digital platforms that sit well outside the enterprise's own ecosystem. Google shows about 25 million results in about 0.62 seconds for any one search. But the discovery process for the customer, while digital, is still linear and lacks the context of the search. The customer has to sift through multiple possibilities, spending time verifying or filtering the proposed links to their individual context before making any decision.

With the Microsoft-backed OpenAI Large Language Model (LLM) bringing generative AI into mainstream use we are already seeing digital-native search providers – Microsoft Bing, Google Bard – transforming into AI-native search engines. As users we are getting spoilt as the search output from these AI-native search engines is more contextual and framed in natural language rather than URLs.

In less than a year since ChatGPT was released to the public, we are also seeing new, AI-native search providers competing, for example PerplexityAI, NeevaAI, You, or Phind.

The Dimensions | The Customer | The Enterprise | The Ecosystem

1 DISCOVERY

Context
The ability to provide precise, integrated and highly contextualized information that drives customer decisions, lowers the time and cost of customer aquistion

Innovation
The ability to surface unknown variables across specializations of science, business, technology, people, economics to create ideas one never thought possible

New Revenue Opportunities
The ability to identify hidden network effects at three levels cross-industry customer spaces, within industry marketplaces or within products, services spaces

2 DESIGN

Experiences
The ability to nudge, recommend and lead customers into new experience categories or have them adopt new ways of using services or products to create brand stickiness

Value Chain
The ability to design hand-offs, processes, integrations, monitor APIs, flow data, integrate services, identify bottlenecks and value creation at each point of interaction

Customer Hand-Offs
The ability to hand-off a customer, their transaction, their context and increase purchase potential across multiple company-owned or third party service integrations

3 DECISION

Make the Choice
The ability to help customers make choices with minimal time spent and with maximum customization to their context

Strategy Choices
The ability to generate a set of choices that range from optimum to transformative so leaders can made decisions on a complex set of variables both known and unknown

Value Pricing
The ability to drive high contextual pricing that delivers personalized value perception to customer but also protects/enhances profitability for the company and ecosystem partners

4 DEXTERITY

Physical+Digital
The ability to design products, services, solutions and business models with an intentional seamless mix of physical and digital go-to-market approaches

Capabilities
The ability to predict, identify and design paths to build organization capabilities — technology, people, process, organization models in an integrated way ahead of time

Rapid Integrations
The ability to integrate new product ideas, new business opportunities, new acquisitions, new technology, new APIs, etc. with speed to create competitive advantage in the marketplace

5 DEDUCTION

Personalization
The ability to offer deep on-demand personalization as an outcome of context, experiences, choice recommendations and fulfilment capabilities

Boundryless Intelligence
The ability to break down data, information, knowledge islands in the organization and integrate them with data from the ecosystem to create boundaryless insights

Intelligence as a Service
Creating compelling and deep business intelligence to offer it as a service to all players in the ecosystem including to the customer to understand their own habits better

Figure 3.1   The five dimensions.

An LLM-powered search engine is an area of adjacency, but services or product companies deploying these advances in AI to help customers discover tailor-made services is a new capability for them. Instacart has been one of the early adopters. 'Ask Insta' is a feature to provide customers with 'shoppable' answers, specific recipes, or ingredients and so on that the customer is looking for in a given context. Shopify added Gen AI to their customer-facing app Shop, as did Kayak and many others. In addition to retailers and marketplaces, even regulated industries like financial services are launching customer-facing LLM-powered contextual services. BloombergGPT, Morningstar's Mo and Moody's Research Assistant are three 2023 such examples.

2. Innovation for the enterprise

Innovation is time consuming, costly and often a laborious process, especially for larger companies. At the ideation and discovery level, the biggest challenge leaders face is how to drive institutionalized and continuous innovation.

For smaller companies it is often easier to discover and implement new business ideas. Quip is one such company, a toothbrush manufacturer with an Apple grade design, founded in 2015. In 2019, they grew into a services company after launching a dental insurance product based on their understanding of their customers' dental habits.

An argument could be made that their transformation from a product to a service company took too long. An AI-powered systematic approach to innovation would have created the dental insurance business idea along with other new business ideas much faster. Scaling or streamlining innovative business ideas for research and development is core to an AI-first business. Most leaders do not have a company-wide view of all the moving parts and data. Partly due to data security concerns and partly due to the significant time-consuming effort required to compile, synthesize and contextualize all the data and analytics to build an innovation narrative.

A powerful example of AI-first enterprise innovation is the R&D process in pharmaceutical companies. R&D is costly (lab equipment, human and material resources) and time consuming as the typical pre-clinical stage drug discovery takes 3 to 6 years.[18]

Exscientia, an AI-powered drug discovery and development company, is an example of the first ever AI-designed drug molecule that is placed in a human body in clinical trials in just 12 months. Large pharmaceutical companies like Bayer, Merck and Bristol Myers Squibb are coming on board to leverage these capabilities.

3. New revenue opportunities for the ecosystem

Amazon sells more than 12 million products in the United States with more than 50% of all Amazon sales coming from third party sellers.[19] There are over two million third-party sellers on the Amazon seller marketplace.[20] While the Amazon platform gives access to a large marketplace, it is also competitive for sellers to get the best of their product placement and prices. Amazon so far has created revenue funnels through advertising, live shopping experiences, featured products and more. However, like any retailer, the category-management structure in merchandizing limits Amazon's ability to see revenue opportunities across the ecosystem of the Amazon sellers for both the platform company as well as the platform participants. While the old fashioned 'person who bought a tomato and onion also bought a yogurt' is still valid, it is still limited by traditional algorithms that analyse the shopping basket. Traditional AI deployment typically means one AI algorithm for conversion metrics, another one for payment options, another one for customer feedback and so on.

An AI-first marketplace would run on a platform that is not task specific and would contextualize all the relevant dimensions, merchandizing, pricing decisions, supply chain issues, customer feedback, product materials and so on.

Design

Thinking and acting like an AI native affects the business design at the customer, the enterprise and the ecosystem level.

1. The customer experiences

There are few, if any, like Apple when it comes to design even after considering the slow decline in the years after Steve Jobs and Jony Ive. But it continues to be formidable as it is one of the few companies that have been able to combine software and hardware into an ecosystem experience. McKinsey's design index found that design-centric companies increased their revenues and total shareholder returns faster by 32 percentage points than their industry peers over a five-year period.[21]

But what if every company had a minimum level of design centricity? What would be the next competitive advantage? We have seen a proliferation of apps that use text, voice or a drawing to convert to images, sound, music and even video. Dall-E, Midjourney, Stable Diffusion, Vizcom and many more fall into this space. The power of applying AI to industrial design is beginning to take shape. Automobile design, architecture, process mapping and even business dashboards with platforms like Olli. With AI, the economic value of design can be a central principle of a customer-centric business.

Ikea has demonstrated AI application to customizing design for customers. It offers customers, through its digital platform and app, a way to visualize life-like designs of their living spaces with a combination of their products. While AR/VR is a base technology, the AI model offers customers curated suggestions integrated into ecommerce platform to complete the idea-to-buy experience.[22]

2. The enterprise value chain

Over the years, we have seen conglomerate business models either morph into platform business models or break up into highly focused entities to compete in focused market spaces. United Technologies, GE, Siemens all have been through this journey. The core challenge in any multi-industry enterprise is the ability to have a value chain that drives growth and effectiveness at every point of interaction or hand-off. Companies have long tried to map this through various methods including Lean and Six Sigma. But the question of great value chain design is as much a matter of mastering organizational complexity as of understanding the market forces. Often this involves multiple teams with different specializations coming together in projects.

That is where AI comes in. Take Microsoft's Automate AI. You can type in a sentence on what you would like to automate in your processes, and the AI tool will build a flow in a few seconds. This is compared to the time-consuming activity to think, determine and draw a process flow.

While business gets increasingly complex, digital has simplified many decision interfaces used by customers or employees. With AI to design value chains, identify opportunities, drive efficiencies or effectiveness, such tools or applications power up value creation across functions, processes and ecosystem to deliver amazing experiences to customers or employees.

Imagine applying AI to drive a post-acquisition or post-merger integration of businesses, processes, teams, financial ledgers, product codes, customer profiles and more?

3. Customer hand-offs in the ecosystem

All companies are part of a loose or a more connected ecosystem.

What percentage of time do companies in an ecosystem lose out to customer service from imperfect interfaces, hand-offs, incomplete product information, faculty payment integrations or just simply an unsatisfied customer returning a product? And what if all these take place across multiple players including third parties who participate in an ecosystem?

Even single product or service companies struggle with this, for example SouthWest airlines. The brilliance of simplicity to book or rebook your travel is offset by the complexity or pain to get a refund through their app.

The platform orchestrator is often at the centre of such complex transactions trying to make sense of it all and present a cohesive positive face to the customer. This involves extensive data mining by teams collecting data to solve complex problems across the value chain of the business. This is often done in a fragmented data set up.

But the complexity of customer service is not just for multi-sided platform businesses. It could also apply to a simple two-sided linear platform like Uber. These companies operate on the assumption that 95% of the time their processes and fulfilment work as planned. So, they build capability and capacity only for the 5% out of norms. But therein lies the distraction. The 5% of the issues that involve so many internal and external players is loss of brand experience to the customer. IBM's Watson X applies AI to customer service for contextual customer interactions for resolution or revenue generation.

Decision

So far, in the digital transformation era, we have seen humans firmly in control of both data and decisions. The linearity of digital allowed humans to understand, map, design and use how data flows resulted in the analytical outcomes. But with AI, the decision-making is augmented with choices being driven both for the customer and the company in a highly contextual manner.

1. Customers making the choice

Will a customer ever buy without comparing prices or options? A key feature in the digital world is the ability for the customer to compare the price of products or services, and customer reviews.

This information has been key to how Google presents choices in their search results or apps like Yelp showing customer ratings on restaurants where the businesses reply to customer comments. There is an entire psychological process of choosing a product or service that generations of people have grown up with – comparative mindset. This has been a core of all value pitches where each business compares and shows how they are different to others. How will highly-contextualized recommendations or discovery change the way a customer makes the choice?

As AI narrows down what a customer should buy by a deep understanding of the customer's context, we will begin to see a change in customer habits. For some products where the value differentiation is negligible, the customer probably will prefer to go with the recommended solution to save time. Time saved is a buying influencer in these cases. In complex or high-value purchases, it will probably be more where the AI application can customize or drive a decision through a layered interactive process before handing over to a human.

2. Choice of strategy in an enterprise

Companies spend significant time to combine intuition, experience and data to make strategy choices for the enterprise. Many of the assumptions also change in real time during this process creating redundancies in conclusions. Planning scenarios is often a process that is not taken seriously. Digital has solved the data-capture problem but has had mixed success in breaking down the islands of data spread across the enterprise.

Where should we plan the next manufacturing facility? What is the best way to deliver to this country while keeping our margins at 40%? Of all the areas of adjacency, which one will add to our competitive advantage? If we were to invest in a new business, knowing what we know from our customers, what would be those options?

JAB holdings is a Luxembourg-based family-run conglomerate with an estimated value of US$20 billion which includes Peet's Green Mountain, Stumptown, Caribou, Panera Breads, Dr Pepper, and more. The coffee giant moved into Pet Clinics in 2020 and in 2023 acquired a pet insurance company in the United States. Why would a coffee, restaurant business conglomerate step into a completely new business area? This is best explained in the Bloomberg article, 'It's easy to see why JAB would be attracted to veterinary investments. Just as many coffee drinkers can't imagine starting each morning without their daily dose of caffeine, hundreds of millions more can't imagine living without their pets.'[23] The pet care business is estimated to be a US$130 billion market in the United States alone.

This is exactly the kind of insights AI would help companies identify brilliant opportunities to shape disruptive strategies.

3. Value pricing

Pricing strategy is one of the hardest parts of the business with an immediate impact to the bottom line – good or bad – that shows up on the P&L. Consider retail, a fast-moving environment with multiple SKUs with different margins, shelf life and product storage conditions. While ensuring availability is a key factor, it could also easily wipe out margins if not managed well. In traditional retail, 'comping' or competitive price benchmarking was a very human-led process on which store management teams were extensively trained. This involved a physical check of pricing in competition stores once or twice a day to return and adjust pricing in the store systems. When you run this process on 1,000 stores with billions in revenue, it becomes more a financial-diligence process than a customer-acquisition process.

The sophistication involved in dynamic pricing can be both simplified and impactful with optimization and adaptation to consumer patterns while protecting the profit margins. This could also be integrated into the distribution centres or procurement team strategies, as AI would continuously learn to make smarter decisions.[24]

Dexterity

AI-native businesses can deal with high levels of complexity with dexterity at the customer, enterprise and ecosystem level.

1. The physical+digital mix for customers

It is easy to mistake Amazon as a B2C platform business. It is but only in part. A significant part of the business is also a platform model on the back of their web services. But it would be an oversimplification to explain Amazon as just another platform business model.

There are four quadrants to this company. First, a digital business that drives massive scale, which has Amazon retail with Prime members, Prime Video, Twitch, Music, Pay, Kindle plus MGM Studios creating content. In 2023, they added Amazon Clinics to this massive customer reach. Second, a physical part of the business, which drives customer interaction experiences on the back of its digital scale; Whole Foods and Amazon logistics that has made the brown box in front of home doors symbolic of ecommerce. Third, the infrastructure drivers, Prime Membership and AWS. Fourth, is the innovation on the back of all the above, Amazon GO, Palm Pay and so on, while developed for in-house use, now become SaaS products that Amazon sells to other retailers.

While these businesses all have their own individual flywheels, they are also interdependent to drive both scale and innovation. Amazon has been on the forefront of automating warehouses while at the same time creating millions of jobs on the distribution side.[25] All these businesses need a level of integration and balance between physical and digital design mix. Businesses with AI can unbundle this complexity to deliver precision experiences across services or locations to customers.

2. Enterprise capabilities

While digital has given birth to platform business models, we have also seen the birth of Super App business models, especially in Asia with apps like WeChat in China. In India, we have seen the disruptive impact of Reliance Jio in Reliance becoming a Super App business with its low-cost digital offerings.

Grab in Southeast Asia in one of the most visible, nimble, high-growth Super App business models. Its journey started as a ride hailing service. Since then it also added Singapore's first neo-bank business in partnership with Singtel. It has entertainment, gaming, insurance and grocery retail in its mix. Their drivers can sell customers personal insurance while they take a ride in their service.

Super App businesses need to build their organization models and capabilities in a radically different manner from even classical platform businesses. Their ability to go deep into a service vertical while collaborating for cross-sell across their portfolio of services, needs not just fast data but the ability to predict the next types of capabilities they need to be building to grow. This is where AI plays a significant role in capturing points of value in an organization, pinpointing bottlenecks, identifying the right performance metrics and getting the productivity equation right.[26]

3. Rapid integrations in the ecosystem

Shopify is a terrific example of a simplified online store platform which in 2017 was building a global ecosystem enterprise through multi-pronged partnerships. They have one of the best API strategies in play, resulting in the wide range of integrations available for any online B2B platform. The Shopify App Store has over 8,000 apps that give flexibility and context to every type of business customer needs. Their fee strategy has been different from every other SaaS player. They are a developer first app and do not charge app store fees for developers of apps with less than $1 million in earnings.

With the volume of partnerships each needing its own API for specific functionality, how does Shopify identify the opportunities for integration? Importantly, how does the speed of such integrations keep up with the app developers on the platform?

Shopify has embedded Generative AI through Shopify Magic to create product descriptions of uploaded images.[27] The real magic, however, could be to deploy AI to identify how the end customers are using the app integrations and provide developers with insights to keep innovating. This rapid loop of integrations, insights and innovation using AI will continue to help businesses find more ways to engage their customers and cross-sell.

Deduction

AI intelligence will bring customer service and enterprise and ecosystem intelligence to another level.

1. Personalization

Personalization has been a promise of digital. It did accomplish personalization to the extent of offering services based on customers' behaviour or past preferences. There have been many attempts at predictive personalization, but they have fallen short of any meaningful value to customers. Instacart offers suggestions on price offers on the customers' past purchase items while Amazon through its app and voice assistant Alexa remind customers of products to reorder.

The chatbot revolution was supposed to deliver this intuitive, conversational experience for customers on discovery to resolution. But it is safe to say that the chatbot era brought in more customer pain than any real wow experience. Companies have unleashed on customers poorly designed and half-responsive chatbots.

Will this change with AI? What if Amazon Alexa had generative AI? Would it be able to understand the customer context better to give predictive personalization? An interesting example is from Duolingo Max that is transforming how people learn languages. Its two AI-based features, 'Explain My answer' helps learners understand why they make the same mistakes in the learning process and 'Role play' where the chatbot role plays real life conversations and scenarios for learners to practise.[28]

2. Boundaryless Intelligence

It is projected that the spending on automating brain power – data, technology, people – will be an estimated $2 trillion by 2030. The Large Language Models are exponentially growing their computing power, from 3,000 words per minute by Chat GPT in 2022, to 25,000 words per minute in 2023 and to 75,000 words per minute with Claude AI.[29]

But will companies be open to having their enterprise data used for training enterprise-captive Large Language Models? While Microsoft has made strides into this segment with the enterprise version of ChatGPT where the company information stays inside the company, it is still early days to know how well companies will deploy generative AI internally on their data.

But the opportunity to breakdown silos, create insights and eliminate blind spots is compelling enough to deploy AI to redefine knowledge management. Very rarely do you see 100% of all company data in a single warehouse. This is partly because to legacy systems and other regulatory issues that have prevented a full-enterprise single system of records. However, with Generative AI, this is no longer a constraint. Just as ChatGPT is trained on trillions of data points that sit on different webpages, sources and systems, an enterprise version of generative AI can be deployed to be trained across connected or unconnected databases inside the company.

3. Intelligence as a Service

All management consulting companies are services versions of SaaS business models with the exception that revenue generation principles are different. However, they represent intelligence as a service model. The assumption so far has been that humans, through either experience or exposure over a period, have assimilated information and through their brain power have synthesized it into knowledge. So, in principle, a single consultant in front of a client brings to bear all the years of collective intelligence in a consulting company. One the causalities of the Arthur Andersen debacle was a tool called Andersen K-Space. It was a global knowledge repository of projects, papers, insights and people that could be found by any consultant anywhere in the world. This allowed them to be truly global in knowledge and localize it to the client's context.

AI is the new management consultant on the block. The difference is that AI will in the future have depreciating cost with appreciating value of knowledge. Humans, conversely, will have depreciating knowledge with appreciating costs.

We will see a new breed of consulting firms that will have tailor-made AI applications that can be deployed to find solutions for different problems or create plans for new opportunities. The new-age consulting firms will offer intelligence as a service with humans heavily augmented with highly specialized AI models. This will also probably lead to new AI-driven marketplaces offering specialized solutions to companies. Gravity AI and Akira AI are two such examples.

The Era of Super-morphable Businesses: AI Natives

To start the AI-driven transformation of a business, companies need to accomplish two things: (1) Ensure their leaders develop a foundational understanding of AI and its impact across customers, enterprise and ecosystem; and (2) Develop a common understanding of its implications for their business – our framework in the chapter helps them do that.

The ability to transform at the speed of AI is constrained by finite resources in companies' budgets, time and people. Therefore, for a company to build a clear intent to roadmap thinking, using our framework, leaders in companies can make choices on where to start and how to progress on the AI journey across the five dimensions and three segments.

Companies that become AI natives have one distinct winning differentiator – rapid experimentation. This is not to be confused with setting up pilots or agile teams. It is the ability to experiment and learn fast so that it can be scaled fast. The journey from experiment to exponential scale capability is not easy and needs a combination of leadership will and execution capability. Execution is actually the critical factor in AI transformation.

Companies that will be born AI-natives will be thinking in nonlinear ways, empowered by the contextualizing capabilities of the advancements in AI. AI-native companies, unlike digital natives, will be able to deal systematically with the complexity and the interconnectedness of their entire business which includes all five dimensions and three levels we suggest in our framework.

AI-native companies will resemble operationally the complex intelligence of a galaxy. AI-native businesses will 'hack' the complexities even digital-native businesses face at each of the three levels – the customer level, the enterprise level and the ecosystem level. They will even 'hack' the complex interdependencies across these levels.

Linear thinking can't grasp the complexity, the intelligence and the interdependencies in any one galaxy. Recent scientific estimates claim that there are as many as two trillion galaxies in the observable universe.[30]

Think of our global economy as a universe, with the potential of encompassing over 400 million small galaxies (estimate of the number of global small businesses) and 350,000 large galaxies (2021 estimate of large companies employing more than 250 employees). What a wonderful world!

Currently, a medium-size business has easily 100 key performance indicators (KPIs) it measures and tracks using all sorts of digital tools. Larger businesses or businesses that are more advanced in their digital transformation use more advanced analytics and track more KPIs. However, the cumbersome task of business decision making is left to the processing capabilities of humans. As a result, leaders typically select a few of these KPIs to focus on. Their top picks frequently are not even balanced amongst customer-focused KPIs, enterprise-focused KPIs and ecosystem KPIs.

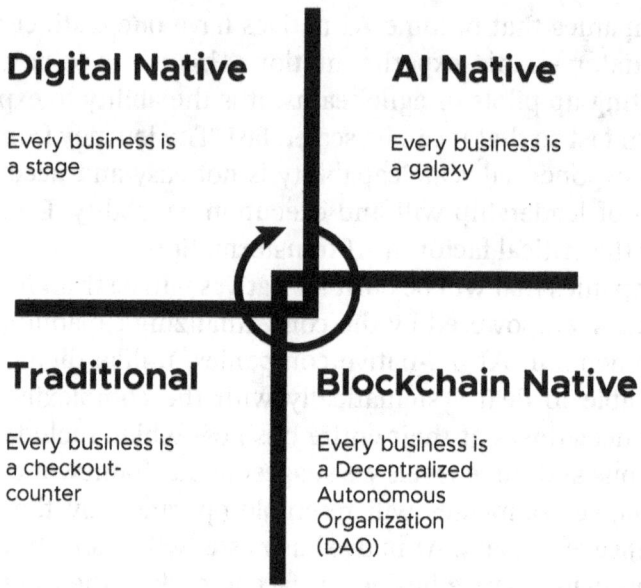

Digital Native

Every business is
a stage

AI Native

Every business is
a galaxy

Traditional

Every business is
a checkout-
counter

Blockchain Native

Every business is
a Decentralized
Autonomous
Organization
(DAO)

Figure 3.2   Four business types.

Business leaders are also often faced with tough trade-offs amongst their short list of KPIs, as their linear thinking can't incorporate for example, breakthrough thinking at the same time as running their business as usual. Linear thinking falls short of dealing systematically with the increased complexity of businesses and this where AI-native businesses will excel.

Although digital-native businesses have hugely improved the feedback loops at all levels; they haven't been able to 'hack' the complex interdependencies they face at the customer level, the enterprise level and the ecosystem level. No one of these levels is more important than the others, at any time. No one level is independent of the others, at any time. The relation of each level to the others is continuously changing. In practice, leaders can use our five-dimensional framework to grasp the penetration at all levels and dimensions. To execute on an AI-driven transformation roadmap, they will have to make choices and prioritize similar to a digital transformation map. The core difference, however, is that even if an AI transformation roadmap starts at the *Customer Discovery* level for example, the training, feedback loops and contextual learnings, should be swiftly used as input for the *Enterprise Discovery* level AI transformation or vice versa.

If an AI transformation roadmap starts at the *Enterprise Decision* level; the training, feedback loops and contextual learnings from that should be used in parallel for the Customer and *Ecosystem Decision* level training. Think of this as AI-driven agility which leverages the contextual capabilities of AI advancements. It is about 'hacking' the complex interdependencies in a business and in the metaphor of operating as a galaxy.

Thinking and operating like an AI-native company at the enterprise level would mean that the strategic decisions between optimum choices and transformative choices are based on incorporating and leveraging contextual AI capabilities. Digital-native companies base such strategic decisions solely on a few leaders combining their experience, data analytics provided to them, and their intuition. AI-native companies will be able to harness contextual AI capabilities and make strategic decisions empowered by insights drawn from a complex, non-linear set of information and in a dynamic and continuous way. The galaxy never sleeps and is intelligent 24/7 at the enterprise level.

Thinking and operating like an AI-native company at the ecosystem level, means having the AI-powered capability to discover potential network effects in a marketplace platform, in a systematic and continuous way. This can be achieved without needing an AI algorithm for each KPI (e.g. gross merchandise metrics, average order value, customer acquisition cost) and without having to wait for this discovery to occur once a year. The discovery of new revenue opportunities will be upgraded to a level that can process the complexity of the galaxy in which the marketplace platform operates. The galaxy never sleeps and is intelligent 24/7 at the ecosystem level.

Thinking and operating like an AI-native company at the customer level, includes systematic dexterity capabilities to serve customers in both physical and digital touch points. No trade-off compromises are needed as the contextual capabilities of AI enable a high level of customization based on the context rather than groupings like by age or education level.

Galaxies are intelligent at all levels and 24/7; at the level of the stars and planets, at the level of dust and gas, and at the level of gravity and expansion.

Galaxies are intelligent in very complex ways. AI-native companies will mimic that built-in level of intelligent complexity as they build and grow their businesses. AI-native companies will not only use data and analytics (similar to digital natives) but will also integrate contextual insights at scale and in every corner of their galaxy.

The suggested five-dimensional framework is a blueprint towards an AI business-wide transformation that facilitates our current understanding. It maps the complexity of businesses and the value of unlocking the interconnectedness in systematic and continuous ways.

While the first cohort of AI-native businesses is not yet born, it is clear that the new archetype of AI-native businesses will push the boundaries of intelligence at the enterprise and ecosystem level, while serving customers in a far superior way than digital natives have.[31]

AI-native businesses will be able to 'hack' the complex interdependencies across the galaxy in which they operate.

Chapter 4

Deconstructed and Decentralized Work: At the Interconnection between the Future of Work and Blockchain

Ravin Jesuthasan and Alun Evans

The last 5 years have seen significant advancements in digitalization and automation. The rapid advances in artificial intelligence (AI), cloud-based computing, 5G, low-cost sensors and processing power have transformed every aspect of human life. When coupled with the democratization of work, i.e. our growing ability to increasingly decouple work from its traditional confines of space, time and structure, the impact has been an exponential acceleration towards the future of work. While many might limit the definition of work to be largely about where it is done and when it is performed, given the focus over the past 3 years on the space and time dimensions of work as organizations grappled with working onsite versus hybrid working versus working remotely, it is important to remember that work is actually defined by six dimensions. In addition to 'where' and 'when' it is performed, there is the 'how' work is done (like job/work sharing, among other things), 'what' the work is (such as the tasks that make up a job, the underlying skills requirements and how rapidly these are changing), 'who' does the work (including automation, gig talent, talent in agile pools and so on) and 'why' work is done (asking questions like 'Why should I engage with your mission? Does it align with my own sense of purpose?').

The traditional 'closed' work operating system with jobs as its basic currency and limited permutations and variations of these six dimensions is increasingly insufficient in delivering the resilience, agility or flexibility required of the twenty-first century organization. As Ravin Jesuthasan and John Boudreau illustrated in *Work Without Jobs*,[1] a fundamental shift is underway. Accelerated change; demands for organizational agility; work automation; efforts to increase diversity, equity and inclusion (DEI); and emerging alternative work arrangements are exposing cracks in this old work structure, revealing it as too cumbersome and ill-suited for the future. In its place, a new work-operating system is emerging, based on deconstructed work (tasks, activities and so on) and workers (skills, interests and so on) that can be perpetually recombined and reinvented within an open ecosystem. Those granular elements are the foundation for more human-centric organizations, where work and talent rather than jobs and processes are the building blocks and the blockchain becomes ever more critical as a mechanism for powering a more decentralized, accessible future of work.

But first, let's cut through the hype and misinformation to clearly define the blockchain.

What is the Blockchain?

What many people refer to as 'the blockchain' is more accurately titled 'blockchain network technology', for there are many different implementations. However, all implementations share three core concepts. The first is *decentralization*. A *centralized* system relies on one network node to be a single source of authority to store data and be the ultimate decision maker (or source of truth). An example of this might be any one of the web 2.0 social media networks – the network owner has full control over who may join, it can censor or remove posts, and all of the data are stored on a server which belongs to the network. This latter point is one of the weaknesses of centralized systems, in that they have a single point of failure. If, for example, the server of the social media network is taken down (for whatever reason), then all the data are lost. To protect against this, most modern centralized systems are implemented in a *distributed* manner, where the same data are stored in multiple nodes (for example, across multiple servers), which means that if one node is lost, hacked or otherwise compromised, it can be safely removed from the network, as the data are still available at the other nodes. However, the network is still conceptually centralized, as it relies on a single source of authority (in our example, the owner of the social media network). A fully *decentralized* system takes the distributed approach to an extreme, in that it provides autonomous decision-making power to each of the nodes of the network. While the nodes may agree on the correct way of communicating with each other (the 'protocol'), they act independently, and are not subservient to any single source of authority.

This leads us to the second core concept of blockchain technology, *trust* – or more specifically, a lack of it. If each node in our network is fully autonomous, how can any node trust that another will behave as it should – or even, as it claims? To generate this trust, the protocol must implement some form of *incentive system* – nodes that are shown to be honest get rewarded, while those that are dishonest either get nothing, or are punished. If the incentives are scarce, this means that nodes will compete to receive them, in other words if a given node is acting honestly to receive a reward, it is in its interest to demonstrate that the other nodes are *not* honest (thus maximizing its chances of being rewarded). Thus, in any blockchain network, the nodes are competing against each other to receive a reward, and doing so by both demonstrating their own honesty, while attempting to prove that others are dishonest – a *trustless* system.

One key component of a trustless system is proof of identity, for without it, none of the nodes has any guarantee of the identity of the author of a given message. For this, blockchain technology relies on cryptography – the process of encoding and decoding messages in a manner that is mathematically guaranteed to be accurate. In particular, *asymmetric* cryptography is fundamental to all blockchain protocols. Asymmetric cryptography permits nodes to 'sign' messages sent to other nodes in a way that proves the identity of the author. Specifically, a node signs a message using its 'private key', a very long number used as a cipher text, which is kept as a closely guarded secret and known only to the author node. Other nodes use a paired 'public key' – known to all and highly distributed – to prove that a given message *must have been signed* by the paired private key. Private/public key pairs are uniquely linked to each other by advanced cryptographic mathematics which are, to all practical intents and purposes, impossible to reverse engineer (e.g. attempting to brute-force extract a 256-bit private key from a given message would take a modern computer over a billion years of non-stop calculation). Key pairs are usually stored and managed within a 'wallet' application, which could be a mobile application, a plugin for a web-browser, or even a hardware device that plugs into a computer via USB. Such wallets, where the user is 100% responsible for the key pairs, are known as *non-custodial* wallets. By contrast, some companies offer services that will store and manage the key pairs on the user's behalf, allowing them to restore access in case of loss via other identification means. These services are known as *custodial* wallets.

This final concept of signing messages (or, to use the more common blockchain term, 'transactions') leads to the third and final core concept, that of *immutability*. A regular store of data (a standard computer database, for example) is freely mutable, in that all the data can be edited or deleted at any time (although modern databases frequently implement a series of protections against this – for example, different access levels for different users – there will always be at least one user with the 'master password' who has complete control over the data). By contrast, blockchain networks are *immutable* – once a record is added to the end of the list of transactions (the 'ledger', to use again the common blockchain parlance) then it can never be edited or deleted without breaking the entire ledger. This is accomplished by leaning again on cryptography. Transactions can be added to the end of the ledger by cryptographically linking any new transaction to the last, most recent, transaction – the new message will, in essence, contain a little bit of the previous message. This creates an unbreakable *chain* of transactions, each referring to the previous one that was added to the end of the chain. If any transaction in the middle of the chain is somehow tampered with, it will invalidate not only the immediate next transaction, but *every single one* of the following transactions. Thus, any tampering is simple to spot. For reasons of efficiency, transactions are usually added to the end of the chain in groups, or 'blocks', thus creating a chain of cryptographically linked blocks, from which we derive the name.

A Practical Example: The Bitcoin Network

Blockchain technology was invented in 2008 (via a white paper whose pseudonymous author, 'Satoshi Nakamoto', remains unidentified to this day) as a potential solution to a task of creating a purely virtual currency which is independent on any central authority. It is useful, then, to use this initial implementation as a case study of how blockchain technology works, and perhaps more importantly, why it is required.

While much of the regular financial system has embraced digital money (many people pay for goods with credit/debit cards, and use online banking systems), most currencies still retain an underlying physical component (for example, the dollar bill). *Virtual* currencies, by contrast, are those that only exist digitally – there is no physical money equivalent. A core problem for implementing a virtual currency is that of 'double spending'. For example, if User A transfers 10 units of currency to User B, how can User B be certain that User A has removed those ten units from their balance?

Or not transferred those same 10 units simultaneously to multiple users, 'spending' the same amount of currency multiple times?

The first implementation of blockchain technology is a network that uses the three threads mentioned earlier, *decentralization*, *trust* (or lack of it) and *immutability* to create a network that functions as a store of a virtual currency – a 'cryptocurrency' (which, in this case, was named 'bitcoin'). The network comprises a decentralized cluster of nodes which can receive and relay transactions (for example, 'User A wishes to transfer 10 bitcoin to User B'). Once a transaction is submitted to the network, the nodes may compete to verify that transaction, and add it to the end of the chain. If a node wins the competition to verify the transaction, it is rewarded (with bitcoin) – this process is called 'mining'. Other nodes are free to verify the transaction themselves, and accept it as a valid addition, that is, it will be used as the root for the next transaction to be added to the chain. (Note: if a majority of nodes think that a transaction is not valid, they are free to ignore it and create a new chain of transactions – this is called a 'fork'.)

As each transaction references the previous one, the double spending problem is eliminated. For example, if User A tries to transfer the same 10 bitcoin to two different users simultaneously, one of those transactions will be valid and be added to the chain, whereas the other will be marked as invalid and not accepted, as the miner can see from the immutable chain history that those 10 bitcoin have already been 'spent' by this user.

The Bitcoin network (note: the network name is capitalized, whereas the currency title is not) has now grown sufficiently to have demonstrated that it is an effective and secure method of retaining and transferring virtual currency. In order for the network to be 'hacked', that is for fraudulent transactions to be included in the chain, a single actor would have to control more than 50% of the mining nodes of the network, in order to force the network to use their fraudulent fork. As there are now over a million miners (anyone can create a node and start mining), and mining is expensive (see later), it would now be prohibitively expensive to attempt to control the majority of the network – the costs would outweigh the benefits.

Mining: Proof-of-Work vs Proof-of-Stake

Many headlines have been written about the energy consumption of blockchain mining. This is due to the manner of the competition that miners use to validate a transaction and add it to the chain. The basic mining implementation is the 'proof-of-work' method – miners use computing power to race to solve an arbitrary mathematical problem. The first miner to demonstrate that they have solved the problem 'wins the race' to add the transaction to the chain, and thus receives the reward. As a result, miners employ ever greater computing power to better compete; this computing power uses electricity, which of course has a cost. The advantage of this scenario is that it means each miner must be willing to spend their own money to have a chance of being rewarded (in colloquial investor parlance, they must 'have some skin in the game'). The disadvantage is that proof-of-work mining uses vast amounts of electricity. As the world is still heavily reliant on non-renewable source of electricity, this has justifiably created negative headlines.

As a result, an alternative method for mining has been developed: 'proof-of-stake'. In this protocol, rather than compete to solve an arbitrary computing problem, miners must 'stake' some of their cryptocurrency as collateral, which is then locked up in a deposit. If the network determines that a transaction is invalid, then a proportion of that stake is lost. A miner's chances of winning the competition are directly proportional to the size of its stake – a larger stake means a greater chance of reward, but also a greater risk. Proof-of-stake requires around 99.95% less energy usage than proof-of-work, and as such is now being used in all modern blockchain protocols.

Blockchain Beyond Cryptocurrency

While cryptocurrency was the motivation for the development of blockchain protocols, the applications of the technology have since been greatly expanded to many other areas of business. Figure 4.1 illustrates some of the benefits of the blockchain.[2]

Benefits blockchain can bring to business

1. Trust
Enables trust between participants who don't know each other.

2. Decentralized structure
Enables real-time data sharing among businesses like suppliers and distributors while reducing points of weakness.

3. Improved security and privacy
Creates an unalterable record of transactions with end-to-end encryption, which reduces fraud and unauthorized activity.

4. Reduced costs
Creates efficiencies by reducing manual tasks such as aggregating and amending data and by easing reporting and auditing.

5. Speed
Eliminates intermediaries so transactions are handled faster than conventional methods.

6. Visibility and traceability
Tracks the origins of a variety of items, such as medicines, to confirm they're legitimate instead of counterfeit and organic items to confirm they're indeed organic.

7. Immutability
Ensures transactions can't be changed or deleted.

8. Individual control of data
Gives entities the ability to decide what digital data they want to share, with whom and for how long, with limits enforced by smart contracts.

9. Tokenization
Converts value of an asset into a digital token recorded and shared via blockchain. Non-fungible tokens are used to sell digital art.

10. Innovation
Leaders across multiple industries are exploring and implementing blockchain-based systems to solve intractable problems and improve long-standing cumbersome practices, such as verifying the info on a job resume.

Figure 4.1 Blockchain benefits.

Now that we have defined the blockchain, let's explore the three ways it is shaping the future of work (Figure 4.2).

1. **Transactional:** The most straightforward and perhaps obvious application would be to use blockchain to enable the distribution of value to non-employees (individuals and organizations who contribute to the mission of a company).
2. **Organizational:** In this scenario, the blockchain creates opportunities to power a more democratized and open work ecosystem through Decentralized Autonomous Organizations (DAOs).
3. **Strategic traceability and verification** across all aspects of the organizational value chain; from logistics and supply chain to decentralized identity management to human resources.

Let's explore each of these in turn.

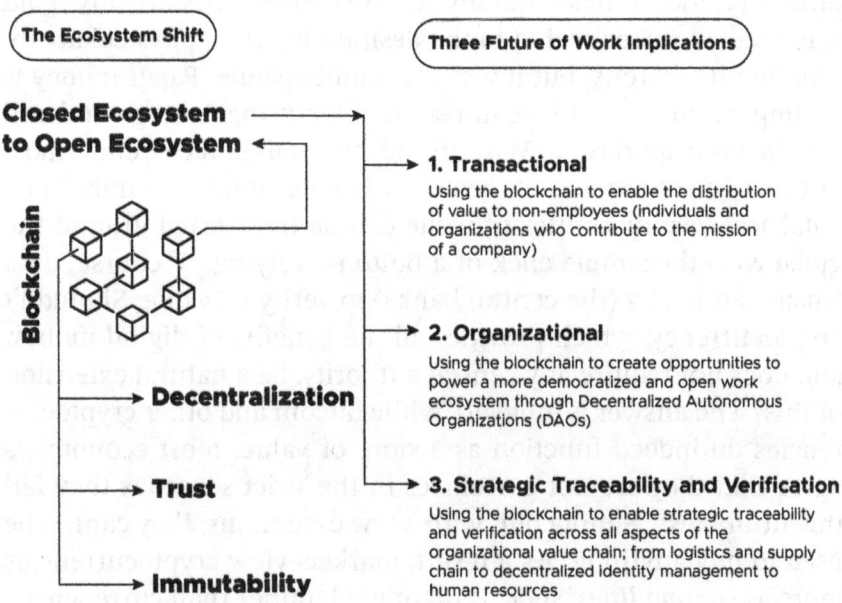

Figure 4.2 How the blockchain is shaping the future of work.

Transactional

As established earlier in the chapter, the first use-case of blockchain technology (indeed, the initial reason for which it was invented) was to carry out transactions via a purely virtual currency (a 'cryptocurrency'). With the rise in popularity of bitcoin and other cryptocurrencies, there has been an equivalent rise of exchange services that allow individuals or businesses to exchange fiat currencies (regular currencies such as the US dollar, or euro) for cryptocurrencies such as bitcoin. Such exchanges are *centralized* services and rely on maintaining their own liquidity pools in each currency to provide an efficient service to the end-user. They are a key part of the ecosystem in that they provide a gateway for fiat currency markets to access cryptocurrency markets. Thanks to the presence of these services, cryptocurrencies such as bitcoin now have an equivalent value in fiat currencies and have now become an established part of the currency trading market.

There is, however, some legal debate as to whether bitcoin and other cryptocurrencies qualify as 'currencies'. Historically, gold was used as currency due to the desirability of its physical attributes and its scarcity, but it was also cumbersome. Paper money is an improvement, but it requires manufacturing, storage and still requires transportation. With the advent of digital currency, most of the value of the world's economy is now simply a number in a database. Vast quantities of value can be transferred around the globe with the simple click of a button – relying, of course, on a trusted authority (the central banks) to verify its value. Shouldn't cryptocurrency, which provides all the benefits of digital money, and does not require any central authority, be a natural extension of this? The answer is 'not yet'. While bitcoin and other cryptocurrencies do indeed function as a store of value, most economists agree that they are not currencies in the strict sense, as they fail the 'utility test'. Simply put, with a few exceptions, they cannot be used to buy anything. As a result, markets view cryptocurrencies more as *commodities*, such as oil or gold, rather than currencies.

Where, then, does this leave the value of blockchain transactions in the future of work? If cryptocurrencies cannot be spent, what is their value? The answer lies in our increasingly distributed and decentralized world, and particularly the developing world. Xapo Bank,[3] an established private bank very tightly integrated into the crypto ecosystem, exists precisely because one of its founders was struggling to transfer currency from the United States to his native country Argentina – and so turned to bitcoin to solve the problem. While it is not yet a common option to pay for goods in store or online with cryptocurrencies, increasingly it is becoming possible to pay for services – with the recipient of the cryptocurrency being free to exchange it into any other currency they like.

Following bitcoin's launch, there are now dozens if not hundreds of blockchain protocols, and the technology has expanded beyond simply being able to store and move value, to being able to store and execute instructions programmatically once certain conditions are met. These 'programmable blockchains' – of which the largest is the Ethereum blockchain – can be thought of a decentralized computer, employing so called 'smart contracts' to generate decentralized applications, or 'Dapps'. Smart contracts have revolutionized the use of blockchain in the business world, extending its utility far beyond simple transactions. It is to these applications that we turn next.

Organizational

Most organizations, such as companies, clubs, cooperatives, charities and so on tend to feature governance structures that enable stakeholders to participate in decisions that affect the future of the organization. For example, a typical company will have shareholders, who can vote (based on the percentage of their shareholding) to have their say on how the company operates. Decision-making power is then delegated to a board, to a leadership team, to management, and so on. Structures like this often result in high agency cost as the interests of each entity may diverge from those of shareholders. The recent situation with OpenAI highlights the significant potential for disruption when governance and decision rights are not clear and transparent.[4]

The proliferation of blockchain technology has seen the rise of a new approach to organizational management and participation, the

Decentralized Autonomous Organization, or DAO. DAOs exploit smart contract architectures and digital tokens verified on public blockchains, such as Ethereum, in order to give members of a DAO the possibility to participate directly in its governance. Decision making thus becomes collective and based on how many votes – expressed in the number of tokens – a certain proposal in the DAO gets. There are no barriers to entry and owning tokens in a DAO is permissionless. Since all rules are coded in smart contracts and all transactions are recorded on a blockchain, a DAO is fully transparent to its members. If the DAO is purposed with developing ideas, or software, then the IP is open-sourced, at least for now.

As DAOs are adopted more widely, new types of businesses will emerge that would look more like digitally native cooperatives and less like traditional centralized corporations, significantly reducing agency costs. In such decentralized organizations, leadership will rely on soft power and empathy, using culture and shared values to align the interests of disparate stakeholders to a common mission and purpose.

In a DAO there are no officers, directors or managers, and therefore leadership roles are more fluid and impermanent, giving more opportunities to members to rise up. DAOs may decide to prioritize social goods – such as job security – above operational efficiency. This shift from hierarchical structures to flat, widely distributed networks and ecosystems run by stakeholder communities instead of boards and executives, will have a profound impact on work too. Figure 4.3 illustrates the fundamental differences between traditional organizations and decentralized autonomous organizations.[5]

In *Work Without Jobs*, Jesuthasan and Boudreau describe three ways in which talent is connected to work (fixed, flex and flow) within the context of a new work operating model for companies organized within the context of a more traditional corporate structure. With the introduction of decentralized autonomous organizations, we see a fourth option with even less friction and much greater agility, one where work flows to talent. Figure 4.4 illustrates these four options and the potential gains as we move from left to right.

Within the context of work being increasingly organized as DAOs, the traditional hierarchical mix of roles within a corporate

	Traditional Org	DAO
Decision making	Centralized	Collective
Ownership	Permissioned	Permissionless
Structure	Hierarchical	Flat / distributed
Information flows	Private and gated	Transparent and public
IP	Closed-source	Open-source

Figure 4.3 Traditional and DAO organizations.

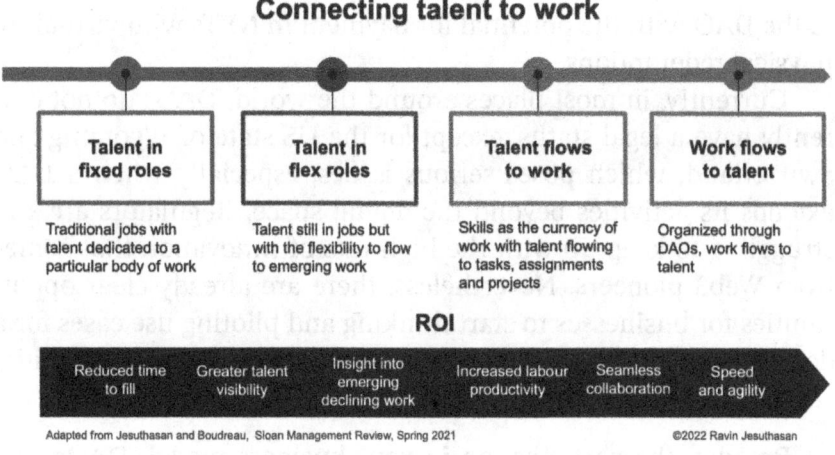

Connecting talent to work

Talent in fixed roles	Talent in flex roles	Talent flows to work	Work flows to talent
Traditional jobs with talent dedicated to a particular body of work	Talent still in jobs but with the flexibility to flow to emerging work	Skills as the currency of work with talent flowing to tasks, assignments and projects	Organized through DAOs, work flows to talent

ROI

Reduced time to fill	Greater talent visibility	Insight into emerging declining work	Increased labour productivity	Seamless collaboration	Speed and agility

Adapted from Jesuthasan and Boudreau, Sloan Management Review, Spring 2021   ©2022 Ravin Jesuthasan

Figure 4.4 Connecting talent to work.

structure (leader, manager, employee, contractor and vendor) and functions will morph significantly into a flatter construct comprising:

- A core group of individuals responsible for the coordination of work and delivering on the value proposition of the DAO.
- A broader contributor group that provides specific services to execute the mission of the DAO. This includes other DAOs that provide services like HR, finance and accounting and customer service on an ongoing basis and individual contributors (gig workers or contractors) that take on projects as needed.

- An even broader group of 'members' who will promote brands, support continued crowdsourcing of ongoing product innovation or otherwise contribute to the advancement of the DAO's mission.

Each of these groups will be compensated quite differently. The core group will share in the total value created by the DAO less payments to the other two groups. The payments to the contributor group will vary between fixed payments for ongoing services in the case of a DAO providing HR services and more episodic payments to individual contributors as they take on and execute specific projects. Members will be rewarded as they make various contributions to the DAO with the potential for payment in NFTs with virtual-to-physical redemptions.

Currently, in most places around the world, DAOs do not currently have a legal status, except for the US state of Wyoming and Switzerland, which poses serious issues, especially when a DAO extends its activities beyond the digital space. Regulators are still struggling to keep up with the high rate of innovation that comes from Web3 pioneers. Nevertheless, there are already clear opportunities for businesses to start thinking and piloting use cases for a decentralized future. Here are a few ways to prototype your initial steps into this new world of work:

- Broaden the participation in your business model. DAOs present us with an opportunity to increase the agility of the enterprise by enabling work to flow to talent beyond the traditional 'walls' of the organization. Consider creating a DAO that enables the broader community of stakeholders in your business to participate in promoting your brands or crowdsourcing ideas for innovation.
- Experiment with taking the idea of a DAO further, by outsourcing ESG goals to a DAO governed by your company's stakeholders, such as employees, contractors, suppliers and impacted communities.
- Identify opportunities and use cases in your core processes where the gradual transition to a blockchain-enabled future will add value and include them in your digital transformation agenda.

Strategic traceability and verification across all aspects of the organizational value chain

Many features of blockchain technology make it ideal for use in organizational value management. Note that in these scenarios, there is a key difference to the examples that have been discussed so far in this chapter. Cryptocurrencies, DAOs and Dapps are usually seen on *open, permissionless* blockchains (i.e., anybody can view and interact with the application), whereas an organization's value chain may need to be *private.*

Although one of the principal tenets of public-facing blockchain technology is that is open and permissionless, use-cases exist where a *private, permissioned* blockchain may be of great benefit to a business or organization, and this section explores several of those use-cases. A *private* blockchain is still decentralized, may still work with incentive systems to reach consensus, and its data will still be immutable; however, access to it is restricted to accredited members of the owning company or organization. A *permissioned* blockchain extends this even further, creating access levels (for example, perhaps only certain accredited nodes may become miners, and there may be different user-access levels that are authorized to submit transactions of different types). Finally, it is also possible to implement an *open, permissioned* blockchain, which allows anybody to view the data, but only accredited users to add transactions.

Logistics and Supply Chain

The supply chain logistics industry is a complex ecosystem that involves the movement of goods, information and finances across the globe. This intricate network is constantly faced with challenges related to transparency, security, efficiency and trust. One of the most significant benefits of blockchain in logistics and supply chain management is enhanced transparency and traceability. Traditional supply chain systems often struggle with limited visibility, making it difficult to track the movement of goods and verify their authenticity. With blockchain, every step of a product's journey can be recorded and made accessible to authorized parties.

Each participant in the supply chain can view the entire history of a product, from its origin to its current location, in real-time. This transparency helps to identify inefficiencies, reduce errors and build trust among stakeholders.

- *Delivery logistics*: The services offered by shipping companies such as DHL and UPS depend on being able to deliver parcels quickly and efficiently around the world, via multiple transport methods, and through multiple hubs. Many logistics companies are turning to blockchain as a way of transparently securing an immutable record of transportation, which can be shown to their customers. Many leading companies are pushing for more open standards and interoperability, with UPS joining an alliance for the development of blockchain usage in the freight industry.[6]
- *Food logistics*: The sourcing, harvesting, transportation and selling of food is clearly an essential part of our modern economy. There are two areas here in which blockchain technology is being used. The first is to accurately verify the source of a particular food package. Many food sources boast of organic farming, fair-pay conditions to employees, strict anti-contamination procedures and so on. Signing on the blockchain that a particular package does indeed come from a given source provides transparency and guarantees authenticity. The second area is in food logistics, particularly for perishable food. By combining blockchain with other areas of technology, such as the Internet of Things, companies such as IBM[7] are creating solutions that enable full traceability and transparency within the supply chain.
- *Automation with smart contracts*: Programmable blockchains (such as Ethereum) permit the use of *smart contracts* (self-executing contracts with the terms of the agreement directly written into code). In logistics and supply chain management, smart contracts automate various processes, reducing the need for intermediaries, and minimizing errors. For instance, when goods arrive at a distribution centre, a smart contract

can automatically trigger payment to the supplier based on predefined conditions such as quality inspection and delivery confirmation. This not only accelerates the payment process but also reduces disputes and administrative overhead.

While blockchain technology offers numerous benefits for logistics and supply chain management, its usage does come with some risks. Principal among these is *security*: although blockchain technology by default is highly secure, it is not immune to security breaches such as private key theft, hacking of blockchain nodes, and vulnerabilities in smart contracts. Any compromise of security can result in data breaches, financial losses and disruptions in the supply chain.

Another potential risk is with regulatory compliance. The regulatory environment surrounding blockchain and cryptocurrencies is still evolving, thus making the technology an integral part of a company's supply chain management is assuming that any changes to the relevant authorities' regulations regarding the technology will not affect the functioning of the business.

Decentralized Identity and Ownership Management

In the early days of the internet, typical usage was much more decentralized than it is today. An email address might be provided by a user's internet service provider, but many enthusiasts ran their own servers. Social media was dominated by Internet Relay Chat (IRC), an open-source client-server chat protocol that doesn't necessarily require creating an account or logging in. While such methods and technologies were adequate for the early adopters, as the Internet developed it became clear that more user-friendly applications were required to drive adoption.

The cost of this was increased reliance on centralization and a ceding of user authority and identity to third parties. The modern digital world relies on centralized permission for almost any and every service. If a user wishes to access their email, they must 'log in' to their provider service. The same for social network access, television services, media access, video gaming, e-commerce and more. At any moment, any of those centralized services could decide to block or cancel their service to a particular user; at which point all the information and data that the user has provided to the service is effectively lost.

Decentralized identity is a futuristic approach to try to invert the power dynamic of access to services, by giving the final user more agency as to how their identity and data can be used. For example, rather than logging-in to an online service by registering with a centralized database, a user demonstrates their identity by digitally signing a transaction, with a signature that could only have been generated from a given private key. This means that the user has full control over where and how their data is being stored and used.

To understand the concept of decentralized identity, we must first start with the reminder that, by default, identification on the blockchain is both *open* and *anonymous*. An 'account' on any given blockchain is simply a public address, and everyone viewing the blockchain can see the full history of every transaction that that account has made. But there is no default way of linking a public address to the identity of a person or organization – indeed any given individual could control multiple accounts. Public identification of a person or organization can be identified by some other means, and through that means provide a signature that only the holder of the private key could generate (for example, a governmental authority could use their regular publication methods to publish a signature to prove that they controlled a given address or addresses).

This method of identification is not feasible at scale, however, and decentralized identity is an attempt to solve this problem. The key approach is based on the idea of allowing any address to make a *claim* about another address. The latter is then free to accept that claim, or reject it.

For example, a government account (verified by other means, as mentioned earlier) might make a claim against a certain address, stating the owner's full name, nationality, and ID number (they might do this having verified the address owner's identity via other means). The owner of the address may accept this claim, and thus show the world an immediate proof of identity – by the authority of the government that made the claim. Any number of other addresses may make claims. For example, a university may claim that this address owner has earned a degree; a country may issue a visa for a limited amount of time, a company may claim the address owner is an employee; local gym may claim that the address is a member and so on.

One of the risks of using decentralized identity is the potential *lack of privacy*. While in many situations, account owners will want to have all their accepted claims made public, once a claim has been accepted it is forever stored with that address – it is not possible to maintain any of that information private, and that information could be used against the account owner (for example, an individual travelling to a given country might not want to advertise accepted claims made by another country that is hostile to the first country).

The major use-case for decentralized identity so far has been in Know-Your-Customer (KYC) and Anti-Money-Laundering (AML) checks for the purchase and sale of blockchain-based assets with fiat (i.e. US dollar, euro) currency. This leads us to the concept of *digital ownership*. Until blockchain technology was invented, 'owning' anything digital did not make conceptual sense. For one point, any file can be copied an infinite number of times; and for another, it was impossible to prove any user's identity in the digital world. Blockchain has solved both these issues. While a file can be copied an infinite number of times, a file's unique identifier (for example, its 'checksum') can be associated to a unique record (or 'token') stored on the blockchain. The most basic category of tokens of ownership is that of cryptocurrency – tokens which are each functionally identical and thus fungible. By contrast, *non-fungible tokens* (NFTs) are unique records that demonstrate that a given user is the owner of a given unique piece of digital content. While the early applications of NFT technology have been to use this unique ownership as a driver of speculative investment (of digital art and collectibles), resulting in typical boom-and-bust cycles, the concept of digital ownership has many logical applications that are now being developed for videogames, store loyalty programmes, ticketing and more.

Human Resources (HR)

Like other organizational functions, there are numerous opportunities for the HR function to leverage the power of the blockchain. These are the most common applications we are currently seeing:

- *Direct compensation of employees*: Payroll through blockchain-based technologies is the strongest use case and probably the most straightforward implementation. An employee can be given a choice of receiving payment either through traditional direct deposit or through a cryptocurrency asset. Early applications were for cross-border payments, especially remittances. Traditional electronic payments can sometimes be stymied by local regulations and IT security protocols that blockchain-based payroll systems can overcome. Use of the blockchain is particularly critical when employees lack bank accounts.
- *Streaming earnings*: The blockchain enables streaming earnings to employees to reduce the rising need for early wage access (EWA) and dangerous pay-day loans. The cost-of-living crisis and the uncertain macroeconomic conditions have resulted in increased cash flow management problems which can be addressed by streaming money (only possible on blockchain) instead of the usual bi-weekly or monthly payrolls.
- *Rewarding contractors and vendors*: The increased use of freelancers, remote contract workers and other non-employee labour creates another potential application for the blockchain. Blockchain token rewards can be used to pay such labour for the execution of agreed work or to reward for over-performance.

- *Recruitment*: Candidates can use the blockchain to tokenize their identity and provide virtual credentials, such as college transcripts, training certificates, resumes and work histories that recruiters and hiring managers can trust have not been tampered with. Recruiters spend a significant amount of time gathering and transmitting documentation. The blockchain can streamline much of this work. Most companies typically use third-party vendors to conduct background checks and verify information. They could eliminate this expense by using blockchain verification. While HR use of the blockchain for this particular purpose is at an early stage, a number of universities are already providing their students and alumni with records in blockchain format.

- *Employee data*: Personal information can be encrypted and stored on the blockchain, providing immutability and a secure governance system for private information. However, as with educational records, the veracity of information stored on the blockchain depends heavily on the methods and integrity of the entity creating the initial record. As a result, some experts believe that it is more realistic for blockchains to be the database of record for employee data going forward than a reliable repository of past information which may not be verifiable.

- *Contract management*: The smart contracts that are enabled by blockchain can replace traditional paper contracts with immutable and transparent digital contracts. Employers can use them to enforce the terms and penalties outlined in agreements with employees and contractors. These include enforcement of non-competes, verification of deliverables in statements of work and monitoring of various covenants.

- *Recognition programmes*: The use of blockchain tokens as recognition awards for employees is growing. Companies are getting creative in their use of such programmes to motivate employees to take on additional projects and assignments, collaborate with colleagues and others and expend more discretionary effort. Companies are more able to tie recognition awards to achievement of specific objectives or dates, in the case of holiday bonuses or related rewards. All of this with the security and reliability of running on the blockchain.

- *Learning and development*: As skills increasingly become the currency of the labour market, the ability to reliably and objectively track skill acquisition and development is becoming critical. More and more companies, edtech providers and traditional educational institutions are providing learners with non-fungible tokens that can be used to track and verify the acquisition and expression of various skills.

Now that we have explored some of the use cases, what are some of the risks we need to consider? The operational risks associated with these applications typically fall into four categories. These include:

- *Cyber security*: Blockchains are still susceptible to data vulnerabilities from endpoints that hackers can exploit to intercept data during transmission. This poses a significant risk to HR professionals and others who deal with personal information and financial transactions.
- *Compliance risk*: Blockchains still lack regional regulatory standards, which expose organizations to financial losses and legal penalties for failing to respect employee data rights and comply with legal frameworks, such as the European Union's General Data Protection Regulation.
- *Counterparty risk*: Third-party vendors often have to be enlisted to facilitate blockchain transactions. The trust provided by a blockchain is thus extended to those vendors' applications and websites, which may not be as secure as the blockchain thus creating additional vulnerabilities.
- *Data privacy*: For HR, the biggest internal risk factor is the human component. Employees and other talent may not trust that their personal information can be stored securely and safely on a distributed ledger.

Conclusion

As you can see, the interconnection between the future of work and the blockchain is both significant today and holds much potential for the future. The transactional, organizational and strategic traceability and verification benefits will only increase as they continue to be deployed more systemically. We leave you with five questions to consider as these interconnections play out:

1. While Proof-of-Stake consensus systems are the norm in new blockchain technology, most legacy technology (including the Bitcoin network) uses Proof-of-Work. Is there a path for eventually moving Bitcoin to Proof-of-Stake? Or will another, cleaner, chain take over its mantle?

2. Some custodial wallet services have collapsed, meaning end-users have lost access to their keys. Will we see a greater level of regulatory scrutiny for such services? How will this work across international borders?

3. Some NFTs are being classed as 'securities' (i.e. investments) in the United States by the Securities and Exchange Commission. Will all NFTs end up being classified as investments, or is there space for other applications of the technology?

4. As regulatory frameworks change and acceptance of DAOs increases, what new applications might we see?

5. As the HR applications of the blockchain increase, what opportunities might we see for it to replace or augment the functionalities of traditional enterprise resource planning (ERP) systems?

Chapter 5

Intelligent Health: The Convergence of Data and AI

Vince Kuraitis and Ramanathan Srikumar

AI could be more profound than both fire and electricity . . . It gets to the essence of what intelligence is, what humanity is. We are developing technology which, for sure, one day will be far more capable than anything we've ever seen before.
(Sundar Pichai, CEO, Alphabet [formerly known as Google])[1]

42% of CEOs say AI could destroy humanity in five to ten years.
(CNN headline, 14 June 2023)[2]

In the grand theatre of human existence, Artificial Intelligence (AI) emerges as both the saviour and the potential destroyer, a paradoxical entity wielding the double-edged sword of promise and peril. On one hand, AI stands as the guardian angel of modern medicine, capable of diagnosing diseases with an accuracy that makes even the most seasoned doctors bow in reverence.

133

Imagine AI algorithms in radiology, detecting the faintest whispers of cancer cells long before they roar into a deadly tempest, thereby saving countless lives. Yet, on the other hand, AI is the Pandora's Box that, once opened, could unleash calamities of biblical proportions. Picture autonomous weapons, AI-driven drones that could make human-triggered warfare look like child's play. These mechanical harbingers of doom could, in a moment of algorithmic miscalculation, plunge civilizations into an abyss of destruction from which there may be no return.

(AI chatbot ChatGPT-4).

The path of progress is littered with the road-kill of technologies that were hyped for rapid, mainstream adoption – but have underachieved, at least to date. Examples include: blockchain, crypto, Web3, NFTs, self-driving cars, flying cars, wearable tech, and others. Some underachieving technologies were spawned at individual companies: Apple's Newton, Google Glass, the Google Plus social network, Amazon's Fire Phone, and others.

Despite its long gestation period, today most observers – including us – would put artificial intelligence (AI) in the category of successful and transformative general-purpose technologies[3] similar to steam power, electricity, computers, and the Internet. Venture capitalist James Currier projects that AI is 'going to affect every industry'.[4] AI is a really big deal.

So what happens when AI meshes with healthcare, one of the slowest-moving, regulated and change-resistant sectors of the world economy? That is the topic of discussion in this chapter. The framework in Figure 5.1 encapsulates the content of the chapter.

First, we start with a brief recap of the history of artificial intelligence. Then we put health and healthcare into context – examining how healthcare is different, describing six dynamic dimensions of world health systems, and exploring the complexity and uniqueness of health data. We then explain a three-phase framework for understanding decades-long adoption patterns of general-purpose technologies. Finally, we present three case studies applying this framework to the adoption of AI in healthcare.

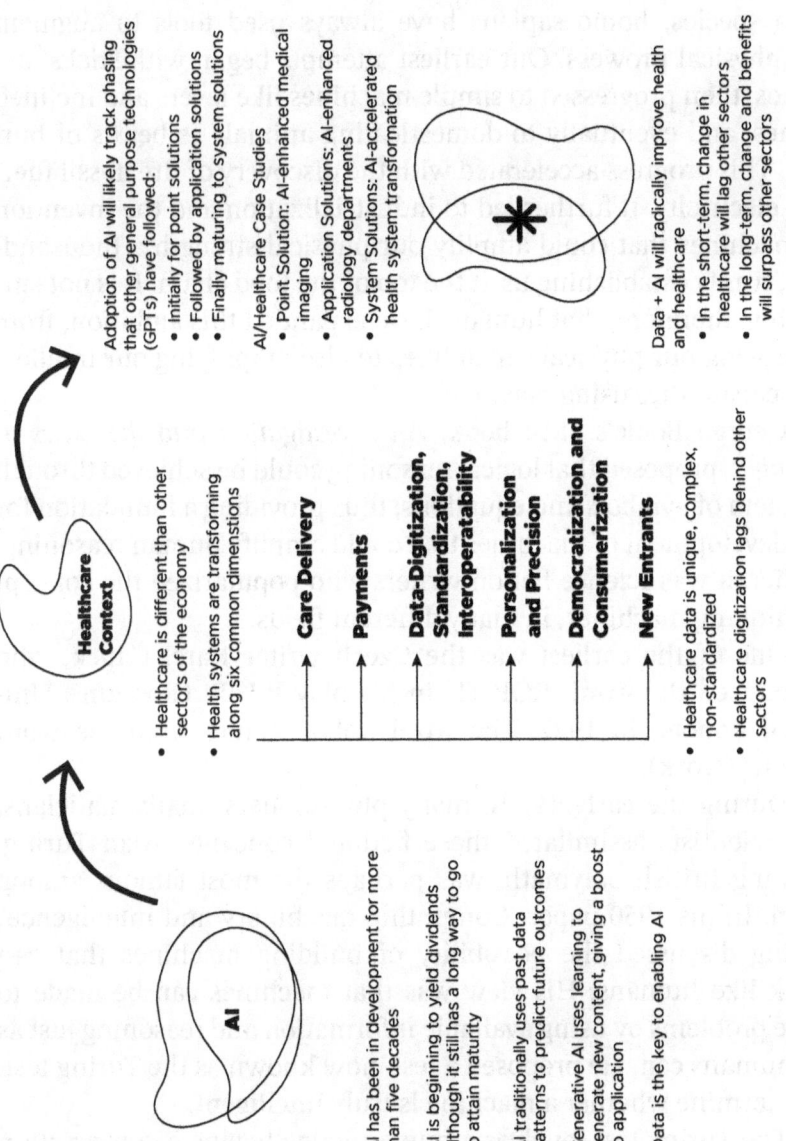

Adoption of AI will likely track phasing
that other general purpose technologies
(GPTs) have followed:
- Initially for point solutions
- Followed by application solutions
- Finally maturing to system solutions

AI/Healthcare Case Studies
- Point Solution: AI-enhanced medical
  imaging
- Application Solutions: AI-enhanced
  radiology departments
- System Solutions: AI-accelerated
  health system transformation

Data + AI will radically improve health
and healthcare
- In the short-term, change in
  healthcare will lag other sectors
- In the long-term, change and benefits
  will surpass other sectors

Healthcare Context

- Healthcare is different than other
  sectors of the economy
- Health systems are transforming
  along six common dimensions

Care Delivery

Payments

**Data-Digitization,
Standardization,
Interoperability**

**Personalization
and Precision**

**Democratization and
Consumerization**

New Entrants

- Healthcare data is unique, complex,
  non-standardized
- Healthcare digitization lags behind other
  sectors

AI

- AI has been in development for more
  than five decades
- AI is beginning to yield dividends
  although it still has a long way to go
  to attain maturity
- AI traditionally uses past data
  patterns to predict future outcomes
- Generative AI uses learning to
  generate new content, giving a boost
  to application
- Data is the key to enabling AI

Figure 5.1 Chapter framework for intelligent health.

Putting AI into Context

As a species, homo sapiens have always used tools to augment our physical prowess. Our earliest attempts began with sticks and stones, then progressed to simple machines like levers and inclined planes, and eventually to domesticating animals as beasts of burden. This progress accelerated with the discovery of fire, fossil fuels and electricity. It further led to industrialization and the invention of machines that could amplify our physical strength a thousandfold, firmly establishing us at the top of the food chain. It is not surprising, therefore, that humans have expanded this ambition, from improving our physical capabilities to also amplifying our intellectual capabilities using machines.

George Boole's 1854 book, *An Investigation into the Laws of Thought*, proposed that logical reasoning could be achieved through a system of symbols and equations, thus providing a foundation for the development of machines that could amplify human reasoning. Earlier, it was science fiction writers who popularized the concept of thinking machines, in many different fields.

One of the earliest was the Czech writer Karel Čapek, who introduced the word 'ROBOT' in his play R.U.R. (Rossum's Universal Robots) in 1927. The word 'robot' comes from the word 'robota' (work).

During the early 1900s, many philosophers, mathematicians, and scientists assimilated these fictional concepts. Alan Turing, a young British polymath, was perhaps the most famous among them. In his 1950 paper 'Computing machinery and intelligence', Turing discussed the possibility of building machines that can think like humans. His view was that machines can be made to solve problems by using available information and reasoning just as we humans can. He proposed a test, now known as the Turing test, to determine whether a machine is truly intelligent.

The Turing test involves a human judge having a conversation with two other parties, one a human and the other a machine. If the judge cannot reliably tell the machine apart from the human, then the machine is said to have passed the test.

However, it was not until 1955 that the term 'artificial intelligence' was coined. John McCarthy (Dartmouth College), Marvin Minsky (Harvard University), Nathaniel Rochester (IBM), and Claude Shannon (Bell Telephone Laboratories), submitted a proposal for a '2 month, 10 man study of artificial intelligence'. In 1956, McCarthy and Minsky organized a conference entitled the 'Dartmouth Summer Research Project on Artificial Intelligence'. The vision for this conference, stated boldly in the proposal read: 'The study is to proceed on the basis of the conjecture that every aspect of learning or any other feature of intelligence can in principle be so precisely described that a machine can be made to simulate it.'[5]

However, the conference was not a great success. The participants attended at different times and worked on their own projects. There was no agreement on a general theory of the field, or even on a general theory of learning. The field of artificial intelligence was not launched by a consensus on methodology, a general theory, or a choice of problems. Rather, it was launched by the shared vision that machines can be made to perform intelligent tasks.

Since then, the journey of artificial intelligence can only be described as a roller coaster ride. AI has been hyped as the 'next big thing' for many years. There have been periods of great hope, followed by periods of AI winter. Between the late 1950s to the early 1970s, there was optimism due to many early successes in AI. However, by the mid-1970s, the field of AI confronted a mountain of obstacles. The biggest impediment was the lack of computational power to store and process large amounts of data needed for achieving proficiency in natural language processing. This resulted in a lack of patience and funding, which caused a slowdown in progress for about a decade.

The revival of interest and funding for AI research began again in the 1980s. Advances in deep learning techniques, which allowed computers to learn through experience, and expert systems, which emulated the decision-making process of an expert, led to significant progress in the field. One of the early expert systems related to healthcare was MYCIN, developed at Stanford University. MYCIN could identify the bacteria causing severe infections and recommend the right antibiotics.

In the 1990s and 2000s, many goals of AI were achieved, which ignited the imagination of the general public. In 1997, IBM's Deep Blue computer beat the reigning world chess champion and grandmaster Gary Kasparov. This was followed by a few more dramatic moments, such as IBM Watson's victory over two champions in Jeopardy in 2011 and Google's AlphaGo's victory over the reigning Go champion in 2016.

This rapid progress has been enabled by multiple factors, such as the increasing availability of computing power, extensive storage, easy availability of voluminous data, and the push by both the private sector and government funding.

Yet AI remained the domain of specialists until the advent of generative AI. The public launch of ChatGPT took the world by storm in November 2022. ChatGPT reached 50 million users within 5 days of launch! Compare this to the telephone, which took 75 years, or the Internet which took 4 years to achieve similar usage.

Putting Health and Healthcare into Context

Healthcare is different

In this section, we will provide an overview of worldwide healthcare systems and delivery. Healthcare is unlike other sectors of the world economy, and health systems across the world are quite disparate. Let's look at some of the specifics about how healthcare is different:

There is disagreement about whether healthcare is a human right or a market good: Is healthcare a human right or a market good? In most developed countries, healthcare is viewed as being much closer to a human right – guaranteed to be available to all citizens. In the United States, however, healthcare is treated much more like a market good.

Healthcare is opaque: Metrics and systems to measure quality in health care are immature and not standardized[6]; thus, today it is virtually impossible to compare health outcomes across clinicians and facilities. Healthcare prices are usually not available to patients to allow for comparisons, and most healthcare services are difficult to 'shop' as patients often lack access to information, lack the ability to interpret medical information, and are not inclined to act as 'consumers' in the face of a serious illness.

Economic incentives are misaligned: It's often the case where a clinician might prescribe a treatment, a patient receives the treatment, and a third-party health plan or government agency might pay all or most of the cost of the treatment. This creates perverse and misaligned incentives. For example, clinicians and facilities maximize income by delivering more services, health plans maximize income by minimizing the quantity of services delivered, and patients are caught in the middle.

Many of the misaligned incentives are tied to current fee-for-service payment systems, which incentivize care providers to 'do more' and provide payments that are not tied to quality or positive outcomes.

Healthcare is fragmented and complex: Healthcare is a complex tapestry of services, clinical providers and payment systems. The range of clinical providers is long and confusing, for example, primary care physicians, specialists, nurse practitioners, physician assistants, pharmacists, optometrists, therapists and many more. The range of medical facilities also is long and confusing, for example, general hospitals, specialty hospitals, ambulatory surgery centres, urgent care centres, skilled nursing facilities, rehabilitation centres, dialysis centres, imaging centres and many more. This can create confusion and gaps in care for patients. An older patient might be seeing over ten different clinicians and be on a regime of a dozen or more medications.

Healthcare is highly regulated: Healthcare is one of the most heavily regulated industries, driven by the life-and-death potential of its services and the ethical imperatives of clinical care. Regulatory bodies impose guidelines on almost all activities – data privacy, clinical protocols, drug and device approvals, billing practices, licensure – to name a few.

The culture of healthcare is conservative, risk-averse, and resistant to change: Healthcare prizes stability over innovation. The

Hippocratic Oath requires that clinicians 'first do no harm'. Thus, systemic improvements do not occur rapidly; one meta-analysis found that it takes an average of 17 years for validated clinical research to be widely adopted into routine clinical practice.[7]

Six dimensions of health system transformation

Healthcare moves slowly. It has been one of the last sectors to enter the digital economy.

However, to those familiar with the industry, change is apparent and inevitable – albeit taking place over the course of decades. Let's look at six dimensions of world health systems that are in flux. While there are many differences across world health systems, they do have elements of change in common. Figure 5.2 summarizes six common dimensions of health system transformation that are underway. The left column displays the 'rear-view mirror' perspective – where health systems have been in the past; the right column displays the 'out-the-windshield' perspective – where health systems are transforming for the future.

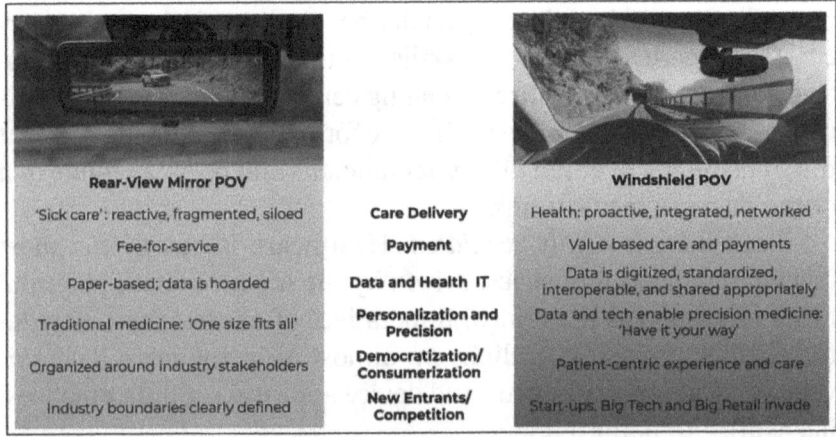

Figure 5.2 table content:

Rear-View Mirror POV		Windshield POV
'Sick care': reactive, fragmented, siloed	**Care Delivery**	Health: proactive, integrated, networked
Fee-for-service	**Payment**	Value based care and payments
Paper-based; data is hoarded	**Data and Health IT**	Data is digitized, standardized, interoperable, and shared appropriately
Traditional medicine: 'One size fits all'	**Personalization and Precision**	Data and tech enable precision medicine: 'Have it your way'
Organized around industry stakeholders	**Democratization/ Consumerization**	Patient-centric experience and care
Industry boundaries clearly defined	**New Entrants/ Competition**	Start-ups, Big Tech and Big Retail invade

Figure 5.2   Six dimensions of worldwide health system transformation.

SOURCE: Vince Kuraitis, Better Health Technologies, LLC, 2023

1) Care delivery

From – 'Sick Care': reactive, fragmented, siloed

To – Health: proactive, integrated, networked

Healthcare systems have stood ready, willing and able to care for sick patients – which in one way is a description of the problem. By the time patients are sick, the damage has happened.

The world view of 'healthcare' is shifting toward a broader understanding of human 'health'. Over the past several decades, it has become increasingly well-understood that a person's and a population's health is attributable to many diverse factors. Only about 20% of 'health' is attributable to the clinical care that a person receives,[8] i.e., access to care and quality of clinicians, hospitals, drugs, and so on. Figure 5.3 is from the County Health Rankings Model[9] developed at the University of Wisconsin Population Health Institute.

Figure 5.3 also shows contributors to the other 80% of health: 30% is attributable to health behaviours, 40% due to social and economic factors, and about 10% due to our physical environment. The responsibility of achieving health extends beyond health systems – it goes to culture, personal responsibility, government policy to incentivize health and other factors.

The health systems of tomorrow will be proactive – the goal will be to keep patients healthy in the first place and to avoid high-intensity, high-cost care; a hospitalization will be viewed as a failure to provide adequate preventive care and treatment.

2) Payment systems

From – Fee-for-service

To – Value-based care and payments

As described in a World Health Organization study,[10] in most healthcare systems in the world, a major change currently is underway – how healthcare is paid for. The shift is from fee-for-service payment systems to value-based payment.

Healthcare has traditionally been reimbursed by fee-for-service payments, that is a specific service is provided, and a specific fee is

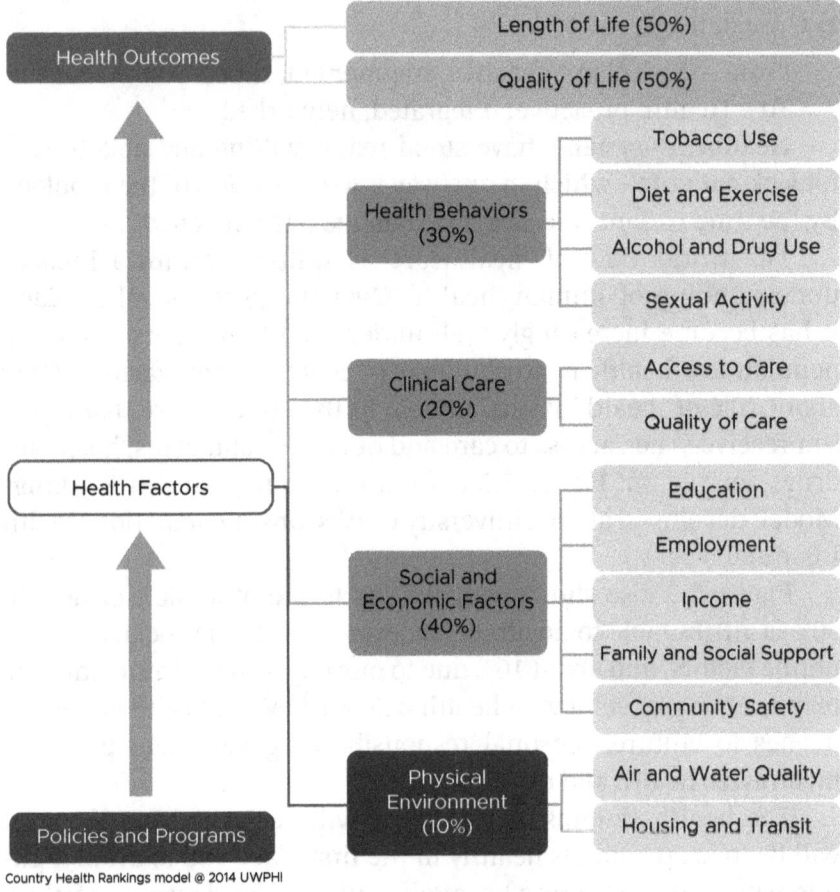

Country Health Rankings model @ 2014 UWPHI

Figure 5.3 Contributors to 'health' From the County Health Rankings Model.

paid to clinicians or facilities. While fee-for-service works relatively well in other sectors of the economy, it is problematic in healthcare. Some of the criticisms of fee-for-service are that it encourages excessive use of low-value services, that it does not provide incentives to improve quality, and that there are insufficient incentives to coordinate care, for example for patients with multiple chronic conditions who might be on a dozen medications and routinely see multiple care providers.

There are many variations of value-based payment models. At the extreme is 'capitation', where care provider organizations receive fixed payments and assume full financial risk for the care of a population of patients. Other value-based payment models will provide some financial incentives and/or penalties tied to providers meeting quality, cost and/or outcome measures, in other words risk is shared between payers and providers.

Using the United States as an example, the shift toward value-based care and payment has been ongoing – albeit slowly – for several decades. As of 2023, about 41% of payments in the United States remain pure fee-for-service, 34% are in early-stage alternative payment models (APMs), and only about 25% of payments are in advanced APMs.[11]

3) Data and health information technology

From – Paper-based, data are hoarded

To – Data are digitized, standardized, interoperable and shared appropriately

Prior to the early 2000s, almost all healthcare data were paper-based. Speaking metaphorically, your healthcare data were 'frozen' – akin to being stuck inside a giant glacier. It existed in a file folder 'somewhere', but it rarely was shared with other healthcare providers.

A landmark study published in 2003 in the *New England Journal of Medicine* documented that clinical care in the United States was delivered according to guidelines only 55% of the time.[12]

Take a moment to think about the implications here. In many industries, the goal of quality improvement programmes is to achieve a level of '6 Sigma' – where quality in a process is achieved more than 99.9% of the time and defects occur at a rate of about 3.4 per million. US healthcare is at '1 Sigma', where a defect – the failure to deliver care in accordance with guidelines – occurs 450,000 times per million.

There is a growing recognition of the value of healthcare data. In the following sections of this chapter, we will go into much more detail about the unique nature of healthcare data. We will describe a 30-year journey to make health data digitized, interoperable and easily shareable. Much progress has occurred, but we are only about two-thirds of the way through this 30-year journey.

4) Personalization and precision

From – Traditional medicine: 'One size fits all'

To – Data and technology enable precision medicine: 'Have it your way'

In the past, 'one size fits all' healthcare was the norm – all patients with the same condition were treated in the same way. We did not have data or technology to individualize diagnoses and prescriptions for unique patients.

The evolving treatment of cancer is one example to illustrate the difference between traditional medicine vs. precision medicine. Traditional treatments for cancer patients included radiation, chemotherapy, and surgery. These shotgun treatments are marginally effective, have high levels of side effects, and have limited efficacy. Novel approaches are being developed to treat cancer through genetics, immunotherapy, and targeted therapies.[13]

Personalization of medical treatments can increasingly be based on:

- 'omics': various disciplines in biology, e.g., genomics, epigenomics, transcriptomics, proteomics, metabolomics;
- Prevalence of other conditions;
- Patient lifestyle; and
- Patient preference.

5) Democratization and consumerization

From – Care organized around industry stakeholders

To – Patient-centric experience and care

In the past, health systems have been organized around the convenience of industry stakeholders; as an example, even today most hospitals are organized around a five-day-a-week operational schedule, with far fewer resources being available on weekends. However, patient illnesses are not limited by Monday through Friday schedules.

A survey by Ipsos examined citizen satisfaction with their country's health system; results were reported for 30 different countries. On average, only 34% of citizens were 'very/fairly satisfied' and 39% were 'not very/not at all satisfied'.[14]

The trend toward democratization and consumerization is illustrated by many aspects. For example, there is a movement to provide care in settings that are more convenient for patients. COVID-19 demonstrated that much care could be provided through telehealth or home-based healthcare. Patients are demanding better experiences and are willing to switch providers. Many new competitors are much more sensitive in catering to the needs and preferences of consumers. Advances in technology are allowing patients more access to their health data and enabling them to become more involved in care decisions.

But . . . many barriers remain. Until recently, patients have not routinely had access to their own health data. The complexity of medicine can limit patient involvement in decision making. Quality and outcome metrics about providers and facilities are difficult to come by and are not highly standardized. Fee-for-service payments by third-party payers can skew incentives and limit patients' desire to treat healthcare purchases like they might treat other consumer purchases.

6) New entrants/competition

From – Industry boundaries are clearly defined

To – Start-ups, Big Tech and Big Retail invade

Today, healthcare is becoming increasingly characterized by new entrants from outside the industry – ones that often are competitive with the doctor down the street or the hospital across town. This trend is reshaping the industry.

A 2023 report by Galen Growth and Finn Partners documents that at the end of 2022 there were over 9,000 digital health ventures worldwide.[15]

Almost all of the Big Tech companies have initiatives in healthcare.[16] Many large retailers and pharmacy chains also have entered healthcare in a big way.[17]

Healthcare data are unique and complex

Unlike other industries, healthcare data are complex and diverse. The data are typically fragmented across different systems and formats, making it difficult to consolidate, standardize and exchange the data. Sensitive patient data are subject to stringent privacy and security regulations.

A simple example can shed additional light on the complexity of healthcare data. You might say 'I have a headache.' A clinician, however, will need much more information from you to begin to consider an appropriate diagnosis and course of treatment. Consider this non-exhaustive list of diverse types of headaches:

- Tension headache
- Migraine headache
- Cluster headache
- Sinus headache
- Rebound headache
- Exertion headache
- Hypertension headache
- Hormone headache
- Caffeine headache
- Allergy headache
- Post-traumatic headache
- Spinal headache
- Thunderclap headache
- Hemicrania continua

Another illustration of the complexity of health data is the Healthcare Information and Management Systems Society (HIMSS) listing and description of the four levels of interoperability for healthcare data[18]:

Foundational (Level 1): Establishes the interconnectivity requirements needed for one system or application to securely communicate data to and receive data from another

Structural (Level 2): Defines the format, syntax and organization of data exchange including at the data field level for interpretation

Semantic (Level 3): Provides for common underlying models and codification of the data including the use of data elements with standardized definitions from publicly available value sets and coding vocabularies, providing shared understanding and meaning to the user

Organizational (Level 4): Includes governance, policy, social, legal and organizational considerations to facilitate the secure, seamless and timely communication and use of data both within and between organizations, entities and individuals. These components enable shared consent, trust and integrated end-user processes and workflows

Healthcare digitization lags other sectors

As of 2023, the United States was roughly two-thirds through a 30-year journey to achieve interoperability and data sharing. We will recap some of the high points and describe some of the remaining obstacles.

The goals of electronic health record (EHR) adoption and health data interoperability have been a bipartisan effort for several decades. The journey began in 2004 when President Bush declared that every American should have an EHR by 2014.[19]

A study by the Office of the National Coordinator for Health Information Technology (ONC) found that in 2008, the adoption of EHRs by hospitals and physicians was below 10%.[20]

After the financial crisis of 2008, a bipartisan Congress was looking for 'shovel-ready' projects to fund recovery. In 2009, the US Congress passed the Health Information Technology for Economic and Clinical Health (HITECH) Act. The HITECH Act aimed to accelerate the adoption of EHRs and health information technology infrastructure by providing financial incentives to hospitals and doctors. Over the next decade, HITECH provided over $35 billion in federal subsidies.[21] By 2014, 95% of hospitals had at least basic EHRs and nearly 80% of physicians had EHRs.[22]

While HITECH was successful in incentivizing hospitals and physicians to *adopt* EHRs, by about 2013 it was becoming obvious that it did *not* guarantee interoperability of data *across* EHRs. One study found that there was only 22–68% interoperability across EHR platforms.[23] A 2015 McKinsey study[24] examined digital adoption across 22 industry sectors. Healthcare was ranked nineteenth.

In 2016, Congress passed the 21st Century Cures Act. In essence, the intent of this legislation was to *mandate* interoperability and data sharing. It took several years for draft regulations to be passed, commented on and revised. Providers, vendors and health plans were then given several more years to implement the regulations. The bulk of these regulations were just starting to take effect in 2021 and 2022.

The 21st Century Cures Act regulations prohibit 'information blocking' by EHR vendors and care providers. The legislation mandates that patients have electronic access to their data – but the question is still open as to whether and how patients will be able to utilize their health data. The legislation also mandated the adoption of standardized application programming interfaces (APIs) to share data across healthcare organizations.

While substantial progress has been made toward the interoperability of health data in the United States, even after the passage of HITECH and the 21st Century Cures Act, many gaps and questions remain, for example:

- Changing the culture of (lack of) information sharing.
- Uncertainties about levels of enforcement.
- Lack of bi-directional data exchange – data can be acquired *from* EHRs, but outside clinicians and patients themselves have limited ability to provide data *to* EHRs.
- HITECH only subsidized physicians and hospitals to adopt EHRs. There are many other healthcare stakeholders that were not included, e.g. long-term care facilities, behavioural health providers, home health agencies.
- The 21st Century Cures Act also does not directly apply to many healthcare stakeholders, e.g. pharmaceutical companies, medical device manufacturers, non-clinical support staff.
- Differing medical vocabulary standards. Outside the United States, this issue has been much more directly addressed by the adoption of the openEHR (pronounced 'open air'), which specifies 'open, interoperable and computable patient-centric health information systems'.[25]

One way of measuring the progress of data interoperability in healthcare is simply to ask clinicians about their experience. In a 2022 survey of physicians by the Medical Group Management Association, 50.4% of physicians responded that the 'lack of EHR interoperability' was 'very or extremely burdensome', and another 26.4% of physicians responded that it was 'moderately burdensome'.[26]

The experience of US physicians mirrors that of clinicians in other countries. In 2023, GE Healthcare surveyed clinicians in seven countries – Brazil, China, Germany, India, New Zealand, South Korea and the United States. They found that only between 48% and 71% agreed with the statement that 'clinicians have timely access to reliable patient records'.[27]

Clinician access to patient data is increasing in importance and complexity as the quantity of medical knowledge and data increase exponentially. The doubling time of total medical knowledge is estimated to be 73 days.[28] RBC capital markets found that '30% of the world's data volume is being generated by the healthcare industry'.[29]

While much progress has been made, in our judgement, it will take another 10 years to achieve true data interoperability and widespread data sharing in healthcare.

AI in Health and Healthcare

The potential of healthcare data + AI

We believe AI holds great promise in healthcare to assist in prediction, decision making and automation. In turn, AI will improve clinician and patient experience, lower costs and improve outcomes and quality.

There is wide-ranging AI development underway in healthcare. According to the US Food and Drug Administration (FDA), as of January 2023, there were more than 520 market-cleared AI medical algorithms available in the United States.[30] An analysis by Tracxn estimated that there are over 2,664 AI startups in healthcare in the United States alone.[31]

Some studies have demonstrated the potential of AI as being more successful in predicting and diagnosing certain illnesses than humans. For example, researchers from Cedar Sinai's Smidt Heart Institute showed that AI proved more successful in assessing and diagnosing cardiac function when compared to echo cardiogram assessments made by sonographers.

AI has also proven itself to be more reliable for predicting patients' future development of some conditions. Researchers at the University of Nottingham in the United Kingdom created a system that scanned patients' routine medical data and predicted which of them would have heart attacks or strokes within 10 years. When compared to the standard method of prediction, the AI system correctly predicted the fates of 355 more patients.[32] These studies are promising and demonstrate the potential value of AI in augmenting the effectiveness of care providers.

Patients generally are not yet comfortable with clinicians relying on AI in their treatment. A 2023 Pew Research Center survey explored this topic.[33] While the headline of the study showed that 60% of Americans would be uncomfortable with providers relying on AI, the details are more nuanced. For example 38% of the respondents believed that AI would lead to better health outcomes while only 33% believed that it would lead to worse outcomes. The same study also reports that younger and more educated adults are more positive than other groups. We anticipate that patient acceptance of AI will increase as AI becomes more precise.

According to a Brookings analysis, the adoption of AI in healthcare is lagging behind that of other industries.[34] For example, an analysis of US job advertisements that require AI-related skills showed that while 1 out of every 100 jobs in information technology required AI skills, in healthcare only 1 out of every 1,850 jobs required AI skills.

There are many factors that contribute to the late adoption of AI in healthcare. We have previously described some of the limitations of healthcare data – they are unique, complex and not yet interoperable and standardized. Machine learning and other AI applications are not programmed in the traditional manner. Instead, they are built by providing samples of input data and corresponding output data, allowing the computer to 'learn' from these samples. The more comprehensive and accurate the training data, the more intelligent the system becomes. The limitations of healthcare data complicate the development of optimal AI algorithms.

Many of the deep learning models and neural networks are like 'black boxes', making it difficult to explain how a particular decision was made. This lack of transparency limits trust and adoption by healthcare providers and facilities. This problem is not unique to healthcare and many technology companies are focusing on addressing this problem.

There are also issues of biases creeping into the models because of inherent issues in data collection. A prominent example of this is data collected by wearables. To understand the perpetuation of bias, consider the method used to collect heartbeat data. Wearables use green LED lights to penetrate the skin, and the reflection of this light is used to measure blood flow. In turn, this helps to measure the heartbeat – when the heart beats, there momentarily is less blood and hence more light is reflected. However, since green lights have a shorter wavelength, it is less able to penetrate melanin. The darker a person's skin is, the less accurate the readings are. If the data collected using these devices is used to train models, one is likely to create biases.

There are many forums focused on providing tools for organizations and AI practitioners to build and supply trusted and responsible AI systems, such as the Responsible AI Institute, IEEE the Center for Human Compatible AI (CHAI), and others. The Artificial Intelligence Code of Conduct (AICC) project is an initiative of the National Academy of Medicine (NAM) to provide a guiding framework to ensure that AI in healthcare and biomedical science performs safely, reliably and ethically.

Every decision has two components to it. One is prediction and the other is judgement. For example, a prediction that a course of medication will be 40% effective, tells only half the story. Whether a patient should take the medication based on that prediction is a judgement call that includes the severity of the disease, the possible side effects, and other factors. AI can help in increasing the accuracy of the prediction, but the judgement remains with humans.

A framework for the adoption of AI in healthcare

Any technological breakthrough goes through different phases of hype and adoption. AI is no exception. In a previous section, we explored the journey AI has taken thus far. With advancements in generative AI – especially the release of ChatGPT, an application built on top of a large language model – AI has become mainstream. Every business and even the public have started harnessing AI to address their problems and opportunities. What led to this seemingly sudden interest?

The exponential growth in processing capacity combined with seemingly unlimited storage and access to data are some of the primary reasons. Even with all of this, until the so-called democratization of AI, AI remained accessible only to specialized data scientists and experts. Only recently has AI been made more accessible, affordable and user-friendly, allowing more people to participate in its creation and application.

This is just the beginning of the AI wave. The initial use of any new general-purpose technology – steam power, electricity, computing, the Internet – is never an indication of the profound ways in which it ends up impacting life as we know it. The fundamental way in which general purpose technologies have changed our lifestyles and the way businesses are conducted were not obvious at the time of the introduction of the technology.

A useful framework for understanding adoption patterns of general-purpose technology was provided by Ajay Agrawal, Joshua Gans and Avi Goldfarb in their book *Power and Prediction*.[35] They explain that there are three phases in which these are adopted; these phases take decades to play out. They label and define the three phases as:

1. *Point solutions*: A point solution improves an existing procedure and can be adopted independently, without changing the system in which it is embedded.
2. *Application solutions*: An application solution enables a new procedure that can be adopted independently, without changing the system in which it is embedded.

3. *System solutions*: A system solution improves existing procedures or enables new procedures by changing dependent procedures.

Many of us have lived through the adoption of the Internet. Consider the evolution of the Internet as an example to explain the general-purpose technology adoption framework in greater depth. Before the Internet, there were special-purpose networks that were established for specific purposes. 'SABRE', for example, was designed and built in the 1960s for airline reservations. ARPANET was one of the first general-purpose networks that was established to connect the various timesharing computers of government-supported research sites, principally universities in the United States.

One of the first *point solutions* developed in this new networked environment was the Simple Mail Transfer Protocol, or SMTP. It enabled sending short messages to users across the network. It took one particular task – writing mail to people – and enabled it in the new network environment, without changing anything fundamental. The advantages were obvious – when compared to writing a letter, this took much less effort and was faster to deliver.

It was the effort to connect the various research institutes in the United States and Europe that resulted in the Internet. From the origins of the Internet in the early 1970s, control slowly moved from government stewardship to the private sector with government supervision. The commercialization of the Internet accelerated with the introduction of personal computers and some key applications built to run on these.

As an example of an *application solution*, one of the most important was the new type of computer program called the browser. The Mosaic browser was first introduced by the University of Illinois in 1993. It provided a new point-and-click interface to access, retrieve and display files through the Internet. The browser running on your personal computer made it easy for you to access information across the network. Browsers enabled people to adopt new ways of sharing information, enabling collaboration across geographical distances and creating new procedures – but still working within the same system. Nothing else needed to change to adopt this new application.

We fast forward to today and see many *system solutions* in how the Internet has evolved. It changed the way we do things, from being able to summon a mode of transport (Uber, Lyft and so on), to ordering any desired product to be delivered to your front door, or even pandering to your exotic palette by ordering food from any cuisine of choice.

The restaurant business itself has changed significantly. For a person who has the skills to cook good food, one can just rent a kitchen, prepare the food and market it on the web to be delivered directly to the consumers, without owning a restaurant. For this to become reality many things needed to change in the system – the advent of 'cloud' kitchens, third-party delivery companies and social media for promotion, to name a few.

Thus, point solutions improve an existing process and can function independently of changes to the process and coexist in the existing system. An application solution may introduce new processes but does not require changes to the overall system. Only in system solutions do we see significant impact to the way things work and system solutions bring about the most significant changes.

In the next three sections of this chapter, we will apply the general-purpose technology adoption framework to AI in healthcare by considering three case studies:

- A point solution – AI-enhanced radiological imaging. We narrowly focus on radiologists' interactions with medical images.
- Application solutions – AI-enhanced radiology departments. We focus more broadly on how AI will improve both clinical and administrative processes in radiology departments in hospitals and imaging centres.
- System solutions – AI-accelerated health system transformation. We revisit the six dimensions of health system transformation that have been in progress for over a decade. We discuss our anticipations that AI will synergistically impact each of these six dimensions.

A point solution – AI-enhanced radiological imaging

Radiologists are medical doctors who specialize in diagnosing and treating diseases and injuries using medical imaging procedures. They interpret images from modalities such as X-rays, CT scans, MRIs and ultrasounds. They play a crucial role in patient care by providing critical diagnostic information and treatment guidance.

Medical imaging was expected to be one of the first areas in healthcare that would get traction with AI

There are several reasons why imaging was expected to be an area for early adoption of AI. First, radiological images are highly standardized, much more so than in almost all other areas of healthcare. Adopted in 1993, Digital Imaging and Communications in Medicine (DICOM) is a global standard for the storage, transmission and processing of medical imaging information. DICOM defines both a file format and a networking protocol. It facilitates the transmission of medical imaging data to devices such as scanners, servers, workstations, printers, and picture archiving and communications systems (PACS).

Second, radiology has a well-established and highly structured digital workflow.[36] For example there are specified sets of examination types and views. Standardization of workflow is increasingly important to assure the highest level of interoperability across images.

Third, radiology image reporting is also highly standardized. The Radiological Society of North America (RSNA) provides resources to help standardize reporting practices by radiologists. They offer a library of templates based on best practices.[37]

Finally, imaging was viewed as particularly well suited for neural network analysis, which began to get traction in the 2000s. The explanation often given to explain how neural networks work is that the AI algorithm is presented with pictures of 10,000 dogs and 10,000 cats. The algorithm is not trained externally – in effect the algorithm becomes able to discern the salient features that distinguish dogs from cats. When picture number 20,001 is presented to the algorithm, there's a high probability that it will correctly be able to predict that it is a cat or a dog.

Initially, simplistic thinking applied this reasoning to radiological images. Present the algorithm with 10,000 images of a 'tumour' and present it with 10,000 images of 'not a tumour'; when presented with image number 20,001 it should be able to distinguish between 'tumour' and 'not a tumour'.

There were high expectations of early and rapid adoption of AI in imaging, much of which came to a head in 2016.[38] Two Harvard Medical School professors wrote that 'machine learning will displace much of the work of radiologists and anatomical pathologists.'[39] Computer scientist and Turing Award Winner Geoff Hinton proclaimed that 'If you work as a radiologist, you are like the coyote that's already over the edge of the cliff but hasn't yet looked down . . . People should stop training radiologists now. It's just completely obvious that within five years deep learning is going to do better than radiologists.'[40] Writing in the *Harvard Business Review*, two Oxford economists wrote that 'when professional work is broken down into component parts, many of the tasks involved turn out to be routine and process based. They do not in fact call for judgement, creativity or empathy.'[41]

As we'll see below, the expectation for rapid adoption of AI in medical imaging has not been met.

What is the current status of AI in medical imaging?

AI has been shown to be effective in interpreting many different types of medical images.[42] For example, studies have demonstrated efficacy in interpreting plain radiographs,[43] computed tomography (CT) scans,[44] magnetic resonance imaging (MRI) scans,[45] mammograms[46] and others. AI has also been found to be effective in tumour classification, detecting neurological abnormalities and lung cancer screening.[47]

In some studies, AI systems have outperformed radiologists.[48,49,50] ChatGPT-4 was able to pass a radiology board exam with a score of 81%.[51]

We previously documented that as of January 2023, there were more than 520 market-cleared AI medical algorithms available in the United States. More than 75% of these are in radiology. The next closest clinical area is cardiology – with 11% of approvals – many of which are specific to cardiac imaging.[52]

The current state of AI in radiology has been focused on 'narrow' algorithms – those that can perform one specific task rather than fully interpret diagnostic imaging studies. Dr Steven L. Blumer, Associate Medical Director of Radiology Informatics at UPMC, explained the challenges in going beyond today's narrow algorithms:

> Such algorithms are a long way from completely interpreting imaging studies. This ability requires incorporating a wide array of imaging and clinical findings and synthesizing this information to determine the most likely diagnosis or diagnoses. These 'human-like' abilities are what many people think about when they believe that AI has the potential to replace radiologists. However, these human-like capabilities require a higher level of AI known as Artificial General Intelligence (AGI). AGI or strong or full AI applications in radiology are still nascent and will likely take many years to fully see any impact on the radiologist workforce.[53]

Adoption of AI in imaging has been slower than expected

AI in medical imaging has not been adopted as rapidly as initially projected. An article in the May 2023 issue of the *New England Journal of Medicine* estimated that the current penetration of AI in the US radiology market was estimated to be only 2%.[54]

Why has adoption of AI in imaging proceeded slowly? Many barriers remain:

Radiology images are not (yet) sufficiently standardized. While we noted previously that radiology images are highly standardized when compared to other medical data, major challenges remain in using images to train AI algorithms.

In a personal conversation, Mircea Popa, CEO of Medicai – a cloud-native medical imaging platform company – described reasons why the analogy of the cat/dog algorithm training methodology doesn't work for medical imaging:

> People sometimes underestimate what the human brain can do. I've been looking at real-world images for the last 38 years. So I've gotten really good at recognizing cats and dogs. An algorithm probably spent three months looking at those pictures.

> Humans don't come with a user's manual. All the values that we believe are normal are just averages. We all have different genes, we all have different habits, nobody's perfect. So how do you establish a baseline?

> Pictures of cats and dogs are a really well-curated database. So we are able to know for sure that in that picture, there is a dog or there is a cat. We do not have that luxury with MRI images. We have to trust the word of a radiologist, or two radiologists, and these experts are not 100%, nobody is. And what if they disagree?

> These images are way less standardized than someone outside of the industry can imagine. Or would imagine. When I started my company, I thought, 'Hey, this is an MRI, right? It's standard? Well, it isn't. In fact, it's so bad that everybody does it in n ways.

There are other areas of concern that limit the 'seeming' standardization of medical images:

- Did the patient move while the image was being taken?
- Was the image taken at the correct angle?
- Is the image quality inferior?
- Were images taken on different generations of machines, e.g. a 1.5 Tesla vs. a 3 Tesla MRI scanner?

- Were the images taken on machines from different manufacturers? There is variability across manufacturers.
- Was data sourced from multiple archiving systems – PACs, VNAs, EMRs and potentially other types as well? The outputs of each of these systems can vary.[55]
- Was the imaging data labelled accurately?

Culture and resistance to change. Healthcare is conservative and change does not come rapidly. Radiologists may resist new ways of working and prefer to continue acquired patterns of work.

While a 2019 survey found that 38% of radiologists feared job loss due to AI,[56] a meta-analysis published in 2023 documented that less than 10% of radiologists and trainees believed that AI poses a threat to the radiology job market.[57]

Difficulty in demonstrating return on investment. Implementing AI can take a substantial investment of time and money. In most regions, fee-for-service payment has been the predominant reimbursement system. With few exceptions, radiologists and the facility do not receive additional revenue for implementing AI. Thus the economic incentives to adopt AI to improve quality are very weak.

Only a small proportion of FDA-approved radiology AI software applications are directly reimbursed. Between 2018 and 2023, 8 of the 200-plus radiology software applications were evaluated for payment by the Centers for Medicare and Medicaid Services (CMS). Six were approved for payment and two were rejected.[58]

There are arguments for and against separate reimbursement of AI in radiology. Dr Bibb Allen, chief medical officer of the American College of Radiology Data Science Institute, explained both sides:

> As a radiologist, I believe it will provide us with safer and more effective care, whether that comes from decreases in turnaround times or decision support capabilities, or the identification of critical findings. On the other hand, the payer might say 'well wait a minute, we are already paying you, the radiologist and the expert, to make those same conclusions, so why should we on a fee for service basis provide additional payment?[59]

Health plans also could be concerned that direct payment for AI will lead to overuse.

An analysis published in *NPJ Digital Medicine* suggested a framework to evaluate whether to reimburse radiology algorithms separately. The authors suggested two aspects that payers must consider: 1) the nature of the benefit that the applications bring, and 2) the availability of evidence to support the existence of the benefit.[60]

Integration of AI into radiological workflows can be challenging. Technical validation of algorithms is difficult as they appear as a black box. Multiple vendors might be considered for a specific application. A contract must be negotiated with the winning vendor. Within a hospital system, there are many levels of approval. Radiologists and departmental staff must be trained on appropriate use and interpretation. Data governance procedures must be established to ensure proper storage of data, sharing of data and protection of patient privacy.

There are other concerns as well: the inability of AI to explain its decision-making process,[61] worries about cybercrime and hacking[62] and fear of potential bias in data sets.[63]

AI will augment, not replace radiologists.

The consensus view at this time – with which we agree – is that AI cannot replace radiologists in the foreseeable future. However, AI can and will augment radiologists, not replace them.[64,65,66]

Radiologists do far more than simply read medical images. A radiologist's job description might list 30 or more tasks that are part of their responsibilities.[67] Broad categories of these tasks include documentation of imaging results, communication and consultation with clinicians and patients, interventional procedures, departmental quality control and workflow optimization, professional development and education, treatment planning for patients, radiation safety and compliance and others.

AI in imaging today is being deployed in narrow, point solution applications. We previously noted that today there are hundreds of FDA-approved algorithms in radiology. However, as observed by

Dr Woojin Kim, 'today's single-task or "narrow AI" models focus on one finding on a single modality. You would need models for thousands of potential findings across multiple modalities in order to mimic the interpretative skills of radiologists.'[68] These don't exist today and won't exist in the foreseeable future.

AI will be able to free radiologists from routine, mundane tasks. The radiologist's job increasingly will be to monitor machine outputs, but the ultimate responsibility will remain with humans. AI has been analogized to being the 'co-pilot' of an aeroplane, helping radiologists be more efficient by pinpointing critical results – or exceptions – and enabling radiology teams to focus attention on patients who need urgent care first'.[69] It has also been analogized to being an 'autopilot' – useful on long stretches when routine prevails, but useless in situations requiring rapid judgement.[70]

Application solutions – AI-enhanced radiology departments

In the previous section, we focused narrowly on AI point solutions that assist radiologists in viewing and interpreting medical images. In this section, we focus more broadly on the next wave of anticipated AI adoption – application solutions – how AI can improve both clinical and administrative processes in radiology departments in hospitals and imaging centres.

Radiology departments provide a range of services, including diagnostic radiology, nuclear medicine and sonography. Their objective is to aid physicians in their efforts to diagnose and treat patients by providing timely and reliable information obtained from radiographic exams. Of patients who enter a hospital, 95% will have some form of medical imaging[71] and the radiology department of a hospital provides services 24/7.

We previously documented that there are over 2,600 AI in healthcare startups in the United States alone; many of these are building applications that might be used in radiology departments, even if they are not exclusively designed for radiology.

We found it difficult to establish how many companies overall are working on AI-assisted radiology applications. A 2023 market analysis report by CBInsights lists 96 AI companies building the next generation of radiology tech.[72] An analysis by GlobalData found that 'there are 870+ companies, spanning technology vendors, established technology companies, and up-and-coming start-ups engaged in the development and application of AI-assisted radiology.'[73]

In any event, there are hundreds of promising clinical and administrative applications of AI that could be used in radiology departments.

The examples we present here are intended simply to be illustrative of the potential of AI in radiology departments. The examples are in various phases of piloting and adoption. As we've noted previously, healthcare delivery is extremely fragmented, and adoption of AI will be uneven within countries and across different countries. As wisely observed by futurist William Gibson 'The future is already here – it's just not evenly distributed.'

AI algorithms will be brought to market in various ways. One possibility is an app store model where multiple vendors offer a menu of AI options. Another is where AI is integrated with vendor picture archiving and communications systems (PACS). Yet another option is AI becoming directly integrated with medical imaging scanners, for example MRIs or CT machines.[74] Some AI companies sell directly to health systems or radiology groups.

In this section, we will look at examples of AI-assisted radiology applications in four major categories:

- Clinical decision support
- Workflow and quality control
- Disease detection and classification
- Benefits to patients.

These examples only scratch the surface in displaying the potential of AI in radiology departments.

Clinical decision support

'Clinical decision support (CDS) provides timely information, usually at the point of care, to help inform decisions about a patient's care.'[75] Examples of CDS tools include order sets for specific conditions or types of patients, databases that provide clinical information, reminders for preventive care and alerts about potentially dangerous situations.

'Artificial intelligence algorithms have tremendous potential to help health care providers diagnose and treat medical conditions', said Robert Ochs of the FDA's Center for Devices and Radiological Health.[76]

AI embedded in scanners can detect incorrect patient positioning and warn radiology staff about errors.[77] Protocol selection is becoming automated, even to the level of suggested breathing instructions for patients. This leads to more consistent image output, improved image quality and reduced scan times.

'Population health is another area where AI can sift through vast amounts of imaging data to identify patients with key incidental findings for things like pulmonary embolism, coronary disease, pulmonary emphysema and hepatic steatosis.'[78]

Workflow and quality control

AI-enabled workflow orchestration systems can improve clinical efficiency and effectiveness. Algorithms can predict volumes of imaging studies on a given day so that the correct number of radiologists and staff are assigned to work during shifts.[79] Prior to scanning, AI can suggest protocols for exams and provide the correct scan range for many scans. AI also can decrease scan times by 30% or more without sacrificing image quality, thus increasing the number of patients scanned per day.[80]

AI algorithms can route studies to radiologists based on their areas of expertise or the urgency of the study.[81] AI can help prioritize the order in which images are reviewed by radiologists.[82] This ensures that critical cases receive immediate attention, thereby saving lives and improving outcomes. This also saves time for radiologists and other radiology department staff.

AI models can generate a full preliminary report for radiologists to review, edit and sign off.[83] A draft report can include information such as the type of scan, the body structures that were visualized, any abnormalities that were detected and their size, location and characteristics. It can also include a comparison with previous scans when available.

AI models can predict the potential for equipment failure.[84] Issues can then be addressed in advance, avoiding unscheduled downtime and lost revenue.

AI adoption likely will be easier in value-based payment models. As explained by Dr Bibb Allen: 'You can imagine in a value-based payment system, any tool that makes you more efficient, if you are getting paid the same, you can pay a little more for AI to become more efficient and it helps your bottom line.'[85]

Disease detection and classification

AI is being deployed in many clinical areas to assist in disease detection and classification. AI algorithms can detect diseases in the lung using deep learning for deep feature extraction and classification.[86] AI models can predict whether breast cancer tissue has been fully removed from the body during surgery.[87] AI algorithms can assist in identifying suspicious regions in prostate MRI scans for the early detection of prostate cancer.[88]

In one study AI was used to predict when a patient was going to die. The researchers analysed CT scans with deep learning algorithms. They were able to predict with 69% accuracy whether a patient would die within five years, which is 'broadly similar' to scores from human experts.[89]

Radiomics is an emerging field of study that spans radiology and oncology. It aims to extract tumour features from medical images that are difficult or impossible to detect through the human eye. These distinctive imaging features between disease forms may be useful for predicting prognosis and therapeutic response for various cancer types, thus providing valuable information for personalized therapies.[90]

Benefits to patients

AI models can be used to personalize patient education materials based on a patient's individual abilities, preferences and medical condition. Materials can explain treatment options and potential side effects. Patients can then better understand their diagnosis and treatment plan, and are able to make more informed decisions about their care.

Not only can AI models create a report for radiologists, but they can also create a separate report customized for the referring specialist physician – and yet another report customized for patients.[91] For patients, the report can be simplified and can include visual aids and layman's explanations of medical terminology and summary results.

Many of the applications described previously also provide benefits to patients, not just to physicians or radiology department staff. Patients will experience less anxiety and discomfort when scans can be performed more quickly. Patients with life-threatening conditions can receive treatment more quickly when scans are triaged based on the severity of clinical conditions and reports are routed to radiologists based on specialized clinical expertise. Physicians and department staff who use AI tools to improve their efficiency can focus more on the human side of medicine – holding a patient's hand, comforting them and explaining diagnoses and treatment options.

In this section, we have provided you with a variety of examples of emerging application solutions in radiology departments. These are broader and more impactful than narrow point solutions in medical imaging. Yet, as we will see in the next section – the broadest penetration and benefits from AI will lie in system solutions.

System solutions – AI accelerates health system transformation

Previously in this chapter, we identified six dimensions of health systems that are being transformed: 1) Care delivery, 2) Payment systems, 3) Data and health information technology, 4) Personalization and precision, 5) Democratization and consumerization, and 6) New entrants and competition.

Healthcare moves slowly and each of these trends has been in development for over a decade. We believe the implementation of AI in healthcare is synergistic with all of these trends – and will dramatically speed up the pace of change for each trend.

In this section, we will examine each trend individually to see how it is advanced by AI. We also acknowledge challenges and barriers.

1) Care delivery

From – 'Sick Care': reactive, fragmented, siloed

To – Health: proactive, integrated, networked

We don't pretend to suggest that moving to a system of health is an easy endeavour. It's a huge, multidimensional undertaking, which we expect will take years of cultural, economic, business and governmental shifts.

One of the barriers to moving toward a proactive system of health has simply been that we haven't had a comprehensive set of metrics to understand and measure 'health'. Researchers at Elevance Health have recently developed the Whole Health Index[92] – a set of 93 measures 'representative of social, physical and behavioural factors of health'. The measures fall into three broad domains: social drivers, clinical quality and global health.

AI's predictive capabilities are central to moving from reactive to proactive care. By analysing patient data, AI can identify patterns that suggest a risk of a medical condition. An AI algorithm could analyse a patient's medical history, lifestyle and genetic information to predict their risk of developing a disease. AI algorithms could create personalized prevention and treatment plans to prevent or delay the onset of disease.

AI can help break down the silos that often exist in healthcare. In the past, different healthcare providers created separate sets of patient data, leading to fragmented care. As interoperability among health IT systems continues to improve, AI can assist in integrating data to provide a more holistic, real-time view of a patient's conditions.

AI can help create a networked health system by facilitating communication and coordination among healthcare providers and patients. AI algorithms could manage referrals, schedule appointments, or coordinate care for patients with complex health needs.

2) Payment systems

From – Fee-for-service

To – Value-based care and payments

While fee-for-service incentivizes the quantity of care, value-based care focuses on the quality of care that patients receive. Providers are rewarded for improving short-term and long-term patient outcomes and for reducing the total cost of care.

AI can be used to analyse large data sets. Thus, it can assess the value of different treatments. Many providers have been reluctant to enter contracts with downside financial risk; AI can identify high-risk patients who may benefit from proactive treatments.

AI can automate clinical and administrative processes, thereby improving efficiency and allowing providers to focus more time on patients and other higher-value activities. Helping clinicians focus on higher-value work can improve productivity by 250% over manual processes.[93]

AI can assist in developing and refining value-based care models. Between 2012 and 2022, the US Center for Medicare and Medicaid Innovation attempted over 50 types of pilot project Alternative Payment Models (APMs).[94] While some have been successful, the science of developing optimal care and payment models is still under development. AI can assist in refining and fine-tuning future models to optimize the right mix of incentives and penalties for achieving cost and quality targets.

3) Data and health information technology

From – paper-based, data are hoarded

To – Data are digitized, standardized, interoperable and shared appropriately

Raw data are the fuel for AI. AI-driven algorithms can quickly process vast amounts of digitized health data, making it easier for healthcare providers and patients themselves to make informed decisions about patient care.

As health data become more interoperable and widely shared over the next decade, AI will be able to contribute more and more value to healthcare and to patients' lives. More and better data – turbocharged by AI – are a linchpin to driving other transformational trends in health and healthcare:

- Enabling a new system of preventive health, wellness and early interventions
- Relieving care providers from their dependencies on fee-for-service payments and facilitating the transition to more proactive health and healthcare
- Enabling personalized and precision care
- Democratizing care – providing patients with access to their health data and to data on healthcare quality and prices – empowering them as consumers
- Enabling innovation and competition based on price and quality among healthcare incumbents and new entrants

4) Personalization and precision

From – Traditional medicine: 'One size fits all'

To – Data and technology enable precision medicine: 'Have it your way'

AI can tailor treatment plans based on an individual's unique health conditions, lifestyle, genetics and personal preferences. This can lead to more effective treatments with fewer side effects.

AI can enable more personalized medicine by analysing an individual patient's data. For example, an AI algorithm could determine how a patient's genetic information would predict their response to different treatments. Doctors can then choose the most effective treatment for each individual patient.

Precision medicine goes a step further by tailoring treatments to the specific characteristics of a disease. An AI algorithm could analyse a tumour's genetic makeup to identify specific mutations that should be targeted with specific drugs.

AI can also help monitor patient responses to treatments. An AI system could analyse data from wearable devices to monitor a patient's response to a drug, allowing for adjustments to the dosage of the drug or perhaps the selection of an alternative drug.

5) Democratization and consumerization

From – Care organized around industry stakeholders

To – Patient-centric experience and care

AI can empower patients by providing them with tools to manage their health. AI-powered apps can help patients track their health metrics, manage their medications and review prices of diagnostic and treatment options offered by different providers. These tools can make healthcare more accessible, convenient and understandable for patients. They can also improve patient engagement and adherence to treatment plans.

AI can also improve patient experience. AI algorithms can be used to optimize scheduling and reduce wait times for appointments.

In the past, healthcare has been centralized around hospitals and physician offices. Healthcare is becoming decentralized, refocusing on care being provided in patient's homes and in the community. COVID demonstrated that a high percentage of care could be delivered virtually.

6) New entrants/competition

From – Industry boundaries are clearly defined

To – Start-ups, Big Tech and Big Retail invade

AI has enabled many start-ups in healthcare – over 2,664 as previously documented by Tracxn. Big Tech, large retailers and pharmacy chains also have been early experimenters and developers of AI in their core businesses. These new entrants don't bring the cultural baggage and old business models that have made healthcare resistant to change.

New entrants disrupt traditional boundaries and bring fresh perspectives to healthcare delivery. For example, one of Alphabet's (Google's) health groups is working on several health projects including an AI system that can predict patient outcomes and wearable devices that can track health data. Apple is leveraging its popular Apple Watch to monitor users' health metrics and alert them to potential health issues. Amazon acquired PillPack – an online pharmacy that delivers medications to patient's homes; Amazon also acquired One Medical, a primary care physician group that serves 800,000 patients.

By offering more efficient, convenient and personalized care, new entrants are challenging the status quo and compelling traditional providers to innovate.

Challenges and concerns

AI in healthcare also presents risks and drawbacks:

- Maintaining the human touch
- Assuring the privacy and security of patient data
- Addressing issues of bias and fairness in algorithms
- Managing the process of workflow and cultural change within healthcare organizations
- Assuring the quality and accuracy of information provided to patients and clinicians
- Assuring ethical use of AI
- Retraining workers whose jobs are eliminated or changed by AI
- Avoiding exacerbating health disparities and the digital divide
- Creating regulatory frameworks that keep pace with technological advancements
- Avoiding monopolistic practices of companies providing AI

Takeaways

We will suggest several takeaway points to glean from our chapter.

First, after a long gestation period, AI is clearly emerging as a general-purpose technology. It will impact our lives profoundly – no individual, business, government or economy will be left untouched.

Second, in the short term, healthcare continues to move slowly. It is different than other sectors of the economy, and healthcare data are uniquely complex and non-standardized. We expect that AI will penetrate healthcare – eventually – and it will be one of the last sectors of the economy to be transformed. Radiology was expected to be one of the first areas for AI adoption in healthcare, yet a decade later the *NEJM* reports only 2% penetration.

Third, in the long run, healthcare will be profoundly changed and improved by AI. History might well show that healthcare was the single-most sector to benefit from AI. There are thousands of new and incumbent companies, clinicians and health systems experimenting with point solutions and application solutions. AI holds great promise for improving patient and clinician experience, improving quality and outcomes, and lowering costs. We remain optimistic.

Chapter 6
Helping Leaders Design New World People Experiences
Using Virtual and Augmented Reality to Advance the Future of Work

Rajan Kalia and Cortney Harding

'As a coinage, *hybrid work* is no beauty. But it will reshape cities, careers, family life and free time. That is ample qualification for a word of the year.'[1] It was *The Economist*'s choice of the word for the year, 2022.

At some point in the relatively near future, a white-collar worker's typical day might look something like this. You wake up in the morning in a rental whose location was determined not by the location of a physical office but by the time zone most of your colleagues work in. Your manager is based in Cape Town and your peer is in

Copenhagen, while you're temporarily in Rome, burnishing your Italian skills and trying to keep the pasta pounds at bay.

You slip on a virtual reality headset and log in for your first meeting of the day – no need to bother with hair and makeup, so you stay in sweats while your avatar sports the latest Prada blouse. Your colleagues, all equally clad in athleisure in real life, appear perfectly turned out as you have your daily stand-up and share the latest 3D model of a product you're all working on. From there, you're in the virtual office, heading to meetings and turning your availability light from red to green as you have time to catch up. A new intern sees your green light and their avatar zooms over; you decide to grab a virtual coffee and answer questions about your career path. During your physical lunch break, you practise Italian with the neighbour's kids, who have been doing math tutorials in a headset all morning. Then back to meetings, a few virtual trainings, which you breeze through quickly, and out to touch grass and enjoy a slice of pizza.

'Oh sure,' you might think as you read this. 'And then I'll just hop in my flying car and my robot housekeeper will vacuum my rug.' But you ignore this technology at your own peril. COVID proved that employees could work remotely and the world wouldn't end; had virtual reality been a few years further along in 2020 it would have been used more widely. Generation Z is already used to learning and working in the metaverse and as they enter the workforce, will expect to be able to do the same. Some businesses will embrace this technology while others will stick their heads in the sand and expect that things will always be the same, and you don't need a dog-eared copy of *The Innovator's Dilemma* to know who will come out on top.

'*Hybrid work*' is now a reality. It is changing the way the world works, lives, commutes and connects with each other. No organization on the globe can escape it, many organizations are finding ways to work around it and sometimes mandating their employees to return to physical offices. Nothing is working. Employees joining new organizations have one prominent question to ask, 'Do you provide flexible working in your company?' Hybrid working is hurting real estate like it never has. In the city of New York commercial real estate is no longer lucrative and office occupancy is down to roughly 50%.[2]

Hybrid work means that most of the leaders in their forties and fifties have to rewire their working styles. These leaders are not used to change and are naturally resisting it. They are asking their employees to return to the office. Change is scary and difficult. Leaders will need to learn new skills to manage employees in hybrid work. Leaders who have assumed that hybrid work is a passing trend are grossly mistaken and will face the music soon. Organizations will need to retrain their leaders and employees for hybrid work and give their best in this new environment.

The purpose of this chapter is to help your organization manage this change. This transition won't be easy and will require upskilling and learning, but not to worry. We will present a framework to help guide you through everything you need to know about the future of work and virtual and augmented reality.

We will start by discussing the three areas of impact, focusing on process, organization and the customer (Figure 6.1). Within the process, we will cover product design, R&D and analytics;

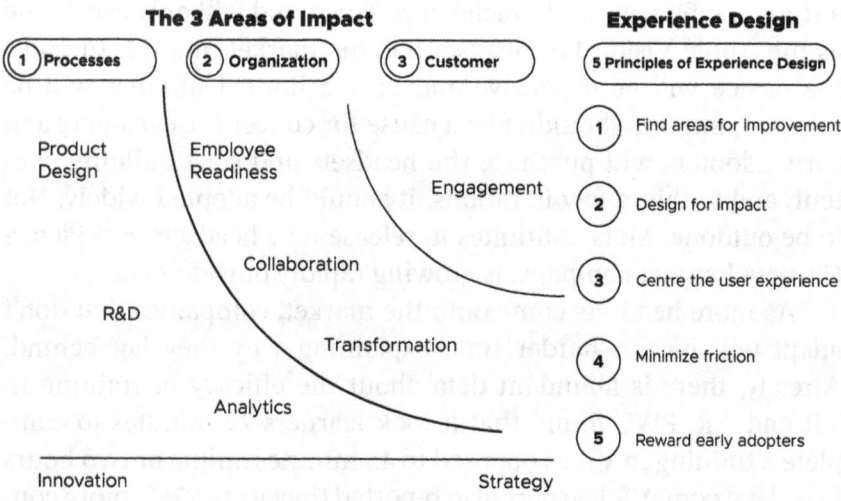

Figure 6.1 The three areas of impact.

within the organization, we'll look at employee readiness, collaboration and transformation; and when talking about the customer, we'll examine engagement. We will then cover the five principles of experience design: finding areas for improvement, designing for impact, keeping the user at the centre of the experience, minimizing friction, and rewarding early adopters.

Trends

Adoption of virtual and augmented reality (VR/AR) for training and education is growing quickly. PWC reported in 2022 that 51% of companies are either in the process of integrating VR into strategy, or have already built VR into at least one dedicated line of business. Of the companies contacted, 34% say that one of the biggest metaverse benefits they currently enjoy or foresee is 'a more effective way to develop and train our people'. Only 9% of the companies interviewed for the report said they weren't doing anything in VR, with the rest in the research or planning phase.

Major companies like Walmart, Exxon and Lowe's are using it to train staff on everything from how to handle an active shooter in a store to safety on rigs to racial bias. This trend will only accelerate as the Apple Vision Pro headset hits the market in 2024. Initially, the device will be expensive and only a limited number will be released, but this shouldn't be a cause for concern. Developers and early adopters will purchase the headsets and start building content, and within a few iterations, it should be adopted widely. Not to be outdone, Meta continues to release new headsets and Pico, a Chinese headset company, is growing rapidly outside Asia.

As more headsets come onto the market, companies that don't adapt will have a harder time explaining why they lag behind. Already, there is abundant data about the efficacy of training in VR and AR. PWC found that it took learners 29 minutes to complete a training in VR as opposed to 45 minutes online or two hours in a classroom. VR learners also reported they were 275% more confident applying what they had learned in real life, and 3.75 times more emotionally connected to the content.

According to PWC, VR training is estimated to be more cost-effective at scale than classroom or e-learning. Because VR content initially requires up to a 48% greater investment than similar classroom or e-learning courses, it's essential to have enough learners to help make this approach cost-effective. At 375 learners, VR training achieved cost parity with classroom learning. At 3,000 learners, VR training became 52% more cost-effective than classroom. At 1,950 learners, VR training achieved cost parity with e-learn. The more people you train, the higher your return will likely be in terms of employee time saved during training, as well as course facilitation and other out-of-pocket cost savings.

The other big trend to focus on is the rise of Gen Z in the workplace. Right now, most of Gen Z is still in school, but once they are in the workforce, they will expect training that mimics how they currently consume content. Many of them are consuming content in the metaverse on platforms like Roblox, which has grown exponentially in the last few years and is only going to grow more as it becomes available on VR headsets. Asking a member of Gen Z to train by watching a video is like asking a millennial to use a record player to listen to music – purely anachronistic.

To keep up with changing norms and trends, leaders will have to learn soft skills like caring, empathy, inspiration and collaboration. These skills were the sissy skills that remained elusive to the most hardened leaders and managers of the 1990s and in the 2000s. But they are facing hard choices now and have little option than to learn these skills. Even millennials, who have taken charge of teams in the last two years, need to learn the people skills of *hybrid work*. All leaders will have to double down to learn these skills or face extinction. Corporate training programmes (like the New World People Leader[3]) are the best way to get to speed with these skills. Organizations need to allocate budgets and include these programmes as essential to becoming a leader. AR/VR tools will help with role playing these skills before going straight into the battlefield of hybrid work, otherwise leaders who are used to fighting with swords risk getting killed by the rifle bullets.

'Soft is hard', said Tom Peters in the 1980s.[4] The soft skills are the hard skills for the current era. Soft skills need a lot of practice.

Training and coaching will soon get baked into routine work of all office goers.

Purpose and connections are the two strongest vectors for employees to remain committed to workplaces. Organizations need to commit to a stronger purpose and help employees build lasting connections at the workplace. Purpose pulls employees to work on their most dreadful days and connections keep them engaged on those days. Innovation happens when people do deep work and are secure when they fail. Psychological safety helps both performance and innovation. It should be an essential subject leaders need to learn when they first assume charge of a team. Leaders need to learn to work with purpose and connections, to innovate and perform in the hybrid work.

Hybrid work will redefine the relationships in organizations, between leaders, their teams and peers. Hybrid work will morph the world.

Product Design

Designing VR and AR training materials is a specialized skill and organizations should consider partnering with an external vendor to produce at least the first few pieces of content. But while the skill set is specialized, it can also be learned, and there are ample resources available if an organization wants to upskill internally to be able to train in VR and AR at scale. Coursera, for example, partnered with Meta to offer a class called 'What Is the Metaverse',[5] which offers best practices for designing and creating interactive experiences. New Mexico State University offers a class called 'XR for Storytelling' which focuses on creating narratives but offers insight into the entire process.

The fundamentals for designing a good VR or AR training course are fairly simple. Choose subjects where learners need this type of training to enhance their learning experience – situations that are unusual, dangerous, hard to replicate, or need standardization. Training someone how to use a computer program like Excel in VR is technically possible but wouldn't add much to the experience; training an employee on how to have a difficult conversation or put out a fire in VR is much more impactful. But even moving dull training programmes into VR or AR and adding a gamified element has been shown to increase engagement and make employees more excited to learn and train.

Product design as a category is experimental in nature. AR/VR offers great opportunities to design products for virtually any industry. The industries it can serve well will be defence, pharmaceuticals, medical devices, automobiles, edtech or any industry that needs humans but can not use them directly to participate. Human safety when threatened is likely to make the product design cycles longer, AR/VR will help reduce the cycles tremendously. Product design with AR/VR will become easier and multiple variations be built and played with without any harm to any human ever.

Sustainable design gains an edge with AR/VR, architectural design and buildings with walkthrough with real time feedback and data points will lead to real time changes in products on the go. Medical devices when used on avatars can give us real feedback on how they are working and how humans are likely to use them. There will always be gaps between AR and real world but these will narrow down with help of better technology and experimentation. A tooth brace on an avatar can give us real feedback on how humans are going to respond to it, helping us study the psychological and sociological impact of products, which might be missing in the realm of product design today. Avatars can emulate humans and the sociological aspect of human interaction and behaviour in the metaverse of that tooth brace will give us insights usually lost to guilt and shame.

R&D

Once you have worked with an external expert in the VR/AR space on initial projects, it is a good idea to upskill people within your organization to be able to create at scale. As those employees start upskilling, they should also start creating – this is the only way to get good at building these experiences. While the hardware will change and evolve, the principles of creating good experiences will remain largely unchanged, so the more opportunities employees have to build, the better.

The first thing to do is get employees a 360 camera and have them shoot test footage. If they want to repurpose existing training in VR or AR, they should first shoot a test version before moving forward. This won't cost much, save for some time on the part of employees who want to act in the piece, but it's also a fun perk and a way to engage team members who are still attached to their high school theatre days. Have them show off the test footage, and make sure the piece actually works to engage the audience. Too often something that sounds great on paper doesn't translate into VR or AR, and you want to determine this sooner rather than later.

It is also worth paying for some interested team members to learn how to use game engines like Unity, if you don't have those people on the team already. If you want pieces to be more interactive and engaging, you'll need them to build and prototype on a regular basis.

Molecular science can gain tremendously from building AR/VR experiences. Hand movements and human moments can be generated in alternate reality and tested over and over again. We can combine AI and AR/VR to deliver research and development.

Imagination and hypothesis drive research and development. Imagine if the whole dream sequence of Einstein on $E = mc^2$ was outlaid in AR/VR, how would it look, how would time travel look, will it help us imagine more vividly, bring out the richness closer, immerse us deeper into the model? Hypothesis can be tested and discarded with speed with AR/VR. Scenarios and algorithms can be drawn out in three dimensions or four dimensions. Instead of one design, scientists can play with tens of designs simultaneously and can morph features of one design into another with gestures and hand movements. Outcome of such scenarios can help companies gain competitive advantage.

AR/VR will help with converting science formulas into likely scenarios and models in the metaverse. Financial aspects, space scenarios, food scenarios and chemistry and biology models – the list is endless to build out in the metaverse. AR/VR will evolve to the next level by feeding outputs of such scenarios into their own LLM/SLM (large/small language models) and a perpetual spiral of improved designs and innovation can be unleashed. R&D efforts take many years and sometimes decades for pharmaceuticals to develop new molecules. With the help of CRISPER and AR/VR technology, the time periods can be slashed. Research done in this manner can be ethical and we can still contain the genie.

Analytics

Using VR/AR for data visualization and analysis can help bring spreadsheets and numbers to life in a new way. Users can be inside the data points and manipulate formulas to see how things change in real time, and data points can be made more meaningful if they are tied to actual human stories that can be experienced.

Think of a city planner who is designing a new neighbour-hood and wants to know where to put stop signs, stoplights and which streets to make one-way. They could build a virtual model of the neighbourhood and put on a headset to see how their decisions would play out – for example, adding and subtracting traffic, changing patterns, and pulling in pre-programmed avatars to account for human behaviour. What works on paper often doesn't work in real life, and this also allows for extreme examples (what if a hurricane hits the neighbourhood and prompts a mass evacuation?) to be included.

Or think of a policy maker trying to decide which state benefits to cut and which to keep intact. When humans are just lines on a spreadsheet it can be easy to run a formula and move on, but when you use a data visualization program in VR/AR, every point can tell a personal story. Cuts will likely still need to be made, but folks will think longer and harder about how they go about that.

Gen AI when trained on converting analytics into insights and ultimately stories is where AR/VR can take us. A whole new generation of employees who can help create stories from analytics with help of AR/VR are sitting on the cusp. Proactive organizations will invest both in the software, identifying the right talent and building their skills on analytics to storytelling. AR/VR will bring these analytics to life with touch and feel. Organizations will enhance their ability to tell stories which evoke the right emotions when the insight hits employees and converts it into a desirable action plan.

Analytics, which has been a lifeless subject and dry by nature, will benefit from the use of AR/VR and become full of life. Imagine a sales employee receiving an email to log into his headset to see the nudge which motivates him. John is a competitive employee and wants to be number one in his group month on month, logging into the AR/VR set he sees an imaginative scenario where he is actually number four in a sprint for the month and also see the bubbles which tell him the action required as he is running the race with milestones popping up in a voice which evokes the emotion in him. We can build similar scenarios for other functions. The secret ingredients for building such a story would be identification of individual behaviour nudges for each employee, conversion of data into insight and a story appealing to the emotional motives of each employee (gathered through his social feeds and achievement data from the past few years).

Analytics and storytelling will ultimately merge and be seamless with the help of AR/VR.

Employee Readiness

Getting a team ready to train using virtual and augmented reality is much easier than many people think. Lots of people have already used a headset, even if it isn't for training purposes, and augmented reality is widely used on smartphones and tablets to play games and add filters to photos. Younger employees are more likely to embrace the technology as it is second nature to many of them, while older users might have more reservations.

One best practice is to allow users to play first and just explore the technology before asking them to do any training or work. People who work with young kids call this 'getting the wiggles out' but it works for adults as well. Being in a headset for the first time can be overwhelming, and letting people virtually teleport around and pick up and explore objects allows them to practice and get comfortable before they have to learn or really engage. Giving clear instructions is also critical – if users feel like they are confused they are likely to give up and report a negative experience and be hesitant to try again.

A design best practice is to always create content with an eye towards the least technical person on the team. Building an experience where someone needs constant hand holding and instruction not only doesn't scale, it isn't generally enjoyable. Finally, as much as you might want to convert everyone all at once, giving folks the option to use more traditional trainings methods for a period of time can help those who are sceptical see the results and make the conversion on their own.

Organizations that are willing to experiment with and who invest early in developing their employees in AI will gain a distinct advantage. Gen-AI will help employees experience work differently than the traditional approach to work. Already a lot of tech employees are feeling more satisfaction when AI is helping them with writing their codes.

AR/VR can help with the whole employee lifecycle:

Recruitment: Managers gain by enacting actual work situations in metaverse to probable candidates and can see their responses and output of work without endangering the actual work. Candidates can ask for tours in the metaverse of the organization before making up their mind to join any organization. A better fit will be inevitable – bringing down the cost of recruitment and early attrition.

Induction: Employees joining in the metaverse can experience work situations, power of purpose of the organization, connect with a wide variety of people joining the organization across the globe and build faster connections within the organization. Employees can benefit from getting training on the job in the metaverse before they are exposed to the real job in the real world.

Performance: Employees can revisit the mistakes they might have made or might make by walking in the shoes of earlier employees with the help of AR/VR. Critical incidents of a job can be enacted in the metaverse and with the help of AR/VR an employee can learn to navigate it well in advance.

Development: Both on hard skills and soft skills, AR/VR is an invaluable tool to develop frontline, middle and senior level employees of an organization. Organizations using AR/VR already include Audi (assemble the right parts), BMW (designing and prototyping), Volkswagen (customer service), DHL (Cargo loading), Bank of America (account opening), Boeing (astronaut missions), Rolls Royce (attaching engines and individual parts to an airplane), KLM (flying choppers for short distances), Siemens (installation of wind turbine blades), DB Sheckner (forklift operations in complex and dangerous scenarios), Myers Police department (life threatening scenarios of dealing with addicts, mental health patients), LA hospital (emergency and trauma situations based on real cases).You can design training around complex, dangerous, life threatening or aggressive customer service scenarios. AR/VR helps train faster and the learning is deeper.

Collaboration/hybrid Work

The increasing complexity of global problems can only be solved when various jigsaw pieces can come together. While most of the employees are super-specialized and know their pieces very well, modern leaders need to see the full picture and nudge people to work with each other, accomplishing impossible goals. When humanity embarks upon goals like climate change, clean energy and a malaria-free world, these complex problems can only be solved with collaboration across boundaries of ethnicity, colour, specializations, countries and other aspects that differentiate humans.

Leaders need to have a mindset to work through problems of collaboration. When employees work together at a set timing and come together to grow apart to do their task, leaders are able to establish rhythms. Rhythms help determine the frequency of working together and the parts of work for which they collaborate and the remaining parts on which they work independently. Weekly connects, morning huddles, zoom calls and so on are helpful in building collaboration to achieve team goals and the organization's mission. Operating systems of organizations often have set routines – annual budgeting exercises, annual retreats, strategic planning workshops, annual sales conferences, quarterly reviews, weekly reviews. Monday morning meetings are a well-established collaboration tool. Organizations have gone back to organizing these with fervour, and leaders want to see people face-to-face once again.

The ostensible reason for this is that offices boost productivity and collaboration. Of course, those are sticky things to prove. Many employees find the ubiquitous open plan offices to be detrimental to their productivity, and companies could very easily just assign productivity targets and evaluate people against those, regardless of where they worked. But in terms of collaboration, it is more difficult to run into people in the breakroom or swing by their desk for a quick chat when everyone is virtual. There are plenty of messaging tools out there, and folks can always book a call, but that feels more formal and folks who just want to chat will likely be dissuaded from doing so.

But the metaverse and virtual reality could provide a solution. You could work in a virtual office from anywhere in the world, although you could keep your calls private so you won't be overheard (a benefit that's harder to get in the office). When you're not on a call, in a meeting, or engaged in deep work, you could mark yourself as available, and another avatar could swing by your virtual desk for a quick chat. Employers could also keep tabs on who is marking themselves as open for collaboration and adjust workloads accordingly.

It's not an exact match to the in-office experience, but far better than our Zoom focused existence now, and offers lots of the same benefits as working from home. Less commuting will lead to less pollution and more time to spend with family and friends, and talent pools will open back up. People can move to places that support their lifestyle rather than being stuck in markets where they have to be just to find work.

Another great benefit of working via virtual reality is the anonymity it can provide. One firm decided to do an experiment – they selected ten people at random, from the C-Suite down to the intern pool, and invited them to a problem-solving workshop in VR. Every avatar looked exactly the same and was randomly numbered, and voices were disguised so no one could tell who was speaking.

The results were astonishing. The interns, who would have never spoken to the CEO in real life, took the lead and offered great ideas. Women and people of colour felt more able to raise points and disagree with each other. In the end, everyone was shocked and excited to see how they all contributed, and the firm plans to keep doing these types of sessions on a regular basis.

These two examples are only the tip of the iceberg when it comes to the possibilities for collaboration in virtual reality. From meetings where people from all over the world can come together without having to travel and sessions where 3D models can be changed in real time, there are endless options.

AR/VR can help take the load off a lot of travel and still give organizations and individuals the opportunity to connect. Organizations need to experiment with using these tools often to see which meetings they can offload to AR/VR. Assessing the effectiveness and impact of using these tools to collaborate will give them a chance to lighten the load and reduce stress while achieving the same impact.

Tools like Zoom and Slack are helping employees to collaborate and connect in real time and respond speedily to workplace problems. When Spotify introduced Agile to solve problems of writing and shipping interconnected and seemingly disparate worlds of technology and music, it established a new norm of solving problems by connecting employees sans their functional boundaries and titles. Customer became the focal point and the rest of the organization became a means to elevate their experience.

Organizations encourage functional silos and deliberately discourage employees to disengage with each other in the name of specialization. Employees actively protect turfs and continuously build moats to protect and enhance the importance of their functions. Leaders need to discover these moats or boundary walls, break them down and create active collaboration methods to reward team members who go out to achieve organization missions rather than functional dominance. Cross-functional teams (CFTs) have been a norm in progressive organizations, these put organization missions above functional goals. CFTs are and should be on repeat loops in any organization. CFTs are one of the most effective collaborative tools in an organization armoury to achieve agility.

Collaboration can be improved through systematic use of rituals, rhythms and rewards within organizations. Leaders need to actively engage in behaviour and role-model collaboration to reap its benefits.

Transformation

Emerging technologies like artificial intelligence, machine learning, spatial computing and robotics will absolutely change the way we work in the next 50 years. As new technologies are introduced into the market, and subsequently into the mainstream, there is almost always resistance, especially among workers who fear their careers will be disrupted or even ended by these innovations. The good news is that these fears are often overblown and new technologies create new jobs that people can do with a bit of retraining; the bad news is that there is often resistance to those opportunities for growth.

Using VR can help smooth over some of these transitions and make the tech handshake more seamless. First off, VR allows people to practice in certain situations before they have to do so in the real world – that's one of the reasons it works so well for training and education. If a factory employee is sceptical about working with robots, for instance, simulations can be built where that worker can practice the tasks they need to complete with the robot to make it seem less strange. The simulations can also be gamified and tell a story at the same time as they educate – the robot that will 'steal your job' can become the robot you partner with to complete tasks in a gamified setting. That robot can even be given a persona to make it seem more human – all of a sudden the worker has a new friend to complete a quest with.

Workers can also see the benefits of automation in action as they interact with AI-powered chatbots in the metaverse. No-one wants to finish a long day at work and then deal with a customer service agent about a late bill or a delayed flight. And customer service agents are increasingly overworked, hard to hire, and even harder to fire, given strong economic conditions. They have no incentive to do a good job and often don't, leaving customers upset and brand reputation damaged. But an AI-powered bot in the metaverse, both for the customer and agent, can solve problems based on very little information or effort. Imagine this – your flight is cancelled at the last minute due to weather conditions. Currently, you have to stand in a long line while an underpaid and overworked human agent tries to help. In the future, your AI powered avatar would work with an infinite number of AI powered agents and get you on the next best flight, all while you read a book in the lounge. And for those rare occasions that require more assistance, a human agent could step in and do the specialized work.

The key idea is to make sure that all these emerging technologies work together to make employee's lives better and allow them to focus on producing the best work possible. There are no 'winners' or 'losers' when it comes to the next wave of tech – all these innovations will depend on one another. In the future, a worker will don a headset and pair up with an AI powered robot to complete work tasks, and that will be as normal as typing an email from the beach is today.

Imagine a co-pilot with you, all the time, whose only interest is your success, happiness and peace. This co-pilot has access to all your interests, your personality, your goals, your likings, your preferred style, it is your wingman, it is your Robert, it is your Jeeves, call it what you might. You are its first and last priority. That is the future one is imagining where humans and technology are on their way to being integrated.[6]

We are at a cusp of history and witnessing it. Technology and Human handshake is turning into a hug where the two blend. Leaders are able to communicate, inspire, direct and engage their teams deeply and richly with help of AI and technology. They have better and richer data available to them about their teams than it ever was. It helps them navigate tricky team situations. AI is helping them match their personal workstyle with their team's workstyle more closely. Technology is able to fix styles almost in real time, giving guidance to leaders on how to deal with their team on a day-to-day basis.

With AR becoming a reality, leaders will be able to don their AR glasses which project holographic displays with intricate data visualizations and predictive analytics. These augmented insights empower leaders to make data-informed decisions about talent management, career development and team optimization. The AR glasses in the near future will have the power to provide a window into the data analysed to link it continuously to the aspirations of each of their team members, allowing them to dialog their personalized growth plans and nurture their unique potentials.

Leaders can immerse themselves in a neural simulation, where artificial intelligence constructs hyper-realistic scenarios for leadership training. As leaders' navigate these simulated worlds, they engage with AI-generated characters who challenge their decision-making skills, emotional intelligence and ability to adapt to unpredictable circumstances. These neural simulations accelerate the growth of the leaders, allowing them and their teams to explore uncharted territories and experiment with innovative approaches.

People leaders will use advanced AI-powered tools to analyse talent data and make informed decisions about resource allocation and career development opportunities. These tools consider factors such as individual skills, aspirations and performance, helping leaders to identify high-potential employees and create personalized growth plans for each team member. Leaders will schedule virtual mentorship sessions and facilitate knowledge-sharing platforms to promote continuous learning and professional development.

Leaders will conduct virtual town hall meetings, where team members from different locations join in real-time to discuss organizational updates, share success stories and provide feedback. The use of AI-powered sentiment analysis during these meetings will help gauge the overall team sentiment and address any concerns promptly.

The co-pilot will keep track of this data, will tag it correctly and keep analysing it while the leaders engage in various other activities. People leaders will multiply their effectiveness with the help of technology. In an era where AI is still being debated with anxiety and question marks, there is a great opportunity to make it work by your side enhancing your skills. Technology as a co-pilot can and should make our lives truer, richer, meaningful and grateful.

Engagement

If there is one metric by which VR and AR excels, it is engagement. Users are more focused in a headset for many reasons, the most basic being that it is much harder to multitask and be distracted. A worker in a classroom will likely be checking a phone or on a laptop; even if they are not allowed to have technology they can daydream and look out the window. An online video training is even worse – a user is likely watching the video in the background while texting a friend about dinner plans, checking the score from last night's game and arguing on social media, likely all at once.

And sure, a user tuning out during a compliance training session likely won't be the end of the world – most people know not to sell trade secrets or do insider trading. But a wise person once said that the way you do one thing is the way you do everything, and by communicating to employees that their education and training is an afterthought, you are subconsciously reinforcing that their career growth is a low priority. When diversity, equity and inclusion (DE&I) and sexual harassment trainings are seen as jokes or just things that have to be done to please a lawyer, what sort of message does that send to women and underrepresented team members?

Actively engaging employees in training can encourage loyalty and make them feel like the company is invested in their progress. And sometimes it can even surface new opportunities – by engaging entry-level employees in immersive training they can demonstrate and learn skills they would otherwise not be able to, setting them up for potential opportunities.

In today's corporate world, the concept of engagement has taken centre stage. Organizations must maintain continuous engagement with all stakeholders. Today is an era where attention is a precious commodity. With attention becoming scarcer and online reels capturing people's focus, AR and VR can prove to be invaluable tools for enhancing training and deep learning. Both customers and employees require distinct and joint engagement strategies to create and deliver value effectively.

AR/VR tools offer a remarkable means to engage with customers and provide immersive experiences. For instance, Lowe's allows customers to test hand tools and work with them in a virtual environment before making a purchase decision, while Walmart facilitates virtual shopping experiences, enabling real-time integration of the shopping list from a customer's phone into their VR environment for a seamless shopping journey.

Engagement serves as a driving force behind purchase decisions and repeat behaviours. One of the most promising applications of AR/VR lies in training employees in critical skills such as empathy, service excellence and essential 'soft' skills without inadvertently causing offence. Companies like Farmers Insurance have already begun using AR/VR to train claim settlement executives, preparing them to interact with customers of varying ages, backgrounds, ethnicities and races sensitively and effectively. By replicating real-life scenarios, AR/VR can foster kinder, more empathetic and emotionally attuned human interactions, ultimately creating a customer-centric approach that ensures repeat purchases and delivers enhanced value to the organization.

AR/VR's role in enhancing engagement will be pivotal in shaping customer interactions, resulting in a more compassionate and customer-focused approach that drives greater value for organizations.

Find Areas for Improvement

Where can VR/AR be used to improve training and education? The list can seem overwhelming at first when companies start to take the plunge into building this type of content. But there are some criteria that can be used to narrow the scope and prioritize initially.

First, look at what isn't working well. If you are running a training programme that is going fabulously, don't mess with perfection. But it is very likely that some of your training programmes aren't going all that well, and there are several ways to drill down on that. For instance, if you work in food service and knife injuries are common in your kitchens, that is probably a good place to start. If your female or underrepresented employees are resigning in droves, sexual harassment and DE&I training via in VR is probably a good first investment.

High employee turnover can be an indication of deeper problems and a good place to start looking for ideas for how to improve your training. Some businesses, particularly those that are seasonal, have high turnover rates baked in, but even then investing in training can help encourage team members to stick around and improve their skills.

That said, there are certain things VR/AR training isn't suited for. Training on programs like Powerpoint and Excel should be done on the computer, because that's the way people will use them in real life. Training on very technical subjects can be started in VR/ AR but will also need to be reinforced in real life – a pilot can get a lot of work done on a flight simulator, for example, but most people wouldn't want to get on a plane piloted by someone who hadn't been up in the air many times.

Many changes can initially appear daunting or unsettling, especially in the realms of AR and VR. When employees first don the headsets and begin to interact with AR and VR technologies, it's natural to feel a sense of unfamiliarity and unease. To integrate AR/VR into an organization's training successfully, it is imperative that the leadership team experiences it first-hand. Once the leadership is on board, most initiatives can be smoothly implemented.

Implementing AR/VR training for a large organization is not an overnight endeavour, and there are a few key challenges that need to be addressed:

Cost and equipment availability:

- Currently, the widespread adoption of AR/VR training in large organizations is hindered by the cost of the necessary equipment. These technologies can be expensive, and organizations need to budget for the investment.
- Availability of suitable AR/VR programs is another consideration. Ensuring that there are programs relevant to an organization's training needs is crucial.

Categorizing training needs:

- To introduce AR/VR training effectively, it is important to categorize the types of training that would benefit most from these technologies. Specifically, areas where human direct engagement might not be safe can greatly benefit from AR/VR training. Such areas include:
  - Repairing deep-sea equipment
  - Space engineering
  - Oil rigs
  - Nuclear plants
  - Wind turbines and more

While the integration of AR/VR training into large organizations may take some time and investment, it is an essential step in ensuring safety and efficiency in various high-risk fields. The leadership's endorsement, coupled with careful consideration of equipment costs and program availability, will pave the way for a successful implementation of AR/VR training in the future.

Designing for Impact

Virtual reality has often been referred to as being an 'empathy machine.' A good VR piece can allow people to experience situations and feelings that they would perhaps never be able to experience otherwise because of their gender identity, skin colour or background. For instance, a VR piece about racial bias for store employees lets workers feel just how awful it is to be followed or accused of stealing unfairly just because of who they are, leading those workers to be more cognizant of their own behaviour and ask themselves about their own biases and blind spots.

This technology also allows for leaders to develop more empathy and understanding by practising difficult conversations in advance of the actual event. While no one should ever lead a challenging conversation based on a script, a VR experience allows a user to practise how it feels to have that hard talk and handle different types of responses and be more comfortable when the time comes for the actual event. Take, for example, a piece called AvenueS. This piece was built to allow new child welfare workers to practise doing a family interview in VR, with the idea being that this training would be more consistent than the approach of having more experienced child welfare workers train new hires. It would also be more replicable, as new hires could repeat the scenario as many times as they needed to feel comfortable, and less potentially harmful – if you chose to leave the children in a problematic situation in VR, there would be no real world impact.

The results were astonishing. In one of the first states to use the piece, Indiana, employee turnover among case workers dropped dramatically, and those same workers reported feeling more confident and prepared going into family meetings.

Virtual reality can also reinforce the purpose of the work that is being done by an organization. Most organizations strive to have at least some positive impact, whether it is a primary or secondary goal, but employees can feel disconnected from this on a day-to-day basis. Even NGOs and government agencies whose entire mission is purpose driven can get lost in the minutiae of sending emails and writing memos and forget about the big picture. A VR experience that reminds them of the impact of their work can bring that back into focus. For example, say an organization is funding a programme to help rural women in Nigeria to learn tech skills. A VR experience allows employees to see the women's day-to-day lives and the impact they are having, and feel like they are actually with the women, not just watching on a flat screen thousands of miles away.

These types of experiences can also be a powerful tool for recruiting new talent. Younger workers often express that they want their work to have a positive impact and higher purpose, and this can help them really understand the difference they could make. Logotherapy school founded by Victor Frankl argues that a person's search for meaning is the central human motivation force. The same is true in organizations – a great purpose engages, motivates and retains team members. Post COVID, the search for meaning has been amplified in the world. Of many, one of the reasons employees are quitting is a mismatch with organizational values and purpose. They do not see their own purpose getting fulfilled by the organization.

Organizations having an appealing purpose are able to attract and engage with employees for longer periods of time. Google's purpose – *Our mission is to organize the world's information and make it universally accessible and useful* – has been attracting college graduates to join it and fulfil their destinies. Most of the technology companies are building purposes far larger than the company can fulfil at present. Microsoft on the other hand wants *to empower every person and every organization on the planet to achieve more*. Most of the purposes are directional in nature. One can always achieve more than their current state and hence the purposes chosen by these companies will always propel their employees to do more and achieve more.

In a retail store, employees sing anthems, in the morning meetings in Japan employees exercise and recite their mottos, share their purpose and the drumroll. Armed forces usually have a motto and soldiers die for their regiment motto rather than for their country. Purpose, belongingness and loyalty all create allegiance. Organizations and organization behaviourists have understood the secret of purpose – it unleashes energy, creates bonhomie and impacts productivity. More and more organizations want to have purposes that defy Milton Friedman's single pursuit of shareholder return. Most organizations and their current employees want organizations to do more for the planet and people than only pursue profits.

People leaders in organizations have the tough task to engage in a dialogue making organization purpose meaningful to their teams. People leaders are the essential translators of purpose to daily work goals. Organization purpose usually does not correlate automatically with the daily, weekly, monthly and quarterly goals of individuals. Individuals and teams regularly struggle to connect their work with organizational purpose. Organizations usually have goals aligned to revenue, profits, and earnings before interest, taxes, depreciation, and amortization (EBITDA), which are mathematical cold numbers, they do not connect well with purpose. Employees find revenue, profits and EBITDA numbers unrelatable, hollow and uninspiring. People leaders often fail to join the disparate dots of purpose and numbers. These seem like two ends of a continuum, never matching and opposite (Figure 6.2).

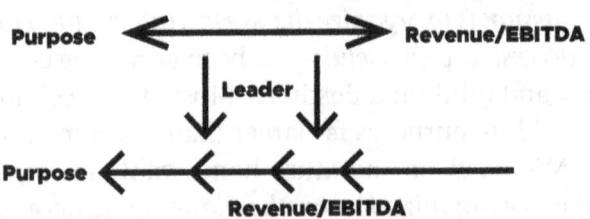

Figure 6.2   Leader aligns Purpose and EBITDA.

Technology can help bridge the continuum gap and bring organizational purpose to life. VR can help employees immerse themselves in an alternate world and build connections physically and visually.

VR designs can create the connection continuum. Induction programmes incorporating VR medium puts the new employee right in the centre of the continuum. When you are in the middle you can pull the two sides together, mix, match and link them to the job description and connect the employee's daily tasks to both. You can play with three or four dimensions and are no longer limited to the two-dimensional screen or paper. You are not going to forget this creation for a long time. You can revisit the connection as many times as you want, modify it when the context changes/company strategy is renewed or you change your function/department.

Centre the Experience of the User

Employee wellbeing is a hot topic, but one that is all too easy to mishandle. No amount of employer-provided meditation apps or discounts on gym memberships will be enough if a workplace is fundamentally toxic. *If workers are not paid a fair wage and able to work in a supportive environment, all of the frills are just window dressing.*

But assuming an employer's proverbial house is in order, new technologies can be used to promote employee wellbeing in a variety of ways. First off, working in a headset allows users to be more focused and present and do deep work more easily than on Zoom or in an office. One of the reasons many employees feel burned out and distracted is because they are constantly dealing with notifications and pop-ups – how many people can honestly say they stay fully focused on their call when a Slack notification pops up? If workers are racing around distracted all day, by the end, they are fried and frustrated, and that's not sustainable.

Many remote workers like the perks of not having to commute but report feeling disconnected from other colleagues, and hosting meetings in the metaverse can help solve these feelings of alienation. Users of metaverse meeting platforms like Horizon Workrooms, Spatial, and Arthur report feeling more connected to their co-workers, even though they are interacting with them in avatar form. While there is no substitute for real-life interaction, these types of meetings can help bridge the gap between days in office or retreats while allowing people the freedom and flexibility of remote work.

The problem of isolation is so pervasive that the US Surgeon General has released guidelines about how to combat it like a public health emergency. While this problem extends beyond work, it also bleeds into work, as the health problems caused by isolation can lead to less productive workers. Building communities in the metaverse can go a long way towards solving this problem for certain populations – people who can't interact with others in real life because of illness or anxiety or certain phobias, or people for whom it is unsafe to be their authentic selves in the physical world.

Extended reality (XR) headsets can also be used for much more than productivity and socialization. There are a number of highly regarded meditation platforms, Tripp and Eunoe among them, that can be used for employee wellbeing and stress management. Engaging with these apps in a headset is more immersive than trying to meditate with an app or in a quiet room, where there are plenty of distractions, and also offer more privacy.

There are also several fitness apps that employers could provide as a benefit to keep workers fit and having fun. Supernatural, for example, can be used by people of all fitness levels, and workers could even have competitions or exercise together. Employers shouldn't monitor or punish those who choose to be active in a different way, but they should encourage employees to participate and make sure their minds and bodies are healthy and balanced.

Robert Waldinger has been leading the longest scientific study on happiness ever conducted (in the last eight decades). One of the discoveries he made is building and keeping connections is a key component of happiness in life. Deliberately working on connections, tending to them, caring about them and spending time nurturing them is one of the key skills leaders need in the new world of work. Connections help leaders drive outcomes. Connections also build better relationships and kinder and more empathetic organizations.

Caring for connections is critical for leaders of the baby boomer generation because this was not as important during their early leadership years. Care was seen as a weak component of leadership in the 1980s, 1990s and early 2000s. In order to work successfully with Gen-Z or Gen-Alpha leaders, leaders need to rewire their mindset to 'soft is hard' (Tom Peters). Without understanding and learning how to care, leaders are most likely to fail with the Gen-Z and Gen-A. This generation refuses to work with managers who do not understand that a pet is as important as a child. Gen-A wants a leave when their pet falls sick, an alien concept for baby boomer and Gen X leaders. Gens Z and A are more in touch with their feelings than earlier generations and want their leaders to be tuned into this reality.

Learning to care can happen through various mechanisms. VR and the metaverse can create care scenarios for learners which can help them learn how to be more sensitive. Leaders can thus learn how to respond to scenarios that they have never been exposed to, for example responding to Gen-Z avatars asking for leave for a sick pet, break-ups, menstrual periods and so on.

Leaders can build deep relations with peers and team members by genuinely caring for their success and well-being. Engaging in a daily routine of check-in into the feelings and emotional aspect of team members helps leaders get the best out of self and team. The leadership mindset in hybrid work needs to shift from 'How do I lead and be successful?' to 'How does my team succeed?' Managers as coaches is a popular training programme offered by organizations like Standard Chartered Bank, SunLife Insurance and many others to upskill their People Leaders. These organizations have successfully helped their managers to build coaching skills enabling them to engage effectively with a multi-generational workforce.

As coaches, leaders ensure that their teams are not continuously under stress. Most organizations in the 1990s and early 2000s had deliberately and successfully created cultures that led to stress. In the post-COVID world, organizations are rethinking their employee engagement model. Caring and well-being have become the mainstay of organizational culture. Leaders need to learn the skills of caring and well-being as much as the other currently popular skills of AI and data analytics. People leaders in the hybrid work world need to be 'gentle leaders'.

When Google promotes psychological safety as the foundation of high-performance culture, gentle leadership gets the place it deserves.

Minimize Friction

Companies are often under the impression that VR/AR devices are cumbersome and hard to deploy at scale, but that's not true at all. Headsets are just like any other device that needs to be managed, but if your organization has a team that distributes laptops and other devices, they can just as easily send around headsets.

Most headsets are not difficult to use, but having a weekly Zoom meeting where people who have just received headsets can dial in and walk through the setup process can be helpful. A good website or paper guide could also work, but the personal touch is nice if there is bandwidth on the team.

When designing VR/AR trainings that will be done remotely, remember that not everyone has access to large amounts of space and build accordingly. Seated experiences are easier to do in confined spaces, but keep the play area small for training where people have to move around – some of them are in tiny big city apartments or have mobility issues.

Managing headsets from afar is not difficult – some platforms have their own multi-device management systems, like Quest for Business, and third party platforms like ArborXR and ManageXR can also be used to keep track of headsets and if folks are completing their training. Training can also be integrated into learning management systems, as long as the learning management system (LMS) has an application programming interface (API).

Efficiency and productivity are the natural results of reducing friction within an organization's processes and systems that have evolved over time. However, change within an organization often meets resistance and organizations need to develop regular coping mechanisms to deal with these scenarios. A key insight is that people tend to learn most effectively when they're having fun. This insight presents an exciting opportunity for the adoption of AR and VR technologies. By incorporating elements of fun and games, organizations can effectively reduce stress and resistance, making it easier to engage employees and introduce AR/VR equipment for work and training.

Let us take the example of a bank operating in rural areas of Africa and Asia. In these regions, both customers and employees may not be familiar with even mobile devices and may be apprehensive about using them, fearing errors that could result in the loss of hard-earned money. Organizations like these will face substantial challenges when it comes to implementing AR/VR technology. It can be a daunting experience for employees of such organizations to don a headset and immerse themselves in alternate realities.

To minimize resistance and build comfort in these situations, a strategic approach would be to introduce games through AR/VR. By starting with engaging and enjoyable gaming experiences, employees can gradually become familiar with the equipment and its capabilities. This initial phase of interaction with AR/VR technologies sets the stage for a smoother transition to training and other job-related tasks, ultimately reducing friction and enhancing overall productivity.

The key to successfully integrating AR/VR technology in traditionally tech-unfriendly environments lies in understanding the importance of making the experience enjoyable and stress-free. By introducing fun and games through these technologies, organizations can pave the way for a more seamless transition to more serious applications and significantly improve efficiency and productivity.

Reward Early Adopters

Likely, the uptake of VR/AR technologies for training will not happen uniformly across an organization, especially in very large companies. By rewarding managers and department heads who are willing to be first movers, it will likely encourage others who are hesitant to make changes.

Early adopters should be recognized and rewarded in a distinctive manner. This reward mechanism should acknowledge that early adopters gain access to the latest technology and tools ahead of their colleagues within the organization. Their pioneering role can shape the path for the rest of the organization, and they should be seen as pioneers in this journey. To facilitate this, early adopters can be elevated to the status of role models and entrusted with the responsibility of training other team members.

Implementing time-tested techniques, such as leaderboards, and providing special badges and prominent name displays, can play a pivotal role in making early adopters feel proud of their achievements. These visual cues serve as powerful motivators, inspiring early adopters to enthusiastically share their knowledge and expertise with their fellow colleagues. This not only benefits the individuals but also accelerates the organization's overall adoption of new technologies and change agenda.

Recognizing and rewarding early adopters through a combination of access, status and visual recognition can be a compelling way to encourage knowledge sharing and expedite the adoption of AR/VR within an organization.

It can be very easy to simply keep doing things as they have been done for years, but that is the type of thinking that sinks companies into failure. *The Innovator's Dilemma* is considered a foundational business book for many reasons, and chief among them is exposing this type of thinking. After all, Blockbuster had never known a world where its video stores weren't packed, and it failed to see disruption on the horizon. Now it is a punchline and object of fond nostalgia when it was once a profitable company.

This type of early adoption will also help attract younger talent. Generation Z is used to the metaverse and virtual reality, and asking them to read manuals to watch videos, is, to use their parlance, 'cringe'. Companies need to change with the times in order to grow, and part of that includes keeping up to date with technology and meeting new people where they are.

Conclusion

Training programmes for the new world leader skills of care, empathy and collaboration are best learnt in a simulated environment as instant reaction of others help us get feedback in real time and modify our behaviours. AR/VR can be simulated to give extreme reactions to various situations. The extreme situations work with the neural system to build a new connection in our brains. The new neural connections are myelin bound and when these simulations are played a couple of times, the connections grow stronger, cementing our learnings. AR/VR avatars can be codified to react in response to the reactions of the participants. The participants also learn in a relatively safe environment without becoming vulnerable to the real-world impact.

Pick from the reflections below to start designing your roadmap for the future new world experiences:

1. What are your organization's biggest challenges when it comes to adopting new technology like VR/AR?
2. What can you do to ensure that your organization will stay current as the future of work unfolds?
3. How can your organization encourage bold thinking when it comes to the future of work?
4. What are the biggest factors that could disrupt your organization in the next year? Five years? Ten years?
5. How are you making sure that your organization values your workforce in a real and tangible way?
6. How would you describe the leaders of the future?

7. What skills will your leaders need in the next 5 years?
8. How will your leaders learn to integrate AR/VR in the day-to-day work of your organizations?
9. Which tasks, functions, processes and responsibilities are better served with AR/VR?

Chapter 7
Designing the Metamobility Future

How Mobility and the Metaverse are Reshaping Industries, Enriching User Experiences, and Paving the Way for a More Interconnected and Inclusive Society

Kristin Slanina and Martha Boeckenfeld

The New Frontier

Unleashing the vast potential of the metaverse heralds a reimagination of mobility – transforming the way people and goods move. Technology will catalyze more efficient modes of movement as well as create new experiences. Imagine a world where borders become insignificant, transportation becomes personalized, spatial constraints fade, and seamless connectivity becomes the new norm. It's about creating new experiences. Welcome to the dawn of a new age where mobility transcends the mere act of movement. It's no longer anchored to the physical world but extends into the realms of virtuality.

Mobility is about the movement of people and goods – and the metaverse symbolizes the transmission of ideas, experiences and engagements across the digital milieu, merging diverse viewpoints, aspirations and possibilities in ways previously unimagined. Metamobility provides accessibility, inclusivity and sustainability. It's how we can be more efficient with our time as well as resources. Visualize attending international conferences, concerts and family gatherings without having to actually travel. The metaverse, a term integral to this narrative, is a dynamic, virtual universe that exists parallel to our physical world. It is an immersive, interactive space enabled by cutting-edge technology where physical and digital entities coexist, interact and evolve. In this realm, users can engage in real-time with multisensory interactions that transcend geographical and physical limitations.

This is the new type of mobility. Metamobility is an experience that is palpably real. The recent launch of the Apple Vision Pro merely scratches the surface of these vast possibilities.[1] The deployment of digital twin technology and NVIDIA's Omniverse, in collaboration with corporate giants like Siemens[2] and the BMW Group,[3] exemplifies the potential for remote simulations and operations. Such technological feats are not only reshaping industries but also promising substantial economic benefits with millions of savings expected. Furthermore, the Emirates Group's collaboration with Amazon Web Services (AWS) to introduce extended reality (XR) for employee onboarding is a pioneering step in the aviation sector, set to debut in 2024.[4] The Metamobility universe symbolizes the digital component, encompassing components like digital twins and in-car entertainment. It is about the value of data, opportunities with autonomous, connected and electric vehicles as well as of multimodal transportation and how smart cities will impact the world. We will have new ways of working that require new skill sets. It is a canvas for the seamless flow of ideas, experiences and engagements across virtual landscapes. In this expansive virtual ecosystem, individuals can traverse digital landscapes, engage in immersive experiences and connect across geographies and cultures like never before. It is a world where virtual and augmented realities merge, enabling real-time interactions across continents and unlocking unprecedented opportunities in various sectors.

McKinsey & Company underscores that by 2030, the economic impact of the metaverse alone could be up to $5 trillion[5] and Citigroup estimates between $8 and $13 trillion.[6] This isn't just a technological revolution; it's a societal transformation where every sector, every industry and every individual is a participant in a new era. The opportunities with connected car data alone could be upwards $400 billion.[7] These are great ways of harnessing new value streams.

It is about inclusivity that can provide a platform for people to connect and collaborate regardless of their physical location, which can help to bridge the digital divide and promote inclusivity that changes the character of mobility. Metamobility can also provide a platform for people to learn about and engage with sustainability issues, such as climate change and renewable energy. As we move into electrification, there are vehicle-to-grid (V2G) and vehicle-to-vehicle (V2V) opportunities that change our thinking about the grid and make it more robust.

Metamobility can provide a platform for people from different parts of the world to collaborate on projects and share ideas, which help promote global collaboration and innovation. The metaverse can also provide a space for people to learn about and engage with different cultures and perspectives, increasing cross-cultural understanding and collaboration.

Metamobility is about sustainability as well. It can help to reduce the need for physical travel by providing virtual alternatives to in-person meetings and events, which can help to reduce carbon emissions and accelerate our goal to net-zero. It provides more efficient multimodal transportation. While the metaverse is still in its early stages, it has enormous potential to improve road safety, increase citizen participation and make mobility more diverse and inclusive. The metaverse will transform our lives and businesses in a profound way, offering new perceptions and experiences when it comes to transport planning and shaping the mobility ecosystem. The metaverse is driving value in the mobility sector by expanding and diversifying revenue streams, enhancing brand loyalty, improving customer experiences and optimizing production. Original equipment manufacturers (OEMs) and other mobility players can already generate substantial value today by adopting the metaverse, even if it delivers only a share of the full experience expected in the future.

The future of mobility promises increased speed and enhanced safety, efficiency and accessibility. From AI-driven smart cities to self-driving vehicles, augmented reality (AR) navigation, and quantum-optimized transportation networks. It's about transportation as a service that is accessible to all and optimized for individual needs. Mobility will be clean, intelligent and inclusive.

Corporate leaders grapple with ethical issues as well as the changing work construct when incorporating AI and mixed reality into their operations. Addressing these challenges demands robust governance structures emphasizing inclusivity, equity and safety. In the age where the Internet of Things (IoT) forms the backbone of digital transformation, its importance is matched by its complexity. With IoT comes challenges, primarily concerning security. Ensuring the protection of interconnected devices, preserving data privacy and ethically managing data are paramount. As we progress into this new digital era, establishing rigorous cybersecurity protocols, ethical guidelines and regulatory frameworks is crucial. These foundations will guarantee that our journey through the metaverse and advanced mobility is steered by ethics, security and privacy, creating an equitable digital ecosystem.

As technology continues to blur the lines between the physical and digital realms, our understanding of these landscapes is constantly evolving. Today's leaders need to navigate these complex terrains, ensuring that they harness the vast potential while staying true to their core focus – the customer. Whether they are crafting experiences in the augmented terrains of the metaverse or developing sustainable mobility solutions, the ultimate aim is to cater to evolving customer needs and forge unparalleled experiences. After all, in today's intricate digital age, customers seamlessly transition between digital and physical worlds, blurring and redefining boundaries like never before.

Leadership in this new age demands more than mere understanding – it calls for foresight, agility and innovation. Our comprehensive framework, rooted in thorough research and insights, aims to guide leaders through these multifaceted paradigms. Central to our narrative, the 'Future of Mobility Experience Model' is designed to demystify the complex interplay between the physical and digital realms. By breaking down this model into four integral axes – Physical, Digital, Hardware and Software – we provide a roadmap for navigating the intricate web of advancements and innovations.

At its core, this model functions as a tactical blueprint, furnishing senior leaders with a panoramic perspective of the confluence of the metaverse and mobility – the Metamobility. It's crafted to guide them through the labyrinth of a rapidly transforming technological and societal milieu. The amalgamation of these innovations and their subsequent effects are reshaping our environment, underlining the significance of responsibly navigating this novel reality, with an emphasis on harnessing its potential and addressing the inherent challenges.

Conclusion

As we delve deeper into the ever-evolving landscape of technological innovations, the interconnection between mobility and the metaverse emerges as a dynamic and transformative force of the Metamobility. This convergence presents a captivating realm of possibilities that are yet to be fully explored and appreciated. The synthesis of IoT, AI, the metaverse and other deep tech innovations is a game changer. It's about creating a world where technology enriches human experience, fosters global connectivity and paves the way for a future where the boundaries between the physical and virtual worlds blur, offering unprecedented opportunities for innovation, collaboration and societal advancement for an inclusive society.

The World Is Your Canvas – let's explore this new reality together, unveiling the opportunities and challenges that lie ahead. Let's work together to create an exciting and amazing new future.

Connected Vehicles and their Data

What does this mean?

The automotive industry is over 100 years old and has evolved over this time. It transitioned from the horse and carriage to internal combustion engines (ICE) – with a brief period of electric vehicles at the turn of the century before ICE vehicles took over. Now we are transitioning to more sustainable transportation. Automotive manufacturers have been continually improving on emissions, fuel economy, features and incorporating new technology. This entails connected vehicle capability as well as harnessing and synthesizing the data.

It's not an easy feat. Automotive manufacturers have traditional processes and different ways of thinking than technology companies. It has a different clock speed. It is an entirely new realm of incorporating fast moving technologies and software into the vehicle – and it's a challenge to modify the structure, processes and thinking accordingly. How to manage the disconnect in the timeline? Think about it: computing power doubles every 18 months and a vehicle development lifecycle is about 4 years. How do the two align?

Acquiring the right skillsets and retaining that talent is also a challenge. As they incorporate connected vehicle technology, they are struggling to figure out what data is relevant and how to make the most of that data. So, what exactly is a connected vehicle? It is one that is equipped with a communication system that allows real-time information to be shared with other vehicles and infrastructure, as well as third-parties that can provide new services that benefit the consumer. The data from these millions of connected vehicles (and there are approximately 1.5 billion vehicles on the road today) is massive and this data can provide insights into driver habits as well as road conditions and many other elements.

A big carrot of connected vehicle data for automotive manufacturers is to address and minimize warranty costs. Warranty costs can be huge. In 2022, Ford, GM, and Tesla together paid out $9.07 billion in claims. In 2022, Ford paid $4.17 billion in claims, a 5.4% increase from the year prior. GM paid $4.10 billion in claims, a 26.1% increase from 2021.[8] Connected vehicle data, if used effectively, synthesized and acted upon quickly, will lower these costs. Data can be gathered real-time and the engineers can assess anomalies and address any issues with a much faster turnaround time. Instead of having recalls with millions of vehicles, recall rates can be significantly less and much more contained.

Connected vehicle data also creates new opportunities for additional revenue streams as well as information for users. Users can see real-time vehicle health reports for all key systems such as tyre pressure and fuel/battery consumption. It can optimize traffic flow, provide usage-based insurance, improved driving safety and roadside assistance.

Otonomo is a company that collects all OEM vehicle data and opens it up for new apps. Figure 7.1 shows the various areas of opportunity.

Figure 7.1   Otonomo connected vehicle data use cases.

How does this relate to the metaverse?

The automotive industry is rapidly accelerating towards a future where the driving experience transcends the physical confines of vehicles, merging with the digital realm to create immersive experiences that were once the domain of science fiction.[9]

Automakers are at the forefront of this revolution, innovating with AR to redefine the driving experience. BMW's iVision DEE concept is a testament to this trend, proposing a future where the windshield becomes a display screen, overlaying digital content onto the real world. This technology promises to enhance driver awareness and safety by integrating navigation cues, speed limits and traffic sign detection directly into the driver's field of vision, effectively reducing distraction and improving information processing.[10]

Audi's Activesphere takes this concept further by offering a glimpse into a future where the vehicle adapts to the driver's needs in real-time, transforming the driving experience into a digitally interactive journey. These in-car displays are not just about information; they are about creating an intuitive interface between the vehicle, its environment and its occupants, ensuring a harmonious and informed driving experience.[11]

The role of the passenger is also being reimagined through the use of mixed reality (MR) headsets, which offer a blend of VR and AR capabilities. Long journeys are transformed into opportunities for entertainment and exploration, as passengers can dive into virtual worlds, enjoy immersive movies, or even overlay educational content onto the passing landscape. This technology turns a vehicle into a mobile entertainment hub, where the journey becomes as engaging as the destination. This is the promise of connected mobility in the metaverse – a promise where travel time becomes a canvas for experiences that are as limitless as the imagination. A few OEMs have already created or plan to launch driver-assistance applications that rely on metaverse tools. For example, WayRay's Holograktor, an upcoming vehicle for the ride-hailing market, is being designed to have metaverse-related applications for both driver assistance and entertainment.[12]

The development of autonomous driving technologies is another area where MR systems are proving invaluable. By capturing vehicle state data and simulating real-world scenarios within a virtual environment, engineers can test and refine autonomous driving algorithms without the need for extensive real-world trials. Waabi has created a virtual world, the Waabi World, supporting driving in the metaverse. The Waabi World is powered by artificial intelligence, a virtual world that can react to what is happening. A (virtual) autonomous car can drive in this metaverse and be subject to a variety of situations, learning from them.[13]

The use of AR for in-vehicle data visualization is a game-changer for both drivers and passengers. By overlaying important information such as navigation paths, points of interest and vehicle diagnostics over the real-world view, AR provides a more intuitive and less intrusive way to interact with data. This technology ensures that drivers can focus on the road while still receiving critical information, and passengers can be more engaged with their environment.

The design and implementation of connected and automated vehicle (CAV) testing scenarios are being revolutionized through MR. Utilizing naturalistic driving data, engineers can create complex testing environments that mimic real-world conditions with unprecedented accuracy. This approach allows for the meticulous crafting of scenarios to test and validate CAV systems, ensuring that these vehicles can handle the intricacies of real-world driving.[14]

What does this mean for companies?

Companies have opportunities of utilizing connected vehicle data to create value in a different way and generate additional revenue streams. This provides personalization, new ways to connect with consumers while they travel as well as being able to offer improved services. Companies like Otonomo are collecting huge amounts of vehicle data from all makes and types of vehicles. This collection of data will allow us to improve traffic safety, reduce congestion and also improve response time for emergencies.

Coupling this with the metaverse has the potential to enhance the use of connected vehicle data in various ways. For example, it can be used to enhance brand loyalty and improve customer experience. OEMs are able to expand their service networks by making it easier to train and license third-party technicians in distant locations, as well as allow OEMS to engage more successfully with customers throughout the lifecycle of a vehicle.

What does this mean for people/the user?

The user receives relevant and tailored information, creating a better overall experience. This new future we are creating is about creating novel experiences as we travel. The vehicle knows its usual routes and stops so that it can tailor ads and coupons appropriately for a more personalized experience that doesn't annoy. People are safer, and their routes are optimized since there is more synthesized data about traffic times and conditions for improved route planning.

Connected vehicles data and the metaverse can provide several benefits to consumers. Here are some of them:

Improved customer experience: The metaverse can allow OEMs to engage better with customers throughout the lifecycle of a vehicle, such as conducting test drives from the comfort of a prospective customer's own home, diagnosing problems with cars from a distance, and providing more accurate predictions of repairs needed before a vehicle is brought in for service. This can lead to greater customer satisfaction.

Improved driver assistance and entertainment: The metaverse can be used to create driver-assistance applications that rely on metaverse tools, such as heads-up-display technology that shows digital information on a car's windshield, and entertainment options that use sensors and cameras to process data and project AR holograms on various vehicle windows. This can enhance the driving experience and make it more enjoyable.

Improved safety: Connected vehicles generate a vast amount of data that can be used to improve the driving experience and safety. The metaverse can be used to test and collect data from networked autonomous vehicles under diverse conditions, allowing companies to learn from a variety of situations and improve their autonomous driving software This can lead to safer roads and fewer accidents.

Improved vehicle design and production: The metaverse can help OEMs improve vehicle design, production and servicing, which can lead to better quality vehicles. Digital twins, which are a key part of the metaverse in automotive engineering, are also now being widely adopted in car design – providing engineers with a virtual twin of a physical car to simulate each step of the design and construction process. This can lead to more reliable and efficient vehicles.

Improved access to vehicle data: Connected vehicles produce a considerable amount of data flow, and the trend will increase in the future since all new models in Europe are connected. The metaverse can help OEMs and other stakeholders better harness this data to improve predictive maintenance, customize vehicle preferences and enhance the driving experience. This can lead to more personalized and efficient use of vehicles.

Overall, connected vehicle data and the metaverse can provide several benefits to consumers, such as improved customer experience, driver assistance, safety, vehicle design and production and access to vehicle data.

Sustainable Propulsion

What does this mean?

Our world is currently in a call to action to lower CO_2 and get carbon neutral. Scientists agree that we must lower global warming to less than 1.5°C by 2050 to prevent devastating impacts. All companies need to take a new look at how they manage their business and 'use less' in all ways: energy, resources and their supply chain. When we look at moving people and goods in these more energy efficient ways, it involves looking at and creating new energy sources for propulsion. It's ironic that in the early 1900s, electrification for cars was a big contender, then it lost out to the internal combustion engine. Now we are back at looking at electrification for vehicles to lower greenhouse gas emissions and improve the environment. Though we also need green electricity for this new revolution.

The lithium ion battery is mainly used today, though there are so many new developments in battery research and technology that leverage common earth elements and a diversity of materials that provide new solutions for the various use cases. It's exciting to see the innovation in this field and it will be required in order for true viability. We are never done innovating.

We also have continued development of hydrogen fuel and hydrogen fuel cells. Hydrogen technology has grown rapidly and many countries are including hydrogen development in their national strategies and implementing measures to promote the fuel cell industry.[15] Green hydrogen can help us meet our 2050 goals as a globe for net zero. It has been looked at for decades. In fact, it was as early as 1966 that General Motors' Electrovan was one of the first fuel cell electric vehicles (FCEVs). It used a fuel cell that combined liquid oxygen and supercooled liquid hydrogen. The emerging green hydrogen market is expected to change the global energy and resource map, creating a $1.4 trillion a year market by 2050.[16]

There are new biofuels that are almost net carbon zero as well as technology such as the hyperloop, drones, eVTOLS (electric vertical take-off and landing devices) and renewable natural gas. Solar technology has developed so that it's now the cheapest electricity in history – lower than coal and gas in most major countries.[17] A report in June 2023 shows that global rooftop solar is rapidly growing, with 118 GW of new rooftop solar installations worldwide in 2022, the equivalent of 36 million more homes globally powered by solar.[18] We are entering a new realm of accelerating more sustainable sources of energy.

We must remember to take a step back and remember that all these new propulsion sources need to be evaluated from the 'wells to wheels' perspective in looking at the entire environmental impact. It's about creating net zero carbon solutions and accelerating these goals. There are so many propulsion options available and it is not a 'one size fits all' solution. We need a diversity of solutions for the diversity of needs that we have today. We will also require new infrastructure solutions and investment.

How does this relate to the metaverse?

The metaverse, in its expansive digital landscapes, offers a unique platform for the simulation and testing of sustainable propulsion technologies. It is here that engineers and designers can iterate and refine electric, hydrogen and hybrid propulsion systems within sophisticated virtual environments that mimic the complexities of the real world. This digital twin technology allows for a depth of analysis that is both cost-effective and expansive in scope.

Consider the research conducted by the Massachusetts Institute of Technology (MIT) on the digital twin concept, which has demonstrated the potential for these virtual models to significantly reduce the time and resources required for the development of new technologies. In the metaverse, the entire lifecycle of a propulsion system, from design to decommissioning, can be visualized and optimized, ensuring that sustainability is woven into the very fabric of innovation.[19] Moreover, the metaverse serves as an experiential platform for consumers and stakeholders to engage with sustainable propulsion in a manner that is both immersive and informative. Virtual test drives and interactive showcases allow for a deeper understanding of the benefits and functionalities of green vehicles. This is not mere speculation; a report by PricewaterhouseCoopers (PwC) suggests that virtual reality (VR) and augmented reality (AR) have the potential to add $1.5 trillion to the global economy by 2030, with education and training being one of the primary beneficiaries.[20]

The implications for the automotive industry and beyond are profound. By leveraging the metaverse, manufacturers can not only accelerate the development of sustainable propulsion but also foster a culture of environmental stewardship among consumers. It is a virtuous cycle of innovation and awareness that propels us towards a more sustainable future.

What does this mean for companies?

This is an opportunity for companies and startups to create more sustainable energy and fuels. For example, the US Department of Energy (DoE) awarded a $2 million grant application to build a pre-pilot scale system to demonstrate the opportunity of a CI (carbon index) score 15 cellulosic biofuel to produce renewable diesel, sustainable aviation fuel, gasoline and marine fuel from forestry residues and other forms of lignocellulosic biomass at dramatically improved yield. It can be a direct replacement to gasoline.[21]

We can create sustainable microgrids for electrification as well as modern nuclear energy. There is new nuclear technology that creates over 110 times the energy density of existing diesel systems. A company called Radiant Nuclear is redefining what nuclear means in the modern age. These are completely self-contained safe units that have a 20 year lifespan and can be refuelled every 5 years. They provide resiliency of energy and are especially useful in more remote areas.

A diversity of energy is a good thing and creates resiliency as well as sustainability. Let's take a look at earth and its elements: sun, wind, water, fire and earth (minerals) as we look ahead to the future of propulsion. These will lead us on our path for a more sustainable world.

Companies now have an opportunity to create a different user experience as well as to capitalize on it. Charging times are longer than filling a tank of gas so how can people be entertained as they charge? They will have time to buy, do work, communicate and exercise.

What does this mean for people/the user?

People are inherently fearful of change so this push for electrification can be daunting to many. There's also a transition time – especially as people hold on to their cars longer. It's now a record 12.5 years in the United States.[22]

Charging times are much longer than filling a tank of gas so there are adjustments in mindset that need to occur. It's about creating a different user experience. The average US driver drives only 37 miles a day so an overnight home charge works for the majority of the time, though there are times when fast charging is needed.[23]

Autonomous Transportation

What does this mean?

Autonomous vehicles have been thought about for centuries, and we now have the technology to make this a reality. LiDAR (light detection and ranging) first came about in the 1960s and was used in space for the first time on Apollo 15 in 1971. It is an active remote sensing technology that uses light in the form of a pulsed laser to measure distance, creating accurate 3-D information about an object in relation to its environment. It works by having the laser light sent from a source (transmitter) and reflected back from objects. The reflected light is detected by the system receiver and the time duration of the laser then creates a distance map of the objects in a scene. LiDAR can also be used to determine velocity. It essentially creates a three-dimensional image of the world. This requires control software and reconstruction software that converts the point cloud to a three-dimensional model. It has an added benefit over cameras in that it detects objects only and therefore protects people's privacy since race and facial features are not captured.

For autonomous vehicles, LiDAR is coupled with sensors and cameras as well as utilizing mapping data. There are many other uses such as being an enabler of smart cities, aerial inspection for things like power lines or infrastructure, precision agriculture, forestry and land management, survey and mapping, smart warehouses/distribution centres and renewable energy, where it can help determine optimal solar panel and turbine placement. It's even being used in archaeology. Every year, costs get lowered, packaging size decreases and capability increases. It's about improving safety and efficiency of transportation.

How does this relate to the metaverse?

Polygon's[24] creation of an autonomous car within the metaverse is a testament to the power of virtual environments in shaping the future of transportation.[25] Polygon built an autonomous car in a simulated environment using computer vision and path-planning algorithms. They integrated a Polygon digital wallet with the car, so that the car is able to extend its autonomy to not only drive itself, but pay for its own repairs, maintenance and upgrades. This simulated space allows for the design, testing and refinement of autonomous vehicles in ways that were previously unimaginable.

Autonomous vehicle companies turned to digital twins and simulation technology to supercharge development in 2023. The NVIDIA Omniverse platform, for example, is being used to unify the 3D design and simulation pipelines for vehicles and build persistent digital twins of production facilities.[26] This allows automakers to develop a unified view of their manufacturing processes across plants to streamline operations. At Carnegie Mellon, researchers are pioneering the use of digital twins to delve into safety-critical scenarios within the metaverse.[27] Real-world data on such scenarios are scarce due to their rarity and the myriad of variables involved. The metaverse provides a fertile ground for generating and testing these scenarios, offering a diversity of data that is both rich and accessible, ensuring that the digital systems safeguarding our journeys are robust and reliable.

The Waabi World represents a leap forward in autonomous vehicle (AV) development.[28] Here, a virtual autonomous car navigates through a myriad of scenarios, learning and adapting in real-time. The Waabi World uses digital twins, automatically created from data derived from the real world. Also interesting, the Waabi World can interact, through its digital twins, with the Waabi drivers pointing to mistakes and ways of avoiding them. Hence, self-learning can take place in the metaverse, with both the autonomous driving software and the metaverse learning from each other. Emergency situations, once a perilous challenge for AVs, can now be encountered and mastered within the safety of a virtual world. This not only accelerates the development of AV software but also ensures that when these vehicles do hit the road, they are equipped with a depth of experience born from a multitude of virtual trials.

Furthermore, the metaverse holds the key to an enriched driving experience.[29] Imagine a 3D map of the vehicle's surroundings, not just a static representation but a dynamic, interactive canvas that enhances navigation and route planning. Moreover, the metaverse invites car buyers into the heart of the vehicle development process, allowing them to engage with virtual models in events that bridge the gap between consumer and creator.[30]

The metaverse is a complementary dimension that enriches our reality. It offers a sandbox for the development and testing of autonomous driving technologies, a canvas for richer navigation, and a platform for immersive user experiences.

What does this mean for companies?

Creating autonomous on-demand transportation is another area of opportunity for new ways of monetization for companies. It opens the door for companies and startups alike to entertain passengers since there are no longer human drivers, offer unique in-vehicle ambiance and virtual experiences at a cost, and new ways to shop and work.

Insurance is another area that will be significantly affected. The reduction in accidents will reduce the total number of claims, reduce fraudulent claims and lower overall costs.

As a global society, we are focusing on decarbonization and ways to activate a more circular economy. Autonomous vehicles are a means that help accomplish this. The technology now exists for creating asset pools of autonomous on demand transportation of all various types – from individual "pod" vehicles to multi-passenger shared vehicles to large buses and eVTOLs. The asset pool would utilize smart contracts and distributed ledger technology to include all parts of the ecosystem: owners, users, insurance per mile, cleaning, maintenance, charging and so on. This will decrease the number of cars on the road and increase overall global asset utilization. On average, a car in the United States sits unused over 95% of the time. If we could get 50%+ asset utilization and meet people's transportation needs, there is tremendous global benefit in utilizing less material and creating more efficient transportation for both people and goods.

What does this mean for people/the user?

We all make mistakes and can get distracted while driving – as well as drive drunk/high, get road rage, and so on. By taking the human driver out of the equation, autonomous vehicles will make our roads safer. There are over 6 million vehicle accidents annually and from 2018 to 2022, the number of fatal accidents in the United States increased by more than 16% – from 36,835 fatal car crashes in 2018 to 42,795 fatal car crashes in 2022.[31]

There is a true societal benefit in regard to overall safety, reduced fatalities and improved traffic flow. Autonomous and connected vehicles can all 'talk' to each other and optimize routes and minimize congestion. There will no longer be the need for longer distances to accommodate human reaction times: autonomous and connected vehicles can have minimal distances. That enables more traffic flow on existing roads. Truck platooning can even reduce fuel economy. Platooning is when aerodynamic drag is reduced by grouping vehicles together and safely decreasing the distance between them via electronic coupling, which allows multiple vehicles to accelerate or brake simultaneously. NREL has conducted several extensive track evaluation campaigns to assess the fuel-saving potential of two- and three-truck platoons. The results show that the lead vehicle saves up to 10% at the closest separation distances, the middle vehicle saves up to 17%, and the trailing vehicle saves up to 13%.[32]

The societal benefits are numerous. Not only more efficient and safe transportation, but it minimizes pollution, reduces insurance costs, and will require less traffic police officers. It provides a lower cost per mile for the consumer and will meet or exceed consumer transportation needs. Cities can use transportation data to look at where the needs are and tailor the right offerings for the right times of day. Parking lots can be repurposed into parks and social areas for increased societal benefit.

Autonomous transportation offers mobility for the elderly and disabled. Autonomous transportation can reshape our lives into something so much better than what we have today.

Multimodal Transportation

What does this mean?

Multimodal transportation is about connecting various transportation modes to allow people to move in more efficient ways. It's how we optimize and mix various ways of moving such as vehicles, bicycles, walking, scooters, rail/train, buses, plane, eVTOL and any other means of transport in order to get to where we need to go in a more expedient way. Imagine landing in a new city and being able to see three or four top options of travel that show all the details: time based on current traffic conditions and cost. We are able to choose the best route – it might only take 5 minutes longer to take public transportation at a cost of $6 vs. other means which might cost $100.

Mobility-as-a-Service (MaaS) is a testament to the power of consolidation, offering users a seamless way to plan and pay for transportation across multiple modes through a single digital service. This innovation simplifies the user experience, making urban navigation intuitive and integrated. The commitment to sustainable urban mobility is underscored by the expansion of infrastructure for electric vehicles.

Multimodal transportation offers flexibility and can decrease travel costs with the improved information on all available options. It provides more choices. Having all these modes tied together in a single app is a powerful new tool that allows us to mix and match various modes that suit our individual needs.

How does this relate to the metaverse?

The concept of multimodality in transportation has long sought to provide a seamless journey for travellers, integrating various forms of transport into a single, fluid experience. From the first mile to the last, the goal has been to create a cohesive narrative in the traveller's journey. The metaverse, with its boundless potential, elevates this narrative to new heights.

Imagine a world where the planning, booking and navigating of a journey are not just at your fingertips but are also immersive experiences within themselves. The metaverse enables a digital twin of the physical world, where one can navigate through a virtual representation of a city, exploring transportation options that blend the physical and digital. This digital twin not only mirrors real-time data but also anticipates and simulates future scenarios, allowing for unparalleled optimization of routes and modes of transport.

Research by Shaheen, Cohen and Martin (2016) underscores the transformative potential of smartphone apps in transportation, revealing that 39% of surveyed users reported driving less due to the availability of multimodal information apps, suggesting a shift in travel behaviour toward more sustainable practices.[33]

Super Apps have emerged as the digital nexus of user convenience, integrating various services into a single platform. These apps are the orchestrators of the user's digital routine, where one can manage finances, social interactions and, pertinent to our discussion, mobility. The metaverse extends the capabilities of these Super Apps, transforming them into more than just tools – they become experiential gateways.

In the metaverse a Super App does not merely facilitate a transaction or a booking; it becomes an interactive space where users can engage with services on a multisensory level. Booking a ride, for instance, could involve a virtual walk-through of the vehicle you are choosing, a real-time discussion with a customer service avatar, or even a preview of the route and its current conditions through a virtual overlay.

A 2021 report highlights the necessity of providing travellers with real-time information on modal and multimodal travel options, integrated e-tickets and payment apps to simplify the process of arranging and paying for multiple modes for a single trip.[34]

The symbiosis of multimodality transportation and Super Apps within the metaverse creates a feedback loop of enhancement. The metaverse provides a rich layer of data and user interaction, which feeds into the efficiency and personalization of multimodal transport. Conversely, the physical experience of multimodal transportation provides tangible data and insights that enrich the virtual representations and simulations within the metaverse.

This interaction is not unidirectional; it is a dynamic, evolving relationship. As users navigate through the physical world, their experiences, preferences and behaviours are captured and reflected in the metaverse, allowing for a personalized and predictive transportation experience. The metaverse, in turn, influences the physical world by enabling better decision making, reducing inefficiencies and enhancing the overall user experience.

Mitropoulos et al. (2023) discuss the planning process for implementing MaaS in Athens, which integrates multimodal transportation services, highlighting the potential for such systems to prepare for the MaaS ecosystem's deployment and market uptake.[35]

What does this mean for companies?

A whole new world for startups and new offerings for the Super App that can integrate globally all the different modes and options. Not an easy feat but a great opportunity for revenue in an area that has never existed.

For the consumer, it creates a seamless and efficient experience. Think about landing in London for the first time, using a Super App where you type in your destination and it gives you the top three options (including multimodal) based on current traffic conditions as well as total cost and time for the end-to-end journey. As we explore the intersection of mobility and the metaverse, it becomes clear that the benefits extend beyond individual convenience and societal sustainability. Companies stand to gain significantly from this convergence, with opportunities for innovation, customer engagement and operational efficiencies that were previously unattainable. The metaverse offers a fertile ground for businesses to reimagine their role in the mobility ecosystem and to redefine the value they deliver to their customers.

In the metaverse, companies can engage with customers in a more interactive and personalized manner. Super Apps within the metaverse provide a platform for businesses to offer immersive experiences, such as virtual showrooms for vehicles or interactive travel planning sessions, which can lead to increased customer satisfaction and loyalty. The study by Shaheen et al. (2016) on the impact of multimodal apps on travel behaviour indicates that users are receptive to digital solutions that enhance their mobility experience.

The wealth of data generated within the metaverse enables companies to gain deeper insights into consumer behaviour and preferences. This data can inform strategic decisions, from service offerings to marketing campaigns. The predictive analytics capabilities of the metaverse can also help businesses anticipate market trends and adapt their services accordingly, ensuring they remain competitive in a rapidly evolving market.

The integration of multimodal transportation options within Super Apps can lead to significant operational efficiencies for companies. By optimizing routes and transportation modes, businesses can reduce logistics costs and improve delivery times. The report by the National Academies of Sciences, Engineering, and Medicine (2021) emphasizes the importance of real-time information and integrated payment systems for streamlining operations.[36]

The metaverse opens up new avenues for monetization. Companies can create and offer virtual services that complement their physical offerings, such as virtual mobility consultations or premium digital content. Additionally, partnerships with other service providers in the metaverse can lead to cross-promotional opportunities and expand market reach.

Companies that embrace the metaverse for mobility solutions can differentiate themselves in the market. By being early adopters of this technology, they can position themselves as innovative leaders, attracting customers who are looking for cutting-edge solutions.

The planning and implementation of MaaS systems, as discussed by Mitropoulos et al. (2023), showcase how companies can lead in urban mobility transformation. The metaverse also offers tools for workforce training and development. Companies can use virtual environments to simulate real-world scenarios for training purposes, reducing the risk and cost associated with on-the-job training. This can lead to a more skilled and efficient workforce, capable of delivering higher service levels.

By leveraging the capabilities of the metaverse, businesses can enhance customer engagement, drive operational efficiencies, create new revenue streams and position themselves as leaders in the mobility revolution.

What does this mean for people/the user?

The integration of multimodality travel within the metaverse, facilitated by Super Apps, begins a transformative era for personal mobility. This triad of technology offers a suite of benefits that cater to the individual's needs, preferences and aspirations, redefining the very essence of personal travel.

Super Apps can leverage user data to offer customized travel suggestions, combining various modes of transport to suit individual schedules, budget constraints and environmental preferences. This level of customization ensures that travel becomes a more integral and seamless part of daily life, as individuals can navigate their journeys with unprecedented ease and efficiency. The concept of integrated marketing communications within the metaverse, as discussed by Kitchen (2016), suggests that a unified approach can enhance user experiences, which is equally applicable to the realm of personalized mobility.[37]

The metaverse's inclusive design principles ensure that multimodality travel is accessible to all, regardless of physical ability or technological proficiency. Super Apps can provide intuitive interfaces and assistive technologies that make planning and executing travel more accessible, empowering individuals with disabilities to move freely and independently. This inclusivity extends the benefits of mobility to a broader segment of the population, fostering a more inclusive society.

Multimodality travel options within Super Apps can optimize routes and connections, leading to significant economic and time savings. By efficiently integrating different transportation modes, such as public transit, ride-sharing and personal vehicles, individuals can reduce travel costs and time spent commuting. This efficiency not only enhances the daily travel experience but also contributes to a better work–life balance.

The metaverse's immersive planning tools and virtual simulations allow individuals to preview and choose their travel experiences before they happen, reducing the uncertainty and stress associated with commuting. This foresight can lead to a more relaxed and enjoyable journey, improving overall well-being. Additionally, the environmental benefits of optimized multimodality travel, such as reduced congestion and pollution, contribute to a higher quality of urban life.

Super Apps in the metaverse can serve as platforms for cultural exploration and lifelong learning. Individuals can virtually visit new destinations, experience different transportation systems, and engage with diverse cultures, enriching their understanding of the world and fostering global citizenship. The use of social networking applications like WeChat for language acquisition, as explored in the study by Pamintuan et al., illustrates the potential for similar applications to enhance learning within the metaverse's mobility systems.[38] WeChat is a multi-purpose service for messaging that also offers transportation services such as ride-hailing, bike-sharing, and public transportation information – just imagine overlaying this with the metaverse experience.

The metaverse facilitates social connectivity by integrating community-driven features into multimodality travel experiences. Super Apps can offer social travel planning, shared experiences and community feedback mechanisms, allowing individuals to connect with like-minded travellers, share tips and build communities around shared mobility interests.

The promotion of sustainable and active travel modes within the metaverse, such as walking and cycling, can have significant health benefits. By making these options more accessible and enjoyable through Super Apps, individuals are encouraged to adopt healthier lifestyles while contributing to environmental sustainability.

The personal benefits of multimodality travel in the metaverse, enhanced by Super Apps, are profound and multifaceted. As this technology continues to evolve, it promises to unlock new potentials for personal fulfilment, societal inclusion and global connectivity.

Smart Cities: Bringing it All Together

In an era of rapid urbanization, current forecasts suggest a significant shift: by 2030, urban locales will become home to over 60% of the world's inhabitants.[39] The potential of smart urban technologies to uplift the quality of urban life could be improved by an impressive 10–30%. Metropolitan areas – such as Shanghai, Seoul, London, Los Angeles, Dubai and Singapore will soon become a reality for other urban areas.[40]

Historically, cities have been the epicentres of ground-breaking innovations. Today, they stand poised to accommodate over half of the global population. And as we approach 2050, the UN anticipates this figure could rise to a staggering 80%.[41] These urban giants are on the precipice of a revolutionary phase. The overarching goal? To architect urban spaces that resonate with their inhabitants with every facet of new pioneering models using the metamobility.

What does this mean?

City governments have been actively working on what smart cities mean and how they could create better societal living for their ever-growing inhabitants. Megacities, cities with populations over 10 million people, are on the rise. In the 1950s, New York and Tokyo were the only two megacities. Now we have approximately 45, most of them in China and India. The largest is Tokyo at a staggering 37.4 million people. These types of density increases are outpacing city infrastructure development, increasing slum areas, creating more and more traffic jams, causing food shortages and insufficient educational facilities.

Smart transportation has been evolving as more vehicles have connected systems. Cameras, sensors, LiDAR, connected vehicle data and the emergence of IoT (internet of things) is allowing a new-interconnectedness for improved traffic flow, safety, smart intersections and less traffic jams. This is the place where connected vehicles, autonomous cars and sustainable technologies in mobility converge to create new places to live.

At the heart of this transformation is the strategic utilization of big data, IoT and smart sensors. By harnessing this data, city planners and policymakers can optimize energy usage, streamline travel logistics and enhance system performance, resulting in a transportation network that is not only efficient but also adaptable to the evolving demands of urban life.

In response to the dynamic needs of citizens, cities are investing in smart mobility solutions. Analysis of traffic patterns, leads to the modernization of transit systems and the creation of new pedestrian routes. The integration of autonomous vehicles into public transportation heralds a significant shift towards enhanced efficiency and safety. The advent of advanced traffic management systems epitomizes the intelligent application of real-time data. These systems dynamically adapt to traffic conditions, optimizing flow and reducing congestion. By providing real-time traffic insights, ITS (Intelligent Transportation Systems) empower commuters with the knowledge to make safer and more informed travel decisions.

Singapore, a global icon of urban innovation, launched the Smart Nation initiative in 2014, a comprehensive plan to harness technology and data for the enhancement of citizen's lives, economic growth and community building. The initiative underscores the seamless integration of technology in urban living, enhancing life and community bonds.[42]

Key goals of the Smart Nation initiative encompass enhancing mobility through the integration of autonomous vehicles, smart urban planning and intelligent transport systems. In the healthcare sector, services are being transformed, enabling aging-in-place through innovations like telemedicine and remote monitoring. Singapore is also poised to become an innovative economy and startup hub, with substantial support channelled toward research and entrepreneurship. Many cities and countries are creating a new framework for improving people's lives.

How does this relate to the metaverse?

The metaverse can be defined as an expansive network of persistent, real-time rendered 3D worlds and simulations that support continuity of identity, objects, history and payments interaction with the real world. In the context of smart cities, the metaverse offers a platform for the creation of digital twins, which are digital replicas of physical entities, processes or services.[43] These digital twins enable urban planners and stakeholders to simulate, model and predict urban dynamics effectively, leading to more informed decision making. The World Economic Forum expects the digital twin market to reach \$48 billion by 2026 and estimates it will save \$280 billion in urban infrastructure costs by 2030.[44]

The metaverse enhances digital twin technology by incorporating live data, allowing for realistic and interactive simulations that mirror the physical world's behaviour. This next-generation modelling facilitates a robust visualization context that can predict and inform policy on urban challenges such as climate change, traffic and energy consumption.

Within urban environments, the application of digital twins, particularly when integrated with the metaverse, is set to revolutionize the way we simulate and model critical events. This includes the forecasting of natural disasters like floods and wildfires, predicting fluctuations in energy requirements due to shifting urban demographics, managing traffic flow and considering various factors associated with climate change.

Sustainability is a fundamental aspect of the smart city framework, and the role of human digital twins is pivotal in this context. By mirroring individual behaviours and preferences, urban centres can craft targeted waste reduction programmes, energy conservation measures and resource management plans that align with their citizens' needs. Such strategies have the potential to dramatically reduce carbon footprints and resource depletion, with estimates suggesting a reduction by as much as one-third.

Human digital twins will not only foster tailored consumer experiences but will also pave the way for novel economic channels. Virtual marketplaces, digitized service offerings and immersive leisure activities are anticipated to inject billions into the economy. Cutting-edge technologies – including AI, Big Data, the IoT and digital twins – offer extensive datasets and sophisticated analytical models of human activity. This wealth of information positions the metaverse to transform urban design and service delivery, enhancing efficiency, accountability and the overall quality of urban life.

However, the spectre of the digital divide poses a significant hurdle. It is imperative that the metaverse emerges as a domain of equal opportunity, where digital replicas of individuals are universally available, transcending economic barriers. Commitment to providing cost-effective access to essential technologies and educational programmes is crucial to democratize the digital twin experience, ensuring it becomes an integral feature of metropolitan life, not a luxury for a select few.

The European Commission's CitiVerse initiative encapsulates a vision for a future where digital twins forge a cohesive virtual-physical existence. This open and equitable platform is meticulously crafted to enhance citizen well-being, establishing a new benchmark for urban evolution in the digital epoch.[45]

What does this mean for companies?

With 5G, LiDAR, cameras, sensors, connectivity, IoT and X2X, there are great gains as a society for safety, efficiency, new experiences and sustainability. Companies who understand this and evaluate how this could change their business model can capitalize on this new area and generate revenue. Frost & Sullivan estimates the worldwide market potential for smart city categories like transportation, healthcare, building, infrastructure, energy and governance to reach \$2.46 trillion by 2025.[46]

The advent of the metaverse is poised to substantially reduce the necessity for travel, both for professional and recreational purposes, as virtual environments increasingly emulate real-life interactions. This trend has been catalyzed by the post-pandemic shift from conventional office environments to augmented virtual spaces for conducting meetings and hosting social gatherings, thereby creating online equivalents of in-person experiences. Such a shift is anticipated to decrease energy consumption due to less vehicle travel and a reduced need for physical infrastructure, potentially balancing out the energy requirements of the metaverse through a deliberate decrease in physical resource utilization and a transition towards renewable energy by leading technology firms.

The metaverse is gaining recognition for its capacity to transfer the production and warehousing of typically tangible, resource-intensive products such as toys, games and holiday decorations into a digital milieu. This move is anticipated to sharply curtail the use of resources and diminish pollution, considering the environmental impact these products have when they end up in landfills and natural settings. By reducing reliance on tangible resources, the metaverse offers an opportunity for urban areas to concentrate on enhancing their natural and cultural heritage and to implement sustainable practices to restore regions that have been impacted by excessive consumption.

Leveraging the metaverse's real-time data, and digital twin technology provides enterprises with a potent instrument for life-like simulations of products and services.[47] This technological leap fosters unprecedented levels of interaction and community involvement, thereby enriching consumer experiences and yielding critical insights for both product enhancement and urban planning. Such technology is crucial for elevating service quality, citizen welfare, sustainable practices and economic prosperity. The strategic insights derived from digital twins pave the way for companies to create higher value for their consumers. A common platform brings diverse voices to the table, fostering transparency and collective action.

Innovation in Santa Monica: A metaverse case study

The metaverse social application FlickPlay merges the tangible with the virtual, rewarding users with real-world redeemables.[48] Concurrently, Mesmerise is at the vanguard of integrating VR into corporate processes, crafting virtual environments for cooperative endeavours and customer interaction – illustrating the vast potential of metaverse platforms to transform traditional business paradigms.[49] These initiatives reflect the broader implications for smart cities, where innovations such as virtual shopping experiences and telemedicine are woven into the offering, thereby providing accessible healthcare solutions and reshaping the dynamics of urban mobility.

What does this mean for people/the user?

Tampere is a prime example of how technology can be a catalyst for change in urban mobility, leveraging cutting-edge advancements such as AI, 6G+ and quantum computing to reimagine transportation. Starting with autonomous vehicles and interconnected devices, advanced sensors driven by AI, these innovations facilitate a fluid melding of the digital and physical worlds, fostering enhanced connectivity and creating intuitive, user-focused transit experiences. This shift towards automated transportation not only promises enhanced road safety and efficient traffic management but also signifies a stride towards environmental sustainability.[50]

Smart cities have a lower crime rate and digital twins of people support early health warnings – in connection with entire populations this can avoid situations we have seen in the last pandemic outbreak. Technology is the cornerstone of a sustainable, proficient and safeguarded transportation ecosystem focusing on the wellbeing of its inhabitants.

Santa Monica's metaverse application is a testament to how digital immersion can invigorate local economies and amplify cultural experiences. In parallel, initiatives like Seoul's digital twin with access to governments[51] and Dubai's[52] urban planning platform with education exemplify the metaverse's capacity to transform urban living, encompassing everything from municipal services to educational ventures.

Impact of Metamobility for Work

What does this mean?

The landscape of work is undergoing a seismic shift, thanks to mobility innovation. New skillsets are emerging and as other jobs phase out, new ones come into existence. Telepresence, autonomous logistics and infrastructure modernization become commonplace. Automated warehouses are now a reality, with drone delivery systems demonstrating the potential of this technology. The integration of autonomous vehicles (AVs) into logistics and infrastructure, equipped with LiDAR, cameras and sensors, is automating manufacturing processes, warehouses, distribution, logistics, trucking and delivery services. This shift is not only streamlining operations but also opening new avenues for efficiency. The workplace is transforming into something very new and different. It offers alternative ways in which to work and flexibility in what that looks like.

How does this relate to the metaverse?

While much of the conversation around the metaverse has focused on its applications in gaming, social media, retail and remote work, it's the fundamental industries such as transportation, manufacturing and construction that are quietly leading the charge. These sectors are adeptly adopting metaverse technologies to refine their operational decision making. It has the potential to become a transformative shift in every industry, signalling the emergence of a fully interconnected digital world. The emergence of the 'industrial metaverse' is a reflection of the physical world, aiming to boost efficiency and safety across various sectors by creating dynamic virtual models of machinery, production facilities, utilities, traffic systems, and other intricate infrastructures using AI, cloud computing and emerging tech.

This virtual modelling grants industries the capability to experiment with and refine operational procedures in a simulated environment prior to their real-world application, fostering enhancements in numerous areas. Consider a multinational automotive manufacturer with a complex network of suppliers, manufacturing sites, logistical centres and distribution spanning the globe. If this enterprise faces the need to halt operations at a particular site due to geopolitical tensions or to integrate new machinery to expand production, the industrial metaverse steps in. It allows the company to model these changes and scale-ups in a virtual space, mirroring its workforce, assets and processes with precision.

This virtual environment is engineered to mimic real-life conditions, incorporating elements of corporate finance, economics, physics, communication and applicable laws and regulations to predict potential advantages and challenges.

The IoT, along with sensors and personnel dispersed throughout the actual supply chain, constantly gather and transmit data back to the metaverse analogue. This enables stakeholders from around the world to collaborate as if they were in the same location. The simulations also empower leaders to retrospectively analyze previous missteps or forecast future results. At the heart of the industrial metaverse lies the concept of the digital twin, which is the foundational technology enabling this virtual innovation.

The industrial metaverse is revolutionizing entire ecosystems, with the automotive industry as a prime example. It's transforming everything from vehicle design and production to maintenance and customer service, altering the landscape of work within the sector and changing the way people are working.

Design and prototyping: Original Equipment Manufacturers (OEMs) are harnessing Extended Reality (XR) tools to revolutionize the way vehicles are designed. Ford's innovative use of Gravity Sketch[53] and Hyundai's integration of 3-D design software and Augmented Reality (AR) tools[54] exemplify the shift towards virtual reality (VR) in automotive design. These technologies are not only speeding up the design process but also fostering better collaboration among teams.

Vehicle testing: Nvidia's DRIVE Sim platform illustrates the power of virtual environments in vehicle testing. By simulating a wide array of driving conditions, it challenges vehicle systems in ways that go beyond the limitations of physical testing environments.[55]

Training and maintenance: The application of mixed reality is becoming increasingly critical for training frontline workers. It offers remote support and enhances collaboration, making it an invaluable tool across various industries.

Virtual factories: The concept of digital twins is revolutionizing manufacturing processes for OEMs. A notable instance is BMW's adoption of Nvidia's Omniverse platform, which allows for highly accurate planning and optimization of factory layouts and operations.[56]

Repair and maintenance: Daimler Trucks North America, for example, recently experimented with a pilot to use AR technology at its dealerships to provide step-by-step training and guidance for service technicians[57] and BMW, are turning to AR to train service technicians more effectively. This approach not only improves the quality of maintenance but also has the potential to significantly boost service-related revenues.

What does this mean for companies?

Companies need to be nimble and figure out how to attract and retain top talent with the new skill sets that are needed. New technologies such as telepresence can help attract talent globally. Companies can leverage the same AV tech such as LiDAR, cameras and sensors to automate manufacturing, warehouses, distribution, logistics, trucking and delivery.

The industrial metaverse emerges as a ground breaking virtual platform, redefining collaboration for executive leaders and their dispersed teams. This digital convergence has the potential to revolutionize the manufacturing landscape, streamlining production, curtailing expenses and elevating efficiency to unprecedented levels.

Enhanced teamwork across borders: The metaverse breaks down geographical barriers, fostering a new era of collaboration. It enables teams to navigate complex manufacturing landscapes and equipment with ease, offering a virtual training ground that is both safe and meticulously controlled. OEMs find in the metaverse a tool to broaden their service networks, simplifying the training and accreditation of third-party technicians, regardless of location. This virtual engagement extends to customer relations, maintaining a consistent and immersive brand experience throughout the vehicle's lifecycle.

Operational excellence and cost-effectiveness: The metaverse stands as a beacon of efficiency in the mobility sector. It reimagines customer interactions by providing immersive and personalized experiences. Imagine customers exploring virtual premises or overseeing their relocation and storage solutions in three-dimensional clarity, witnessing their possessions in transit or storage with unparalleled detail. Furthermore, logistics and transportation entities leverage the metaverse to refine their operational expenditures, enhancing their competitive edge.

Redefining workplace dynamics: The industrial metaverse holds the promise of transforming our very approach to work within the mobility ecosystem. It offers novel perspectives and experiences, reshaping transportation planning and the broader mobility framework. This virtual environment allows organizations to recalibrate the equilibrium between hybrid and remote work models, capturing the essence of team-based interaction – spontaneity, interactivity and enjoyment – while preserving the autonomy, productivity and convenience that remote work affords.

The rise of the metaverse and advanced mobility technologies requires companies to be adaptable and innovative in attracting and retaining talent. Companies need to upskill and reskill their workforce to be able to function in this new environment and realize the benefits. Industry leaders have already voiced some of the challenges: A lack of employees with the right skills, along with the steep learning curve for those who must be trained; and the insufficient digital infrastructure and other resources. The success of the companies will depend on building a culture of innovation, establishing leadership support and starting small by investing in a digital technology foundation.

What does this mean for people/the user?

For individuals, the implications are profound. The new technologies enable global remote working, offering a better balance between personal and professional life. Workers can now shift their focus from mundane tasks to more strategic and engaging activities, thanks to the automation of repetitive processes.

The industrial metaverse increases collaboration and the ability to train in virtual environments with higher safety and efficiency. It will enable teams to resolve design conflicts and align on aesthetics, aerodynamics and features through rapid experimentation with virtual models. This could lead to a more inclusive vehicle development process and continuous feedback for R&D efforts (Figure 7.2).

Hyundai is pioneering a ground breaking initiative called 'Metamobility', which seeks to extend the concept of mobility into VR, transcending the traditional boundaries of movement across time and space – a vision they refer to as 'Expanding Human Reach'. At the heart of this transformation is robotics, a field in which Hyundai has bolstered its expertise with the strategic acquisition of Boston Dynamics. The synergy between robotics and mobility is pivotal for Hyundai, as advancements in one area fuel progress in the other.[58]

The essence of Metamobility lies in using robots to help humans bypass the physical constraints of time and space, enabling new forms of connection and interaction within the metaverse. Hyundai envisions scenarios where workers could remotely operate industrial robots from the metaverse's virtual realm. This capability would empower individuals to undertake hazardous or challenging tasks from the safety of distance, enhancing both safety and operational efficiency.

In the context of this new environment, the industrial metaverse requires the acquisition of advanced competencies among the

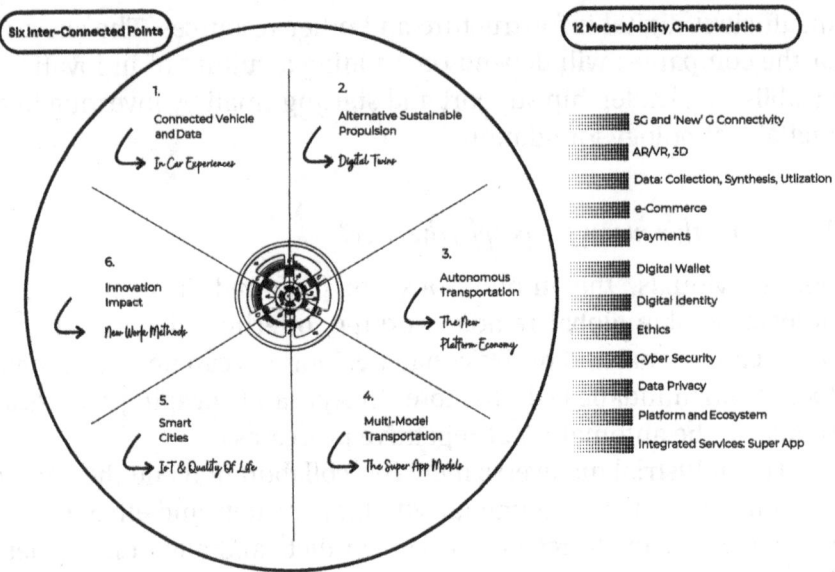

Figure 7.2 The six inter-connected points.

workforces. Skills such as programming, virtual and augmented reality expertise, 3D modelling, design, data analysis and user interface/user experience (UI/UX) design, AI and robotics become critical. Mastery in these areas is crucial for the creation of virtual spaces, the interpretation of complex data sets, and the crafting of engaging user experiences. Furthermore, the ability to work collaboratively in a real-time virtual context is essential, enabling employees to address tangible business challenges more efficiently and cost-effectively. Whilst these skills can be developed, to master the future of work in the new era of Metamobility, workers need to adopt a new mindset that embraces innovation, collaboration and continuous learning.

A Glimpse into the Future

The future will be an exciting realm for both society as a whole and the new business opportunities that emerge with the continued advancement of these technologies. The exponentiality of technology development means that today, we can't even comprehend what will be possible just 10 years from now.

We are already on a path of changing the way people and goods move as we integrate new technologies not only in propulsion but also in regard to how these work together in different ways. Every sector is affected. It brings new questions into play, such as how we ensure the privacy and security of these systems. We must incorporate ethics as we advance technology. With the growth of autonomous and connected transportation, cybersecurity plays an even greater role. The phrase that 'data is the new oil' means that data, like oil, isn't useful in its raw state. Its value amplifies as the data is gathered daily, accumulated together, and connected with other data that makes it relevant and significant. This collection and synthesis of data creates new value streams.

How we leverage the data and determine who truly owns vehicle data will continue to be a question. Is it the consumer – or is it the auto manufacturer who paid for the connected vehicle system? There have been back and forth rulings on that issue and we will continue to see changes in the determination.[59]

Metamobility extends far beyond what we see and do in our physical world. It is boundless and can transcend us to wherever we want in an instant – or provide us with options on whatever experiences we want, when we want them. Will we travel more – or less? How will it re-shape our travel experiences? This will continue to change over time and never sit still.

The role that quantum computing will play in this new Metamobility future is vast. Its computing power is 158 million times faster than today's classical computers. It can solve complex problems in seconds and will be the key in solving our climate change challenge as well as other challenges that we face at this time. It will take us into new realms that today, we only see in the movies.

As we conclude this chapter on the future of mobility, let's embark on a journey of imagination to envision how this rapidly evolving landscape might look in the not-so-distant future.

Picture this: You step out of your home, and there's no need to own a car anymore. Instead, a sleek, autonomous vehicle arrives at your doorstep, customized to your preferences. As you step inside, the car instantly syncs with your mood, music preferences and even the perfect lighting to match your ambiance. It's like stepping into your own personalized bubble.

In this future, you'll experience virtual test-drives, much like what Škoda offers in the Skodaverse. You can explore Škoda's latest models in a 3D world, revolutionizing the test-driving experience. The Skodaverse is not just about displaying cars; it's about crafting an entire immersive world. You can step into a digital Škoda vehicle and embark on various adventures, from exploring art galleries to setting new records on racing tracks. The community aspect is equally remarkable, serving as a vibrant hub where car enthusiasts and tech aficionados converge, connect, share their passion and gain insights from Škoda's experts. It's a future where immersive experiences like the Skodaverse become commonplace.

But there's more to this future than convenience and efficiency. It's a world where the focus has shifted from ownership to experience. You no longer worry about owning a car; instead, you crave a journey that's tailored specifically for you. It's about personalization, connectivity and the seamless integration of Web3 principles into your daily life.

Companies like Mercedes have already laid the foundation for this transformation, connecting your car to your digital identity and allowing you to display your favourite digital art with a simple link to your crypto wallet. Additionally, innovations like the battery passport system powered by blockchain ensure that the journey is sustainable and ethical. The battery passport system tracks the lifecycle of EV batteries, promoting transparency and responsible sourcing within the EV market. Since 2021 the Minespider team has worked to create the most comprehensive Battery Passport on the market and launched the first version in November 2021. During the past two years 15 companies have been onboarded, use the product and provide valuable feedback. Minespider works with industry-leading companies from the EV battery market, including Ford Otosan and Renault. They are also a part of the European Battery Alliance and the EU Commission's funded project BATRAW, aimed to find new technological ways to recycle critical minerals from the EV batteries.[60]

Ownership and content will be crucial within a shared economy where the next generations are not interested in owning a car, but they'll still care a lot about personalization.

The boundaries between the physical and virtual worlds blur as immersive experiences like the Skodaverse become commonplace. You explore new realms, connect with like-minded enthusiasts and attend live events, all from the comfort of your digital Škoda vehicle.

Moreover, companies like Holoride are transforming the in-car experience by strapping on VR headsets, turning mundane car rides into immersive adventures that sync with the car's movements. The automotive industry is no longer just about transportation; it's about creating vibrant communities and unforgettable experiences.

In this future, mobility is not just about getting from point A to B; it's a journey that caters to your desires, anticipates your needs and aligns with your values. It's a future where sustainability, transparency and ethical practices are woven into the fabric of the automotive industry, thanks to innovations like the battery passport system powered by blockchain, digital identity and initiatives like Riddle & Code's car wallet technology that enable vehicles to securely process transactions autonomously.

In summary, last thoughts to highlight on the main 12 characteristics of a MetaMobility world for pondering:

1. 5G / 'New' G – The advent of advanced connectivity, enabling lightning-fast data transfer and communication, essential for Metamobility.
2. 3D AV/VR – The integration of 3D audio-visual and VR, transforming how we experience and interact with mobility.
3. Data collection/synthesis/utilization – The continuous evolution of data, from collection and synthesis to meaningful utilization, shaping the future of mobility.
4. E-commerce – A driving force behind the transformation, enabling seamless transactions and services within the Metamobility ecosystem.
5. Payments – The revolution in payment methods, simplifying transactions and enhancing the user experience.

6. Digital wallet – The digital wallet becomes the heart of Metamobility, consolidating payment, identification and personalization.

7. Digital identity – Establishing a secure and unique digital identity for each individual, a cornerstone of the Metamobility paradigm.

8. Ethics – Ethical considerations guide the development of Metamobility, ensuring responsible and sustainable progress.

9. Cybersecurity – The critical role of cybersecurity in safeguarding Metamobility systems and user data.

10. Data privacy – Protecting user data and privacy in an interconnected Metamobility world.

11. Platform and ecosystem – Building robust platforms and ecosystems that drive innovation and collaboration.

12. Integrated services: Super App – A convergence of services into a Super App, simplifying user experiences within the Metamobility universe.

As we stand on the precipice of this groundbreaking era, one thing remains abundantly clear: we are never done innovating. The Metamobility world is dynamic and ever-evolving. It challenges us to push the boundaries of what's possible continually. It invites us to explore uncharted territories, forging new paths in mobility, and redefining our relationship with technology.

The road ahead is filled with endless possibilities, and as executive leaders and visionaries, you are at the forefront of this transformative journey. Embrace the future of Metamobility with open arms, for it promises to be a thrilling ride filled with innovation, personalization and limitless potential. The future is closer than you think, and it's a future where mobility knows no bounds.

The world is your canvas.

Chapter 8

Conclusion: Living to Love the Fast Future Blurs

Efi Pylarinou

Conventional approaches typically centre on specific emerging technologies and environmental or socioeconomic trends. Artificial intelligence (AI), blockchain, the metaverse, augmented reality and virtual reality (AR/VR), robotics, the Internet of Things (IoT), quantum computing, are all technologies powering what the World Economic Forum (WEF) has termed as the Fourth Industrial Revolution (4IR). Each one merits in-depth exploration of their individual technical advancements, their impact on our economic and social activities, and the policies and regulations that either enable or limit them.

In addition, significant trends driven by these technological advancements such as the future of work, platforms, finance, mobility and health also require individual in-depth analysis.

Recognizing that the future potential of each of these technologies and trends is significantly influenced by policies and regulations is also crucial for each one of these areas. At present, such policies and regulations are either non-existent or limited and lacking harmonization.

Despite these uncertainties, there is a growing recognition of the importance of the dynamic interconnections of these unstoppable and accelerating technological changes, and their increasingly complex impact on organizations, employees and customers, society and the environment. For instance, there is consensus that AI will impact the future of work and health, that the IoT will transform mobility, that blockchain enables disruptive business models, governance and impacts the future of money. Business leaders are starting to recognize the web of interdependencies, the multifaceted nature of these technologies, and their far-reaching implications across various domains.

The focus has often been on identifying and assessing potential risks arising from interdependencies. The WEF has been publishing its annual *Global Risks Report*[1] since 2005, identifying the top global risks over a two-year and a ten-year horizon across five categories of risk – economic, environmental, geopolitical, societal and technological.

From the early editions the WEF recognized that the impacts of interconnected risks can be greater than the sum of their parts. This highlighted that our future is rarely an extrapolation of our past. By 2014, the WEF started publishing a Global Risks Interconnected Map[2] including a visual of the correlations of these risks.

In 2021, the WEF launched the Global Future Council[3] focused on the future of complex risks and by 2023, 'polycrises' (i.e. multiple, deeply interconnected crises) became a major area of focus in assessing risks. The Global Future Council perspective is that *'The biggest threats come from multiple risks, interacting with each other.'* COVID accelerated our collective awareness of the network effects of the interconnections of risks, as we witnessed the aggregate impact of several societal, economic and geopolitical risks all at once.

Such potential global risks and their networks effects keep leaders up at night. The WEF's reports also estimate the likelihood of these risks and the size of their impact. Over time risks change, new ones are added and their likelihood and impact also vary. For example, widespread cybercrime is more likely nowadays and will have greater impact than a decade ago. The risk of a collapse of systemically important supply chains is a new one, ranking at the top of the economic risks and largely connected with technological risks. The adverse outcomes of frontier technologies are also a new risk with high impact and likelihood. Tables 8.1 and 8.2 show a comparison of the technological and economic risks noted in 2014 and 2023.

Businesses have become familiar with the importance of dynamic interconnections through a risk lens. Environmental event risks such as natural disasters and extreme weather events are no longer rare. They affect infrastructure, disrupt trade, destroy food production and severely impact all economic activity. The unprecedented

Table 8.1 Technological risks included in the WEF annual global risk reports.[4]

2023	2014
Adverse outcomes of frontier technologies	
Digital inequality and lack of access to digital services	
Digital power concentration	Data fraud
Widespread cybercrime and cybersecurity	Cyberattacks
Breakdown of critical Information Infrastructure	Breakdown of critical Information Infrastructure

Table 8.2 Economic risks included in the WEF annual global risk reports.

2023	2014
Collapse of systematically important supply chains	Fiscal crises
Failure to stabilize price trajectories	Unemployment and under employment
Debt crisis	Failure of financial mechanism or institution
Asset bubble	Liquidity crisis
Prolonged economic downturn	Oil shock crisis
	Failure of critical infrastructure
	Decline of the USD

monsoon rains in Pakistan in June 2022, submerged parts of the country underwater for several months leading to a climate-induced humanitarian disaster of epic proportions.

Our world is one of growing complexity with dynamic inter-connections across ecological, digital and physical ecosystems. The multi-directional and ever-changing dynamics across interrelated systems, lead to multiple potential risks but also opportunities. Similar to risks, interconnected technological, socioeconomic and environmental trends can yield opportunities exceeding the sum of the individual components. This *Fast Future Blur* book focuses on these opportunities at the intersections arising from our complex, dynamic, interconnected world. Businesses should not only focus on managing downside risks but also harnessing potential opportunities.

The opportunities from the increased complexity arising from the interactions of advanced technologies, socioeconomic and environmental trends; are underestimated.

In this book we chose to discuss the potential impact of select interdependencies between advanced technologies and major aspects of societal and enivormental trends. Our insights can help leaders explore, design and start creating the future from these blurs. We think of them as blurs because some have not yet manifested and some are just emerging. We chose to focus on less-known blurs because they are less-recognized opportunities leaders can ride and pioneer our future.

Acknowledged Blurs

Several blurs have already materialized. Business leaders recognize how traditional industry segmentations are already being challenged. Advanced technologies have entered a phase of impacting all types of industries, economic activity and lifestyle.

Businesses are more frequently revisiting questions like:

- What business are we in and why?
- Who are our partners and why?

- Who are we serving and why?
- What ecosystem are we enabling and why?
- How are we designing our products and services?
- How are we manufacturing our products and services?
- How are we delivering our products and services?

Breaking industry segmentation silos and transforming businesses is being enabled by the technological advancements and their impact on business models, leadership and work. By now, we have recognized the impact of digital on all aspects of our socioeconomic activities.

The blurring of industry boundaries is well documented. Businesses are no longer defined or constrained by their traditional or original categorization but by their current and evolving capabilities and the business models dictating how they manufacture and deliver their products and services.

Traditional manufacturers of engines, rails and other industrial equipment are increasingly becoming service providers and energy solution consultants. They offer services like 'power by the hour', 'machine time as a service' and 'outcome-based contracting' by leveraging connectivity, data analytics and a new business model. The combination of advanced technologies allows traditional manufacturers to blur original industry lines of industrial equipment with the energy sector and the service sector. Such examples are Siemens increasingly offering rail maintenance services including preventative, corrective and predictive maintenance. Rolls-Royce offering their 'CorporateCare Enhanced' service for their jet engines (a fixed maintenance cost per flight hour). Tesla offering a range of energy storage and solar energy systems from home battery storage system Powerwall to solar roof tiles and panel installations.

Traditional automotive industry players are blurring their industry lines and shifting towards positioning their businesses as part of the mobility industry, a service-oriented sector transforming both the logistics sector and how people move. Daimler coined the term CASE – Connected, Autonomous, Shared, Electric – as early as 2016. By now, most traditional automotive industry players have launched car-sharing services for short-term rentals

(MOIA by Volkswagen, Maven by General Motors, SHARE NOW, by Daimler and BMW). New mobility service providers have emerged and are competing with diverse offerings beyond car sharing (e.g. peer-to-peer sharing, carpooling, multimodal transportation services via apps).

One of the most walled sectors, financial services, has been blurring its traditionally impenetrable walls, in more than one way. Grown-up digital-only neo-banks have started diversifying their products and services, beyond financial solutions. Nubank, is a great example of one of the most successful and profitable neo-banks based in Brazil (publicly traded NYSE: NU), which offers its 80 million customers a digital shopping mall with more than 150 partner stores, within its banking app. In 2024, Nubank also plans to launch a travel portal within its shopping marketplace, in partnership with Hopper, a leading North American travel app.

Another way that financial services walls have been blurred, is the delivery at scale by non-banking entities of financial products and services, especially in Emerging Markets (Asia, Africa, Latin America). From basic current accounts, payments, savings, loans, all the way to investment and insurance services, for both individuals and businesses (especially, small business enterprises) are being delivered on lifestyle apps. For example, Super App GoJek in Indonesia which started as a ride-hailing app, now offers banking services, food deliveries and logistics.

Both traditional health players and innovative startups are blurring the lines between healthcare and tourism, to the point that medical tourism has become increasingly competitive. Top destinations include Thailand, India, Turkey, Hungary, and many more countries. Apollo Hospitals is an Indian hospital chain example with a significant international patient base, offering a comprehensive health tourism package that includes treatments, travel and accommodation. Bookimed is a ten-year-old international medical tourism platform connecting patients to top hospitals for their medical needs. Medical tourism is becoming crowded and opportunities for innovation by leveraging advanced technologies are emerging at this intersection.

In addition to the evolving industry segmentation blurs, there are other blurs that have also become mainstream. For example, several *blurs of physical boundaries in different contexts* have already gained traction:

- The *blurring of physical boundaries at work and in business*, as the physical location matters less with remote work setups and advancements in virtual collaboration tools enabled by AR/VR and the metaverse.
- The *blurring of physical boundaries in retail shopping*, as hybrid commerce continues to rise, blurring the lines of brick-and-mortar shopping and e-commerce.
- The *blurring of physical boundaries in healthcare,* as telemedicine and digital health tools are changing delivery models of healthcare services.

Interconnections pose threats and perils but also opportunities and possibilities. Future Blurs are opportunities.

Embracing Interconnectedness

The blurs that are already underway, continue to evolve and are nowhere close to being done. Leaders of traditional, grown-up digital-native and innovative businesses should be continuously on the lookout for future blurs. In this book, we have focused on such emerging interconnectivities and their potential network effects. We have purposely explored less examined blurs that are on the edges of the C-suite's radar screen or out of their current peripheral vision because we strongly believe they present opportunities to lead in designing our future.

An exponentially regenerative world delivered on digital platforms is a future blur with a potential to completely transform every type of platform and its ecosystem. Digital marketplaces, platforms, platform-based ecosystems (PBEs), and Super Apps that recognize this, can evolve beyond the narrow boundaries of their business, and lead our way into the future in service of social, economic and planetary health. Business leaders who don't recognize this potential of digital platform models risk being blindsided.

A regenerative mindset extends beyond integrating sustainability and environment, social and corporate governance (ESG) goals. It is a future blur at the interconnection of digital platforms and the relationships with people, communities, the economy and the ecology. It brings purpose with its holistic mindset of being of service to all these relationships. It requires shifting to the framework of live complex organisms, also known as adaptive cycle thinking, which is also a blueprint for adaptability, resilience and innovation.

Complexity is here to stay and so are future blurs. Embracing the interconnectedness of business, social and ecological activities, can become our future.

The impending business disruption wave of AI on all aspects of business, is a future blur that will have major impact – to an even larger extent than digital. While digital-native businesses have pioneered feedback loops at all levels of business and are increasingly integrating AI tools, their linear thinking falls short of dealing systematically with the increased complexity of businesses. The next generation of AI-native businesses which are not yet born, will become the pioneers of the complexity, the intelligence and the interdependencies of businesses.

Digital-native, blockchain-native, and traditional businesses who are at a mature stage of their digital transformation journey, should start their journey of *thinking like an AI-native business*. This will prepare them for the sweeping future blur of AI on all aspects of business, while in the process of integrating AI tools in various parts of the enterprise.

Embracing complexity and future blurs, is our way forward. An AI-native mindset is the next frontier of intelligence.

The blur of AI with the health sector is already starting to be recognized because of the major socioeconomic significance of health and the consensus that AI is a transformative general-purpose technology, like electricity and the internet.

All businesses in the health industry and those whose platform strategy touches the health sector, cannot ignore this future blur.

Despite the unique complexities and non-standardization of the health sector, that far exceed even those of the financial sector, in the long-term healthcare will be profoundly changed and improved from this future blur. *Intelligent health, leveraging data and the advancements in AI*, will probably become the most impactful development of our era. Even though intelligent health system solutions don't seem plausible in the near future, the direction of travel is being set.

> *Embracing general-purpose technologies like AI in healthcare is inevitable. The social and economic impact of this future blur in the long run is underestimated.*

The future blur of mobility and the metaverse takes us into what may currently seem more futuristic. This new frontier will not only impact the businesses operating already in the mobility sector, but it will transform our everyday lives, work, travel and more. At the intersection of mobility and the metaverse, businesses can design innovative and enriching experiences, enable connectivity and the next level of experiences for digital communities, and create increased inclusiveness. Collaboration in this future blur will reduce substantially physical boundaries. This future blur is about *a metamobility future* that has the potential to reshape industries by combining new hardware and software, fusing physical and digital experiences and opening up collaborative opportunities that we never imagined before.

> *The future blur of mobility and the metaverse are leveraging IoT and AI, fusing physical and digital, and paving the way to our future of smart living.*

The future of work has been in the spotlight since 2020, as the blur between physical business locations and work became normal during the pandemic. Any small, medium or large employer is now aware of these workplace shifts underway. However, the future of work is not limited to just where and when work is done, it includes what the work is, how it is performed, who performs it (including AI, non-employee labour, robotics) and why work is done or needed. The future blur of the technology, culture and governance of blockchain and the future of work, are rarely discussed even though it has an impact on all six of the aforementioned dimensions of work and has implications for all business leaders, not just those in human resources. While some aspects of this future blur are at a nascent stage, others have been in play for years and are approaching broad adoption. This future blur can bring purpose and alignment as it has the potential to reshape every aspect of work and our experience of it. This interconnection – blockchain and future of work – can enable fairer distribution of value to people within organizations and to all stakeholders across the value chain. This interconnection can play a major role in the 4IR evolution by contributing to increased transparency, traceability and reduced centralization in support of participatory, secure and frictionless digital lives.

Deconstructed and decentralized work is a future blur that is currently distant but has sizable potential impact.

Our current reality is characterized by a growing oxymoron. While we fear but slowly adopt advanced technologies like AR/VR headsets that make us look and feel like cyborgs, we also believe more in stakeholder capitalism, purpose in business, and the power of collaboration and openness. It is at the intersection of augmented and virtual reality with leadership and people in the new world, that we can scale digital communities, collaboration and continuous education and training. This future blur can empower people to experiment safely and creatively beyond a traditional innovation lab or a research lab; to learn from each other, to upskill coworkers, to increase engagement. While AR/VR hardware isn't anywhere close to AirPod adoption and appeal, it has the potential to enable leaders to infuse more purpose, increase engagement and facilitate innovation at scale, which all contributed to higher performance.

New world people experiences using augmented and virtual reality are future blurs leaders can embrace and shape the future of work.

The fast future blurs explored in this book (Figure 8.1) highlight the rising importance of non-linear thinking to navigate complexity – both to manage risks and to identify transformative opportunities. As technologies are increasingly accessible, we invite leaders to examine these future blurs as unexplored areas, potential competitors' blind spots, offering first-mover advantage.

The blurs we have discussed reinforce the notion of 'hybrid' beyond the context of work, healthcare delivery, commerce, banking and training. While the impact of any one advanced technology

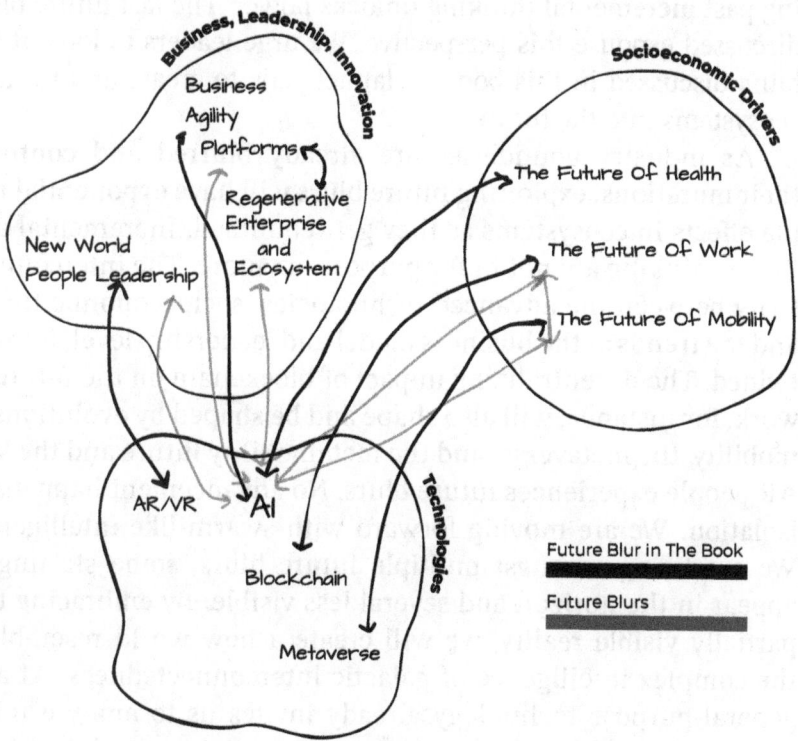

Figure 8.1 The Fast Future Blurs.

and trend is substantial, combinations unlock exponential network effects. The fast future blurs emphasize the power of fusing advanced technologies and societal trends to enable scalability in unimaginable places and in areas that have simply not been economically viable opportunities. Leaders must intentionally apply non-linear perspectives to uncover hidden value at the intersections of technological advancements and societal trends.

Ironically, as complexity increases, the transformative potential of fast future blurs is often underestimated. Linear thinking gets in the way and unless leaders intentionally analyse less-recognized interconnections with an eye to unlock new opportunities, they risk accumulating new blind spots. As Tina Seelig,[5] Stanford Professor of Creativity and Innovation with a Stanford PhD in Neuroscience, advocates, embracing novel combinations and intentionally pushing past incremental thinking unlocks power. The fast future blurs discussed espouse this perspective. We urge leaders to look at the blurs discussed in this book as launchpads to create and reshape ecosystems into the future.

As industry boundaries are already blurred and continue their mutations, exploiting future blurs will have exponential ripple effects in ecosystems as they get rebundled. Incremental and linear thinking are not fit for purpose anymore. The interconnectivity between the advanced technologies, socioeconomic trends and the trends at the business model and leadership level, is intertwined. The decentralizing impact of blockchain on the future of work, for instance, will also shape and be shaped by evolutions in mobility, the metaverse, and the metamobility future and the VR/AR people experiences future blurs. No advancement happens in isolation. We are moving forward with swarm-like intelligence. We are living amongst multiple future blurs, some starting to appear in the horizon and several less visible. By embracing this partially visible reality, we will create a new world resembling the complex intelligence of galactic interconnectedness. AI as a general-purpose technology already invites us to analyse intersections with all facets of socioeconomic activities, and the future of business models, leadership and new people experiences. The adoption of a native-AI mindset is a provocative but necessary invitation to explore opportunities in a future beyond the current spotted integrations of AI tools. The regenerative platform business model we've explored is a future blur requiring yet another purposeful mindset shift to overcome the current narrow vision of platform businesses and become the masterminds of a future we all love to live in.

The future belongs to those who recognize the future blurs before they become obvious, and start preparing for this future.

Notes

Chapter 1: The Fast Future Arsenal: Unbundling, Rebundling and Innovating at the Intersection

1. Coase, R.H. (1937). The nature of the firm: origins, evolution, and development. *Economica*, 4(16): 386–405.
2. Williamson, O.E. (1975). Markets and hierarchies – some elementary considerations. *American Economic Review*, 63(2): 316–325.
3. David, R.J. and Han, S.K. (2004). A systematic assessment of the empirical support for transaction cost economics. *Strategic Management Journal*, 25(1): 39–58.
4. Autio, E., Nambisan, S., Thomas, L.D. et al. (2018). Digital affordances, spatial affordances, and the genesis of entrepreneurial ecosystems. *Strategic Entrepreneurship Journal*, 12(1): 72–95.
5. Adner, R., Puranam, P. and Zhu, F. (2019). What is different about digital strategy? From quantitative to qualitative change. *Strategy Science*, 4(4): 253–261.
6. Yoo, Y., Henfridsson, O. and Lyytinen, K. (2010). The new organizing logic of digital innovation: an agenda for information systems research. *Information Systems Research*, 21(4): 724–735.
7. Zittrain, J. (2008). *The Future of the Internet*. Yale University Press.

8. Siggelkow, N. and Terwiesch, C. (2019). *Connected Strategy: Building Continuous Customer Relationships for Competitive Advantage.* Harvard Business Press.

9. Adner, R., Puranam, P. and Zhu, F. (2019). What is different about digital strategy? From quantitative to qualitative change. *Strategy Science,* 4(4): 253–261.

10. For instance, Uber's algorithms allow control over driver behaviour without requiring Uber to own the cars or employ the drivers. In more industrial contexts, digitization of the supply chain affords similar levels of control without requiring explicit ownership.

11. Zachariadis, M. and Ozcan, P. (2016). The API economy and digital transformation in financial services: the case of open banking. Swift Institute.

12. Hagel, J., III and Singer, M. (1999). Unbundling the corporation. *Harvard Business Review,* 77(2): 133–141, 188.

13. Gao, L.S. and Iyer, B. (2006). Analyzing complementarities using software stacks for software industry acquisitions. *Journal of Management Information Systems,* 23(2): 119–147.

14. Becker, G.S. and Murphy, K.M. (1992). The division of labor, coordination costs and knowledge. *Quarterly Journal of Economics,* 107(4): 1137–1160.

15. Desai, D.R. (2014). The new steam: on digitization, decentralization, and disruption. *Hastings Law Journal,* 65(6): 1469–1482.

16. Dhanaraj, C. and Parkhe, A. (2006). Orchestrating innovation networks. *Academy of Management Review,* 31(3): 659–669.

17. Dhanaraj, C. and Parkhe, A. (2006). Orchestrating innovation networks. *Academy of Management Review,* 31(3): 659–669.

18. Iansiti, M. and Levien, R. (2004). *The Keystone Advantage: What the New Dynamics of Business Ecosystems Mean for Strategy, Innovation, and Sustainability.* Harvard Business Press.

19. Stango, V. (2004). The economics of standards wars. *Review of Network Economics,* 3(1): 1–19.

20. Shankar, V. and Bayus, B.L. (2003). Network effects and competition: an empirical analysis of the home video game industry. *Strategic Management Journal,* 24(4): 375–384.

21. Parker, G.G., Van Alstyne, M.W. and Choudary, S.P. (2016). *Platform Revolution: How Networked Markets are Transforming the Economy and How to Make Them Work for You.* WW Norton & Company.

22. For instance, platforms like Google and Facebook control user relationships and data, which provides them leverage over other ecosystem firms looking to target these users.

23. The media industry, for instance, used to be organized as vertically integrated firms integrating content production, content distribution, and advertising. With the rise of web-enabled content distribution and the

emergence of new content publishing technologies like blogging, the industry has been reorganized into an ecosystem of firms specializing in different capabilities. While the majority of media firms have been relegated to focusing on content production, social media platforms like Facebook and Twitter, and search engines like Google and Bing have taken on the content distribution role and a range of advertising technology firms work together to optimize digital advertising.

24. Parker, G.G., Van Alstyne, M.W. and Choudary, S.P. (2016). *Platform Revolution: How Networked Markets are Transforming the Economy and How to Make Them Work for You*. WW Norton & Company.

25. Cusumano, M.A., Gawer, A. and Yoffie, D.B. (2019). *The Business of Platforms: Strategy in the Age of Digital Competition, Innovation, and Power*. Harper Business.

26. Srnicek, N. (2017). *Platform Capitalism*. John Wiley & Sons.

27. Adigozel, O., Pellathy, T.M. and Singh, S. (2009, 1 June). Why understanding medical risk is key to US health reform. McKinsey and Company. https://www.mckinsey.com/industries/healthcare/our-insights/why-understanding-medical-risk-is-key-to-us-health-reform (accessed 22 Januery 2024).

28. 40%+ consumers use personal technologies to measure fitness in 2020, compared to only 17% in 2013, in Betts, D., Korenda, L. and Guillani, S (2020). Are consumers already living the future of health? *Deloitte Insights*. https://www2.deloitte.com/us/en/insights/industry/health-care/consumer-health-trends.html (accessed 22 January 2024).

29. Alkon, C. (2018). What's behind the growth of urgent care clinics? *Medical Economics*, 95(17).

30. Christianson, J. and Hamilton, J.A. (2017, 30 March). Retail clinics are still here. Now what? AJMC. https://www.ajmc.com/view/retail-clinics-are-still-here-now-what (accessed 22 Januay 2024).

31. Sarasohn-Kahn, J. (2016, 25 July). Retail clinics continue to shape local healthcare markets. *Healthcare IT News*. https://www.healthcareitnews.com/blog/retail-clinics-continue-shape-local-healthcare-markets (accessed 22 January 2024).

32. For instance, Epic Systems had less than 50,000 appointments on its telehealth services in February 2020, but that number had risen to 2.5 million by April 2020. PYMNTS. (2020). Google puts $100M in telehealth provider Amwell. https://www.pymnts.com/news/investment-tracker/2020/google-invests-100-million-dollars-into-telehealth-provider-amwell/ (accessed 22 January 2024).

33. A 2017 report by West Monroe Partners states that 35% of healthcare organizations house more than 50% of their data or infrastructure in the

cloud. https://www.westmonroe.com/perspectives/signature-research/technology-is-transforming-everything (accessed 22 January 2024).

34. Fry, E. and Schulte, F. (2019, 18 March). Death by a thousand clicks: where electronic health records went wrong. *Fortune.* https://fortune.com/longform/medical-records/ (accessed 22 January 2024). Electronic Health Records (EHRs) were originally set up with the goal of achieving data portability across health systems. However, EHR providers evolved their formats independent of each other, increasing data silos.

35. Eliason, B. and Sigafoes, K. (2020, 14 July). Interoperability in health-casr: making the most of FHIR. *Health Catalyst.* https://www.healthcatalyst.com/insights/interoperability-healthcare-potential-fhir (accessed 22 January 2024).

36. For example symptoms, procedures or diagnoses.

37. Darcy, A.M., Louie, A.K. and Roberts, L.W. (2016). Machine learning and the profession of medicine. *Journal of the American Medical Association (JAMA)*, 315(6): 551–552.

38. Napolitano, G. Marshall, A. Hamilton, P. et al. (2016) Machine learning classification of surgical pathology reports and chunk recognition for information extraction noise reduction. *Artificial Intelligence in Medicine*, 70, 77–83.

39. Murff, H.J., FitzHenry, F. and Matheny, M.E. (2011). Automated identification of postoperative complications within an electronic medical record using natural language processing. *Journal of the American Medical Association (JAMA)*, 306(8): 848–855.

40. Buch, V.H., Ahmed, I. and Maruthappu, M. (2018). Artificial intelligence in medicine: current trends and future possibilities. *British Journal of General Practice*, 68(668): 143–144.

41. Prediction is defined as the ability to anticipate future outcomes based on available data.
    Agrawal, A., Gans, J.S. and and Goldfarb, A. (2017). What to expect from artificial intelligence. *MIT Sloan Management Review*, 58(3): 23–27.

42. Agrawal, A., Gans, J.S. and and Goldfarb, A. (2019). Artificial intelligence: the ambiguous labor market impact of automating prediction. *Journal of Economic Perspectives*, 33(2): 31–50.

43. Google workspace: collaboration software for healthcare. https://workspace.google.com/industries/healthcare/ (accessed 22 January 2024).

44. Farr, C. (2020, 20 April). Google unveils tech to make it easier for doctors and patients to share health info. CNBC. https://www.cnbc.com/2020/04/20/google-cloud-health-api-released.html (accessed 22 January 2024).

45. https://support.apple.com/en-us/HT204351.com/healthcare/health-records/ (accessed 21 October 2023).
46. Beckers Health IT. (2020). Apple partners With Epic, Mayo on new health app platform https://www.beckershospitalreview.com/healthcare-information-technology/apple-partners-with-epic-mayo-on-new-health-app-platform.html (accessed 22 January 2024).
47. Shinkman, R. (2019, 23 August). Allscripts touts deal with Apple Health Records. Dive Brief. https://www.healthcaredive.com/news/allscripts-touts-deal-with-apple-health-records/561556/ (accessed 22 January 2024).
48. Farr, C. (2017, 19 June), Apple is working with this small start-up to change how we track our health. CNBC. https://www.cnbc.com/2017/06/19/apple-working-with-start-up-health-gorilla-on-iphone-ehr-plan.html (accessed 22 January 2024).
49. Apple Developer. (n.d.). Health and fitness. https://developer.apple.com/health-fitness/ (accessed 22 January 2024).
50. Healthkit. (2017). Healthkit compatible devices 2017. iSmartliving. https://www.ismartliving.net/healthkit-compatible-devices-2017/ (accessed 22 January 2024).
51. Apple Developer. (n.d.). CareKit. https://developer.apple.com/carekit/ (accessed 22 January 2024).
52. Apple Developer. (n.d.). Empowering medical researchers, doctors and you. https://www.apple.com/in/researchkit/ (accessed 22 January 2024).
53. With access to data on more health indicators, such connected device complements may also deliver clinically tested decision support alerts, enabling users to take remedial action.
54. Cohen, J.K. (2018, 12 September). Apple watch: FDA-cleared for electrocardiogram screening. Beckers Health IT. https://www.beckershospitalreview.com/supply-chain/apple-watch-fda-cleared-for-electrocardiogram-screening.html (accessed 22 January 2024).
55. Some current examples include a portable ultrasound tool by Butterfly Network and an otoscope by Cellscope.
56. Apple is working with third party medical device manufacturers to create such complements. Zimmer Biomet's mymobility – a remote care management system aimed at the pre- and post-operative joint replacement experience – integrates with the Apple Watch to facilitate interactions between patients and their surgical care teams, informed by real-time mobility metrics like gait quality.
57. Ford, O. (2020, 27 January). Verily powers up position in wearables with new FDA nod. MD+DI. https://www.mddionline.com/

regulatory–quality/verily–powers–position–wearables–new–
fda–nod (accessed 22 January 2024).

58. Bohn, D. (2020, 27 August). Amazon announces Halo, a fitness band and app that scans your body and voice. The Verge. https://www.theverge.com/2020/8/27/21402493/amazon-halo-band-health-fitness-body-scan-tone-emotion-activity-sleep (accessed 22 January 2024).

59. http://www.personal.psu.edu/faculty/r/u/rug14/68.Changing%20competitive%20dynamics%20in%20network%20industries.pdf (accessed 10 March 2023).

60. HealthIT.gov (n.d.). Blue button. https://www.healthit.gov/topic/health-it-initiatives/blue-button (accessed 22 January 2024).

61. Health Tech Newspaper HTN (n.d.). Apple, Google, Amazon and Microsoft pledge commitment to interoperability. https://htn.co.uk/2019/08/01/apple-google-amazon-and-microsoft-pledge-commitment-to-interoperability/ (accessed 22 January 2024).

62. Moore, G.J. (2018, 5 March). Google Cloud for Healthcare: new APIs, customers, partners and security updates. https://www.blog.google/products/google-cloud/google-cloud-healthcare-new-apis-customers-partners-and-security-updates/ (accessed 22 January 2024).

63. Apigee, an API management company acquired by Google, was one of the early movers in building FHIR-based APIs. Padmanabhan, P. (2016, 15 September). Why healthcare needs to care about Google's acquisition of Apigee. CIO. https://www.cio.com/article/236092/why-healthcare-needs-to-care-about-googles-acquisition-of-apigee.html (accessed 22 January 2024).

64. Apple Newsroom. (2018, 24 January). Apple announces effortless solution bringing health records to iPhone. Appple. https://www.apple.com/newsroom/2018/01/apple-announces-effortless-solution-bringing-health-records-to-iPhone/ (accessed 22 January 2024).

Chapter 2: Regenerative Innovation: Exploring the Potential of Digital Platforms for Ecosystem Health

1. Howard, S., Schwerhoff, G. and Stuermer, M. (2019, 27 August). Solving a puzzle: more nonrenewable resources without higher prices. Federal Reserve Bank of Dallas. https://www.dallasfed.org/research/economics/2019/0827 (accessed 22 January 2024).

2. International Futures Forum. (n.d.). Three horizons framework. https://www.iffpraxis.com/three-horizons (accessed 22 January 2024).

3. Wikipedia. (2024, 21 January). Timeline of the evolutionary history of life. https://en.wikipedia.org/wiki/Timeline_of_the_evolutionary_history_of_life (accessed 22 January 2024).

4. Simard, S. (2016). *How trees talk to each other.* TED Talk at TED Summit. June. https://www.ted.com/talks/suzanne_simard_how_trees_talk_to_each_other (accessed 22 January 2024).

5. Marshall, C. (2019, 15 May). Wood wide web: Trees' social networks are mapped. BBC. https://www.bbc.com/news/science-environment-48257315 (accessed 22 January 2024).

6. Polman, P. and Winston, A. (2021). Net positive: how courageous companies thrive by giving more than they take. *Harvard Business Press*, 5 October. https://hbr.org/2021/09/the-net-positive-manifesto (accessed 22 January 2024).

7. Fullerton, J. (2015). Regenerative capitalism: how universal principals and patterns will shape our new economy. Capital Institute. https://capitalinstitute.org/wp-content/uploads/2015/04/2015-Regenerative-Capitalism-4-20-15-final.pdf (accessed 22 January 2024).

8. Heading, S., di Battista, A., Cavaciuti-Wishart, E. et al. (2023). Global risks report 2023. World Economic Forum. https://www.weforum.org/publications/global-risks-report-2023/ (accessed 22 January 2024); Harding, S. and Markovitz, G. (2023) These are the biggest risks facing the world. https://www.weforum.org/agenda/2023/01/these-are-the-biggest-risks-facing-the-world-global-risks-2023/ (accessed 22 January 2024).

9. Anthes, R. (2021). Most economists now see climate change urgency. *The Balance*, 22 April. https://www.thebalancemoney.com/most-economists-now-see-climate-change-urgency-5180139 (accessed 22 January 2024).

10. Bussiere S., Halper, J. and Shriver, T. (2022). Asset management industry confronts the challenges presented by climate change transition. *Harvard Law School Forum on Corporate Governance*, 28 February. https://corpgov.law.harvard.edu/2022/02/28/asset-management-industry-confronts-the-challenges-presented-by-climate-change-transition/ (accessed 22 January 2024).

11. Caudle, D., Janson, E., Pozza, M. et al. (2023, 18 July). Generating upside from ESG: opportunities for private equity. PWC. https://www.pwc.com/gx/en/services/sustainability/publications/private-equity-and-the-responsible-investment-survey.html (accessed 22 January 2024).

12. Climate Action Tracker. (2023, 11 November). CAT net zero target evaluations. https://climateactiontracker.org/global/cat-net-zero-target-evaluations/ (accessed 22 January 2024).

13. Wolfe, L. (2023, 28 March). Regenerative industry landscape. HowGood. https://howgood.com/regenerative-industry-landscape/ (accessed 22 January 2024).

14. Consultancy.org (2018, 10 December). Market size of global platform economy surpasses $7 trillion mark. https://www.consultancy.org/news/104/market-size-of-global-platform-economy-surpasses-7-trillion-mark (accessed 22 January 2024).

15. Sangheet Choudhary, S. (2016). What's good for the platform is bad for the ecosystem. Keynote at the Social Business Forum in Milan. https://www.youtube.com/watch?v=N50EJvOGC7o&source_ve_path=MjM4NTE&feature=emb_title

16. Our World in Data (n.d.). Global plastics production. https://ourworldindata.org/grapher/global-plastics-production; based on Geyer, R., Jambeck, J.R. and Law, K.L. (2017). Production, use, and fate of all plastics ever made. *Science Advances*, 3(7). https://www.science.org/doi/10.1126/sciadv.1700782 (accessed 22 January 2024).

17. Snider, M. (2022). Microplastics have been found in air, water, food and now ... human blood. *USA Today*, 26 March. https://www.usatoday.com/story/news/health/2022/03/25/plastics-found-inside-human-blood/7153385001/ (accessed 22 January 2024).

18. Readers can access more information about these companies by accessing their websites: https://plasticbank.com/ (accessed 22 January 2024); https://www.reboundplasticexchange.com/ (accessed 22 January 2024) and https://www.cleanhub.com/ (accessed 22 January 2024).

19. Poore, J. and Nemecek, T. (2018). Reducing food's environmental impacts through producers and consumers. *Science*, 360(6392): 987-992. doi:10.1126/science.aaq0216. https://pubmed.ncbi.nlm.nih.gov/29853680/ (accessed 22 January 2024).

20. Food and Agriculture Association of the United Nations. (2015). Natural capital impacts in agriculture: supporting better business decision making. FAO, p. 6. https://www.fao.org/fileadmin/templates/nr/sustainability_pathways/docs/Final_Natural_Capital_Impacts_in_Agriculture_-_Supporting_Better_Business_Descision-Making_v5.0.pdf (accessed 22 January 2024).

21. Ecosystem services are defined as the direct and indirect contributions of ecosystems to human well-being. They represent emerging asset classes and/or methodologies for valuation of the environment in economics. Readers can learn more here: Pearce, R. (2023, 3 January). What are ecosystem services? Earth.org. https://earth.org/what-are-ecosystem-services/ (accessed 22 January 2024).

22. Peto, J., Reichheld, A. and Ritthaler, C. (2023). Research: consumers' sustainability demands are rising. *Harvard Business Review*, 18 September. https://hbr.org/2023/09/research-consumers-sustainability-demands-are-rising (accessed 22 January 2024).

23. Best Pitch Decks. (2022). HowGood Pitch Deck. Best Pitch Decks. https://bestpitchdeck.com/howgood (accessed 22 January 2024).

24. Statista. (2023, 18 July). Electronic waste generated from 2010 to 2019. Statista. https://www.statista.com/statistics/499891/projection-ewaste-generation-worldwide/ (accessed 22 January 2024).

25. Austen-Smith, C. (2023, 25 January). The environmental impact of refurbished tech. BackMarket. https://www.backmarket.com/en-us/c/news/impact-of-refurbished-on-environment (accessed 22 January 2024).

26. Dillet, R. (2022, 11 January). Back Market reaches $5.7B valuation for its refurbished device marketplace. *TechCrunch*. https://techcrunch.com/2022/01/11/back-market-reaches-5-7b-valuation-for-its-refurbished-device-marketplace/ (accessed 22 January 2024).

27. Gitcoin. (n.d.). WTF is quadratic funding? Gitcoin. https://qf.gitcoin.co/?grant=&grant=&grant=&grant=&match=1000 (accessed 22 January 2024).

28. A4AI. (2022, 28 February). Advancing meaningful connectivity: towards active and participatory digital societies. Alliance for Affordable Internet. https://a4ai.org/research/advancing-meaningful-connectivity-towards-active-and-participatory-digital-societies/ (accessed 22 January 2024).

29. Foy, K. (2023). New tools are available to help reduce the energy that AI models devour. *MIT News*, 5 October. https://news.mit.edu/2023/new-tools-available-reduce-energy-that-ai-models-devour-1005; and Rozite, V., Bertoli, E. and Reidenbach, B. (2023, October). Data centres and data transmission networks. IEA. https://www.iea.org/energy-system/buildings/data-centres-and-data-transmission-networks (accessed 22 January 2024).

Chapter 3: Thinking Like an AI Native

1. Abburi, H. (2018, 29 October). Leading in a world of intangible assets. LinkedIn Newsletter.
2. J.P.Morgan. (2024) Technology at our firm. JP Morgan.com. https://www.jpmorgan.com/technology (accessed 22 January 2024).
3. Knowles, J., Baris, R., Hunsaker, B.T. et al. (2023, 18 May). Best Bath & bankruptcy: lessons for senior leaders. *MIT Sloan Management Review*.
4. ChartMogul. (2023). SaaS growth report 2023. https://chartmogul.com/reports/saas-growth-report/2023/ (accessed 22 January 2024).
5. Zippia.com. (2022). Klarna company history timeline. https://www.zippia.com/klarna-careers-1419599/history/ (accessed 22 January 2024).
6. Abburi, H. (2020, 24 August). Ideas don't die, companies do. Forbes.
7. Schwab, K. (2015). The fourth industrial revolution, what it means and how to respond. World Economic Forum.
8. McNamee, J. (2022). How Marcus by Goldman Sachs met its end in 2022. Insider Intelligence.
9. Mixson, E. (2022). Lessons learned from GE's digital transformation failure. Intelligent Automation Network.
10. Pylarinou, E. (2019). Banks should steal the 2002 Bezos internal memo. https://efipm.medium.com/banks-should-steal-the-2002-bezos-internal-memo-286c489381c9 (accessed 22 January 2024).
11. Pine, J. II and Gilmore, J. (2011). *The Experience Economy*. Harvard Business Press.
12. Daniel, Ch. (2023). Apple pay revenue and growth statistics (2023), www.usesignhouse.com/blog/apple-pay-stats (accessed 22 January 2024).
13. Bank of International Settlements (BIS). (2023). Project Mariana: BIS and central banks of France, Singapore and Switzerland successfully test cross-border wholesale CBDCs. BIS. www.bis.org/about/bisih/topics/cbdc/mariana.htm (accessed 22 January 2024). Foundation models, the new kid on the bloc.
14. Bloomberg. (2023). Introducing BloombergGPT, Bloomberg's 50-billion parameter large language model, purpose-built from scratch for finance. Bloomberg www.bloomberg.com/company/press/bloomberggpt-50-billion-parameter-llm-tuned-finance/ (accessed 22 January 2024).

15. Souze, K. (2023). The supply side: generative AI or ChatGPT next holy grail for retailers, suppliers. Talk Business. talkbusiness.net/2023/06/the-supply-side-generative-ai-or-chatgpt-next-holy-grail-for-retailers-suppliers/ (accessed 22 January 2024).

16. Ingka. (2023). AI and remote selling bring IKEA design expertise to the many, Ingka `www.ingka.com/news/ai-and-remote-selling-bring-ikea-design-expertise-to-the-many/#:~:text=Since%20the%20rollout%20of%20the,million%20in%20savings%20thus%2-0far` (accessed 22 January 2024).

17. Stanford University. (2021). Introducing the Center for Research on Foundation Models (CRFM). `hai.stanford.edu/news/introducing-center-research-foundation-models-crfm` (accessed 22 January 2024).

18. Chun, M. (2023, 20 March). How Artificial Intelligence is revolutionizing drug discovery. Harvard Law Bill Of Health. `https://blog.petrieflom.law.harvard.edu/2023/03/20/how-artificial-intelligence-is-revolutionizing-drug-discovery/` (accessed 22 January 2024).

19. Dayton, E. (n.d.). Amazon statistics yu should know: opportunities to make the mot of America's top online marketplace. Big Commerce. `https://www.bigcommerce.co.uk/blog/amazon-statistics/` (accessed 22 January 2024).

20. eDesk Blog. (2023, 26 June). Amazon marketplace statistics 2022. `https://www.edesk.com/blog/amazon-statistics/` (accessed 22 January 2024).

21. Candelon, F., Reichert, T., Duranton, S. et al. (2020, 28 October). Deploying AI to maximize revenue. BCG. `https://www.bcg.com/publications/2020/deploying-ai-artificial-intelligence-to-maximize-revenue` (accessed 22 January 2024).

22. IKEA, (2022, 5 July). Corporate news. IKEA.

23. Buckley, T. (2020, 3 June). Builders of a $20 billion coffee empire have their eyes on pets. Bloomberg.

24. Drenik, G. (2023, 15 February). Leading retailers lean into AI to satisfy inflation-weary shoppers. Forbes.

25. Amazon. (2022, 10 November). Amazon introduces Sparrow – a state-of-the-art robot that handles millions of diverse products. Amazon News.

26. Fox, L. (2023, 19 May). Grab looks to further efficiency gains via generative AI. PhocusWire.

27. Price, J. (2023, 10 April). Introducing AI-generated product descriptions powered by Shopify Magic. Shopify News.

28. Duolingo Team. (2013, 14 March 14). Introducing Duolingo Max, a learning experience powered by GPT-4. Duolingo Blog.

29. Korn Ferry. (2023). AI in the workplace. Korn Ferry. `https://www.kornferry.com/insights/featured-topics/gen-ai-in-the-workplace` (accessed 22 January 2024)

30. Siegel, E.) 2022, 8 March). How many galaxies are in the Universe? Big Think. `https://bigthink.com/starts-with-a-bang/how-many-galaxies` (accessed 22 January 2024).

31. Quantumrun Foresight. (2022, 18 August). AI marketplaces: Shopping for the next disruptive technology. Quantumrun. `https://www.quantumrun.com/insight/ai-marketplaces-shopping-next-disruptive-technology` (accessed 22 January 2024).

Chapter 4: Deconstructed and Decentralized Work: At the Interconnection between the Future of Work and Blockchain

1. Jesuthasan, R. and Boudreau, J. (2022). *Work Without Jobs*. MIT Press.

2. Baker, P. (2021, 3 December). Blockchain HR technology: 5 Use cases impacting human resources. TechTarget. `https://www.techtarget.com/searchhrsoftware/tip/Blockchain-HR-technology-5-use-cases-impacting-human-resources?Offer=abt_pubpro_AI-Insider` (accessed 22 January 2024).

3. XAPO Bnk. (n.d.). the bank for Bitcoiners by Bitcoiners. XAPO Bank. `https://www.xapobank.com/` (accessed 22 January 2024).

4. Jesuthasan, R. and Zarkadakis, G. (2022, 5 July). How will Web3 impact the future of work? World Economic Forum. `https://www.weforum.org/agenda/2022/07/web-3-change-the-future-of-work-decen-tralized-autonomous-organizations/` (accessed 22 January 2024).

5. Schecter, B. (2021, 17 December). The future of work is not corporate – it's DAOs and crypto future. a16zcrypto. `https://a16zcrypto.com/posts/article/the-future-of-work-daos-crypto-networks/` (accessed 22 January 2024).

6. Henderson, J. (2020, 17 May). UPS joins alliance to create blockchain standards for logistics. SupplyChain. `https://supplychaindigital.com/technology/ups-joins-alliance-create-blockchain-standards-logistics` (accessed 22 January 2024).

7. IBM Food Trust. (n.d.). Food logistics on blockchain. IBM Food Trust. `https://www.ibm.com/blockchain/resources/food-trust/food-logistics/` (accessed 22 January 2024).

Chapter 5: Intelligent Health: The Convergence of Data and AI

1. Prakash, P. (2023). Alphabet CEO Sundar Pichai says that A.I. could be 'more profound' than both fire and electricity – but he's been saying the same thing for years. *Yahoo! Finance*, 17 April. https://finance.yahoo.com/news/alphabet-ceo-sundar-pichai-says-175046683.html (accessed 23 October 2023).

2. Egan, M. (2023). 42% of CEOs say AI could destroy humanity in five to ten years. *CNN*, 14 June. https://www.cnn.com/2023/06/14/business/artificial-intelligence-ceos-warning/index.html# (accessed 23 October 2023).

3. Wikipedia. (n.d.). General-purpose technology. https://en.wikipedia.org/wiki/General-purpose_technology (accessed 2 November 2023).

4. Currier, J. (2023). 3 waves of generative AI startups. NfX, February. https://www.nfx.com/post/3-waves-generative-ai-startups (accessed 23 October 2023).

5. McCarthy, J., Minsky, M., Rochester, N. et al. (1956). Artificial intelligence coined at Dartmouth. https://home.dartmouth.edu/about/artificial-intelligence-ai-coined-dartmouth (accessed 23 October 2023).

6. Akachi Y. and Kruk, M. (2017). Quality of care: measuring a neglected driver of improved health. Bulletin of the World Health Organization, 95: 465–472. https://doi.org/10.2471/BLT.16.180190

7. Morris, Z., Wooding, S., and Grant, J. (2011). The answer is 17 years, what is the question: understanding time lags in translational research. *Journal of the Royal Society of Medicine*, 104(12). https://doi.org/10.1258/jrsm.2011.110180

8. Magnan, S. (2017, 9 October). Social determinants of health 101 for health care: five plus five. National Academy of Medicine. https://nam.edu/social-determinants-of-health-101-for-health-care-five-plus-five/ (accessed 23 October 2023).

9. County Health Rankings & Roadmaps. (2023). County Health Rankings Model. https://www.countyhealthrankings.org/explore-health-rankings/county-health-rankings-model (accessed 23 October 2023).

10. World Health Organization. (2021). From value for money to value-based health services: a twenty-first century shift. WHO Issue Brief, 13 April. https://www.who.int/publications/i/item/9789240020344 (accessed 23 October 2023).

11. Healthcare Payment Learning & Action Network. (2023). APM measurement: progress of alternative payment models. 2023 methodology and results report. HCPLAN. https://hcp-lan.org/workproducts/apm-methodology-2023.pdf (accessed 4 November 2023).

12. McGlynn, E., Asch, S., Adams, J. et al. (2003). The quality of healthcare care delivered to adults in the United States. *New England Journal of Medicine*, 348: 2635–2645. https://doi: 10.1056/NEJMsa022615.

13. New York Presbyterian. (n.d.). What is precision medicine. Health Matters. https://healthmatters.nyp.org/precision-medicine/ (accessed 23 October 2023).

14. Ipsos MORI. (2020). Perils of perception 2020: causes of death. https://www.ipsos.com/sites/default/files/ct/news/documents/2020-02/ipsos-perils-of-perception-2020-causes-of-death.pdf (accessed 23 October 2023).

15. FINN Partners and Galen Growth. (2023, 6 January). FINN Partners and Galen Growth global state of digital health 2022. https://www.finnpartners.com/news-insights/finn-partners-and-galen-growth-global-state-of-digital-health-full-year-2022/ (accessed 23 October 2023).

16. BertelsmannStiftung. (2022, 7 May). Tech giants in healthcare. BertelsmannStiftung. https://www.bertelsmann-stiftung.de/en/publications/publication/did/tech-giants-in-healthcare-en (accessed 23 October 2023).

17. Definitive Healthcare. (2023, May). Retailers in healthcare: a catalyst for provider evolution. Definitive Healthcare. https://www.definitivehc.com/sites/default/files/resources/pdfs/Retailers-in-healthcare_A-catalyst-for-provider-evolution.pdf (accessed 23 October 2023).

18. Healthcare Information and Management Systems Society. (n.d.). Interoperability in healthcare. HIMSS. https://www.himss.org/resources/interoperability-healthcare (accessed 23 October 2023).

19. The White House. (2004). Promoting innovation and competitiveness: President Bush's technology agenda. https://georgewbush-whitehouse.archives.gov/infocus/technology/economic_policy200404/chap3.html (accessed 23 October 2023).

20. Office of the National Coordinator for Health Information Technology. (2022). Report to Congress. ONC. https://www.healthit.gov/sites/default/files/page/2023-02/2022_ONC_Report_to_Congress.pdf (accessed 23 October 2023).

21. Miliard, M. (2019, 30 December). 10 years on from meaningful use, major progress despite the challenges. *Healthcare IT News*. https://www.healthcareitnews.com/news/10-years-meaningful-use-major-progress-despite-challenges (accessed 23 October 2023).

22. Office of the National Coordinator for Health Information Technology (2022). Report to Congress. ONC. `https://www.healthit.gov/sites/default/files/page/2023-02/2022_ONC_Report_to_Congress.pdf` (accessed 23 October 2023).

23. Bernstam, E., Warner, J., Krauss, J. et al. (2022). Quantitating and assessing interoperability between electronic health records. *Journal of the American Medical Informatics Association*, 29(5): 753–760. `https://doi.org/10.1093/jamia/ocab289`.

24. Manyika, J., Ramaswamy, S., Khanna, S. et al. (2015, 1 December). Digital America: a tale of the haves and have-mores. (1 December). McKinsey & Company. `https://www.mckinsey.com/industries/technology-media-and-telecommunications/our-insights/digital-america-a-tale-of-the-haves-and-have-mores` (accessed 23 October 2023).

25. openEHR. (n.d.). Specification program. openEHR. `https://openehr.org/programs/specification/` (accessed 23 October 2023).

26. Medical Group Management Association. (2022). Annual regulatory burden report October 2022. MGMA. p. 5. `https://www.mgma.com/getkaiasset/b7e88b99-8e93-44a9-8144-725ca956089e/10.11.2022-MGMA-Regulatory-Burden-Report-FINAL.pdf` (accessed 23 October 2023).

27. GE Healthcare, (2023). Reimagining better health 2023: quantitative survey data insights. GE Healthcare. `https://www.gehealthcare.com/-/jssmedia/gehc/us/images/insights/reimaging-better-health/reimagining-better-healthdataaddendumquantitative-survey-data-insightsexternaljune022023--jb24942xx` (accessed 23 October 2023).

28. Corish, B. (2018). Medical knowledge doubles every few months; how can clinicians keep up? (23 April). `https://www.elsevier.com/connect/medical-knowledge-doubles-every-few-months-how-can-clinicians-keep-up` (accessed 23 October 2023).

29. RBC Capital Markets. (2018). The healthcare data explosion. PBC Capital Markets. `https://www.rbccm.com/en/gib/healthcare/episode/the_healthcare_data_explosion#content-panel` (accessed 23 October 2023).

30. Fornell, D. (2023, 6 February). FDA has now cleared more than 500 healthcare AI algorithms. Health Exec. `https://healthexec.com/topics/artificial-intelligence/fda-has-now-cleared-more-500-healthcare-ai-algorithms` (accessed 23 October 2023).

31. Tracxn. (2023, 4 September). AI in healthcare startups in United States. Tracxn. `https://tracxn.com/d/explore/ai-in-healthcare-startups-in-united-states/__LDTRt1tGQgT9k_Zm2hqI1s5wlXVn-PwLgIShrk0AXts/companies` (accessed 23 October 2023).

32. Strickland, E. (2017, 1 May). AI predicts heart attacks and strokes more accurately than standard doctor's method. IEEE Spectrum. https://spectrum.ieee.org/ai-predicts-heart-attacks-more-accurately-than-standard-doctor-method (accessed 23 October 2023).

33. Tyson, A., Pasquini, G., Spencer, A. et al. (2023, 22 February). 60% of Americans would be uncomfortable with provider relying on AI in their own health care. Pew Research Center. https://www.pewresearch.org/science/2023/02/22/60-of-americans-would-be-uncomfortable-with-provider-relying-on-ai-in-their-own-health-care/ (accessed 23 October 2023).

34. Goldfarb, A. and Teodoridis, F. (2022, 9 March). Why is AI adoption in health care lagging? Brookings Research. https://www.brookings.edu/articles/why-is-ai-adoption-in-health-care-lagging/ (accessed 23 October 2023).

35. Agrawal, J., Gans, J. and Goldfarb, A. (2023). *Power and Prediction.* Harvard Business Review Press.

36. Kotter, E. (2021). Basic workflow of medical imaging. In: van Ooijen, P.M.A. (ed.) *Basic Knowledge of Medical Imaging Informatics. Imaging Informatics for Healthcare Professionals* (pp. 41–53). Springer. https://doi.org/10.1007/978-3-030-71885-5_4.

37. Radiological Society of North America. (n.d.). RadReport reporting templates. https://www.rsna.org/practice-tools/data-tools-and-standards/radreport-reporting-templates (accessed 23 October 2023).

38. Langlotz, C. (2019). Will artificial intelligence replace radiologists? *Radiology: Artificial Intelligence.* 1(3). https://doi.org/10.1148/ryai.2019190058

39. Obermeyer, Z. and Emanuel, E. (2016). Predicting the future: big data, machine learning, and clinical medicine. *New England Journal of Medicine,* 375: 1216–1219. doi: 10.1056/NEJMp1606181.

40. Creative Destruction Lab. (2016). Geoff Hinton: on radiology. YouTube. https://www.youtube.com/watch?v=2HMPRXstSvQ (accessed 23 October 2023).

41. Suskind, R. and Suskind, D. (2016, 11 October). Technology will replace many doctors, lawyers, and other professionals. *Harvard Business Review.* https://hbr.org/2016/10/robots-will-replace-doctors-lawyers-and-other-professionals (accessed 23 October 2023).

42. Rajpurkar, P. and Lungren, M. (2023). The current and future state of AI interpretation of medical images. *New England Journal of Medicine,* 388: 1981–1990. doi: 10.1056/NEJMra2301725.

43. Nam, J., Hwang, E., Kim, J. et. al. (2023, 7 February). AI improves nodule detection on chest radiographs in a health screening population: a randomized controlled trial. *Radiology*. https://doi.org/10.1148/radiol.221894.

44. Eng, D., Chute, C., Khandwala, N. et al. (2021). Automated coronary calcium scoring using deep learning with multicenter external validation. *NPJ Digital Medicine*, 4: 88. https://doi.org/10.1038/s41746-021-00460-1.

45. Astuto, B., Flament, I., Namiri, N. et al. (2021). Automatic deep learning-assisted detection and grading of abnormalities in knee MRI studies. *Radiology: Artificial Intelligence*, 3(3): e200165. https://doi.org/10.1148/ryai.2021200165.

46. Becker, A., Marcon, M., Ghafoor, S. et.al. (2017). Deep learning in mammography: diagnostic accuracy of a multipurpose image analysis software in the detection of breast cancer. *Investigative Radiology*, 52: 434–440. doi: 10.1097/RLI.0000000000000358.

47. Javaid, S. (2023, 10 April). Top 6 radiology use cases in 2023. AI Multiple. https://research.aimultiple.com/radiology-ai/ (accessed 23 October 2023).

48. Rodriguez-Ruiz, A., Lång K., Gubern-Merida, A. et al. (2019). Stand-alone artificial intelligence for breast cancer detection in mammography: comparison with 101 radiologists. *Journal of the National Cancer Institute*, 111: 916–922. https://doi.org/10.1093/jnci/djy222.

49. Seah J., Tang C. and Buchlak, Q. (2021). Effect of a comprehensive deep-learning model on the accuracy of chest x-ray interpretation by radiologists: a retrospective, multireader multicase study. *Lancet Digital Health*, 3: e496–506. https://doi.org/10.1016/S2589-7500(21)00106-0.

50. Rajpurkar, P., O'Connell C., Schechter, A. et al (2020). CheXaid: deep learning assistance for physician diagnosis of tuberculosis using chest x-rays in patients with HIV. *NPJ Digital Medicine*, 3: 115. https://doi.org/10.1038/s41746-020-00322-2.

51. Fornell, D. (2023, 16 May). Latest version of ChatGPT AI passes radiology board exam. *Radiology Business*. https://radiologybusiness.com/topics/artificial-intelligence/latest-version-chatgpt-ai-passes-radiology-board-exam (accessed 23 October 2023).

52. Fornell, D. (2023, 6 February). FDA has now cleared more than 500 healthcare AI algorithms. HealthExec. https://healthexec.com/topics/artificial-intelligence/fda-has-now-cleared-more-500-healthcare-ai-algorithms (accessed 23 October 2023).

53. Blumer, S. (2023). The current state of AI in radiology. *HealthTech*. https://www.healthtechmagazines.com/the-current-state-of-ai-in-radiology/ (accessed 23 October 2023).

54. Rajpurkar, P. and Lungren, M. (2023). The current and future state of AI interpretation of medical images. *New England Journal of Medicine*, 388: 1981–1990. doi: 10.1056/NEJMra2301725.

55. Richardson, T. (2022). MedTech: transforming healthcare with medical imaging AI. HIT Consultant. https://hitconsultant.net/2022/04/08/transforming-healthcare-medical-imaging-ai/ (accessed 23 October 2023).

56. Huisman, M., Ranschaert, E., Parker, W. et al. (2021). An international survey on AI in radiology in 1,041 radiologists and radiology residents part 1: fear of replacement, knowledge, and attitude. *European Radiology*, 31: 7058–7066. https://doi.org/10.1007/s00330-021-07781-5.

57. Hassankhani, A., Amoukhteh, M. and Valizadeh, P. (2023). Radiology as a specialty in the era of artificial intelligence: a systematic review and meta-analysis on medical students, radiology trainees, and radiologists. *Academic Radiology*, (June). https://doi.org/10.1016/j.acra.2023.05.024.

58. Lobig, F., Subramanian, D., Blankenburg, M. et al. (2023). To pay or not to pay for artificial intelligence applications in radiology, *NPJ Digital Medicine*, 6: 117. https://doi.org/10.1038/s41746-023-00861-4.

59. Fornell, D. (2023, 6 April). What is the ROI on AI adoption in radiology? Radiology Business. https://radiologybusiness.com/topics/artificial-intelligence/what-roi-ai-adoption-radiology (accessed 23 October 2023).

60. Lobig, F., Subramanian, D., Blankenburg, M. et al. (2023). To pay or not to pay for artificial intelligence applications in radiology, *NPJ Digital Medicine*, 6: 117. https://doi.org/10.1038/s41746-023-00861-4.

61. Stempniak, M. (2023, 8 March). More experts weigh in on the use of ChatGPT in radiology: ethical use is 'imperative'. Radiology Business. https://radiologybusiness.com/topics/artificial-intelligence/chatgpt-radiology-ethics-rsna-artificial-intelligence (accessed 23 October 2023).

62. Hagland, M. (2022, 29 November). At RSNA, experts warn of danger from malicious use of AI against radiology. Healthcare Innovation. https://www.hcinnovationgroup.com/imaging/artificial-intelligence/article/21288493/at-rsna-experts-warn-of-danger-from-malicious-use-of-ai-against-radiology (accessed 23 October 2023).

63. Radiological Society of North America. (2022, 24 August). Special report lays out best practices for handling bias in radiology AI. Press Release.

64. Harvey, H. (2018). Why AI will not replace radiologists. *Medium*, (24 January). https://towardsdatascience.com/why-ai-will-not-replace-radiologists-c7736f2c7d80 (accessed 23 October 2023).

65. Mesko, B. (2021, 2 March). 5 reasons why artificial intelligence won't replace physicians. The Medical Futurist. `https://medicalfuturist.com/5-reasons-artificial-intelligence-wont-replace-physicians/` (accessed 23 October 2023).

66. Banja, J. (2020). AI hype and radiology: a plea for realism and accuracy. *Radiology: Artificial Intelligence*, 2(4): e190223. `https://doi.org/10.1148/ryai.2020190223`.

67. O*NET OnLine. (2023). Radiologists. O*NET OnLine. `https://www.onetonline.org/link/summary/29-1224.00` (accessed 23 October 2023).

68. Kim, W. (2019). Imaging informatics: fear, hype, hope, and reality — how AI Is entering the health care system. *Radiology Today*, 20(3): 6. `https://www.radiologytoday.net/archive/rt0319p6.shtml` (accessed 23 October 2023).

69. Areeratanasak, W. (2020, 9 September). How AI in medical imaging is leading the way to better patient care. *The Nation*. `https://www.nationthailand.com/business/biz-insights/30394256` (accessed 23 October 2023).

70. Mesko, B. (2022, 22 September). The future of radiology and artificial intelligence. *The Medical Futurist*. `https://medicalfuturist.com/the-future-of-radiology-and-ai/` (accessed 23 October 2023).

71. Harvey, H. (2018). Why AI will not replace radiologists. *Medium*, (24 January). `https://towardsdatascience.com/why-ai-will-not-replace-radiologists-c7736f2c7d80` (accessed 23 October 2023).

72. CBInsights. (2023, 31 March). 96 AI companies building the next generation of radiology tech. CBInsights Research Brief. `https://www.cbinsights.com/research/ai-radiology-startups-market-map/` (accessed 23 October 2023).

73. Global Data. (2023, 29 May). Artificial intelligence innovation: leading companies in AI-assisted radiology. Global Data Premium Insights. `https://www.verdict.co.uk/innovators-ai-assisted-radiology-technology-ai/?cf-view` (accessed 23 October 2023).

74. Fornell, D. (2022, 2 September). Where are we with AI adoption in radiology? HealthImaging. `https://healthimaging.com/topics/artificial-intelligence/video-where-are-we-ai-adoption-radiology` (accessed 23 October 2023).

75. Agency for Healthcare Research and Quality. (2023, September). Clinical decision support. AHRQ. `https://www.ahrq.gov/cpi/about/otherwebsites/clinical-decision-support/index.html` (accessed 23 October 2023).

76. Kent, J. (2018, 3 August). How is artificial intelligence changing radiology and pathology to enhance care delivery and improve patient outcomes? Health IT Analytics. `https://healthitanalytics.com/news/how-artificial-intelligence-is-changing-radiology-pathology` (accessed 23 October 2023).

77. Potocnik, J., Foley, S. and Thomas, E. (2023). Current and potential applications of artificial intelligence in medical imaging practice: a narrative review. *Journal of Medical Imaging and Radiation Sciences*, 54: 376–385. https://doi.org/10.1016/j.jmir.2023.03.033.

78. Fornell, D. (2022, 2 September). Where are we with AI adoption in radiology? HealthImaging. https://healthimaging.com/topics/artificial-intelligence/video-where-are-we-ai-adoption-radiology (accessed 23 October 2023).

79. Blumer, S. (2023). The current state of AI in radiology. HealthTech. https://www.healthtechmagazines.com/the-current-state-of-ai-in-radiology/ (accessed 23 October 2023).

80. Cowen, L. (2023, 10 February). How artificial intelligence is driving changes in radiology. Inside Precision Medicine. https://www.insideprecisionmedicine.com/news-and-features/how-artificial-intelligence-is-driving-changes-in-radiology/ (accessed 23 October 2023).

81. Blumer, S. (2023). The current state of AI in radiology. HealthTech. https://www.healthtechmagazines.com/the-current-state-of-ai-in-radiology/ (accessed 23 October 2023).

82. Durairaj, J. (2022, 24 May). AI in radiology: changing dimensions and diagnosis for radiologists. Synapsica Blog. https://synapsica.com/blog/ai-in-radiology/ (accessed 23 October 2023).

83. Jeong, J., Tian, K., Li., A et al. (2023). Multimodal image-text matching improves retrieval-based chest X-ray report generation. arXiv, 2303.17579. https://doi.org/10.48550/arXiv.2303.17579

84. Liao, H., Cade, W. and Behdad, S. (2022). Forecasting repair and maintenance services of medical devices using support vector machine. *Journal of Manufacturing Science and Engineering*, 144(3): 031005. https://doi.org/10.1115/1.4051886

85. Fornell, D. (2022, 2 September). Where are we with AI adoption in radiology? HealthImaging. https://healthimaging.com/topics/artificial-intelligence/video-where-are-we-ai-adoption-radiology (accessed 23 October 2023).

86. Priyadarsini, M., Kotecha, K., Rajini, G. et al. (2023). Lung diseases detection using various deep learning algorithms. *Journal of Healthcare Engineering*, 2023: 3563696. https://doi.org/10.1155/2023/3563696.

87. Kennedy, S. (2023, 28 September). AI tool may improve tumor removal accuracy during breast cancer surgery. Health IT Analytics. https://healthitanalytics.com/news/ai-tool-may-improve-tumor-removal-accuracy-during-breast-cancer-surgery (accessed 23 October 2023).

88. Belue, M. and Turkbey, B. (2022). Tasks for artificial intelligence in prostate MRI. *European Radiology Experimental*, 6: 33. https://doi.org/10.1186/s41747-022-00287-9

89. Mesko, B. (2022, 22 September). The future of radiology and artificial intelligence. *The Medical Futurist*. https://medicalfuturist.com/the-future-of-radiology-and-ai/ (accessed 23 October 2023).

90. Wikipedia. (2023). Radiomics. https://en.wikipedia.org/wiki/Radiomics (accessed 23 October 2023).

91. Rajpurkar, P. and Lungren, M. (2023). The current and future state of AI interpretation of medical images. *New England Journal of Medicine*, 388: 1981–1990. doi: 10.1056/NEJMra2301725.

92. Chi, W., Overhage, M. and Sponholtz, T. (2023). The whole health index: a practical, valid, and reliable tool to measure whole-person health and manage population health. *New England Journal of Medicine Catalyst* (30 May). https://catalyst.nejm.org/doi/full/10.1056/CAT.23.0015 (accessed 23 October 2023).

93. Ackerman, J. (2023, 29 September). AI and value-based care. Physicians Practice. https://www.physicianspractice.com/view/ai-and-value-based-care (accessed 23 October 2023).

94. Center for Medicare and Medicaid Innovation. (2022). CMS Innovation Center: 2022 Report to Congress. https://www.cms.gov/priorities/innovation/data-and-reports/2022/rtc-2022 (accessed 23 October 2023).

Chapter 6: Helping Leaders Design New World People Experiences

1. Johnson. (2022). And the word of the year is.... *The Economist*, 14 December.

2. Kastle system, chart in Semuels, A. (2023, 19 May). Return-to-office full time is losing. Hybrid work is on the rise. *Time*. https://time.com/6281252/return-to-office-hybrid-work/ (accessed 23 January 2024).

3. Fast Future Executive. (2022). New world people leader. https://www.fastfutureexecutive.com/neworldpeopleleader (accessed 23 January 2024).

4. Peters, T. (2018). Hard is soft, soft is hard. Blog. https://tompeters.com/2021/10/hard-is-soft-soft-is-hard/ (accessed 23 January 2024).

5. Coursera. (2022). Meta: what is the metaverse. https://www.coursera
.org/learn/what-is-the-metaverse?utm_medium=sem&utm_
source=gg&utm_campaign=B2C_EMEA_ibm-data-science_ibm_
FTCOF_professional-certificates_country-GB-country-UK-
pmax-nonNRL-within-14d&campaignid=20858198563&adgroupid=
&device=c&keyword=&matchtype=&network=x&devicemodel=&ad
position=&creativeid=&hide_mobile_promo&gclid=Cj0KCQiA-
62tBhDSARIsAO7twbbpcezT4EiyrCAJKbRBcPZn0xnoCPKoBnW6i0hg-
3sJHEHMA2QCDOB8aAtI1EALw_wcB (accessed 23 January 2024).
6. Humane Media. (2023, 20 April). Good AI is humane. Humane Media.
https://hu.ma.ne/media/designing-for-the-ai-era (accessed
23 January 2024).

Chapter 7: Designing the Metamobility Future

1. Boeckenfeld, M. (2023, 5 June). The world is your canvas. Linkedin article.
2. Siemens. (2023, 13 June). Siemens to invest EUR 1 billion in Germany
and create a blueprint for industrial metaverse in Nuremberg metropolitan region. Siemens, Press Release.
3. Takahashi, D. (2023, 21 March). BMW Group starts global rollout of
NVIDIA Omniverse for factory digital twin. VentureBeat.
4. *Gulf News.* (2023, 31 May). Emirates inks deal with AWS to create extended
reality platform for airline staff. *Gulf News.*
5. McKinsey & Company. (2022, June). Value creation in the metaverse.
McKinsey & Company Report.
6. Citi GPS. (2022, 30 March). Metaverse and money.
7. Matthey, A., Rupilia, F. Schneiderbauer, T. et al. (2023, 13 September).
How do consumers perceive in car connectivity and digital services?
McKinsey. https://www.mckinsey.com/industries/automotive-
and-assembly/our-insights/how-do-consumers-perceive-
in-car-connectivity-and-digital-services (accessed 23
January 2024).
8. *Warranty Week.* (2023, 23 March). U.S. auto warranty expenses. *Warranty Week.* https://www.warrantyweek.com/archive/ww20230323
.html#:~:text=(in%20US%24%20millions%2C%202003,a%20
26.1%25%20increase%20from%202021 (accessed 23 January 2024).
9. Heineke, K., Khan, H., Möller, T. et al. (2023, 4 January). The metaverse:
Driving value in the mobility sector. McKinsey & Company. https://
www.mckinsey.com/industries/automotive-and-assembly/our-
insights/the-metaverse-driving-value-in-the-mobility-
sector (accessed 23 January 2024).

10. PYMNTS. (2023, 9 February). Augmented Reality Helps German Automakers Drive Future Of Connected Vehicles. PYMNTS. https://www.pymnts.com/connectedeconomy/2023/augmented-reality-helps-german-automakers-drive-future-connected-vehicles/ (accessed 23 January 2024).

11. PYMNTS. (2023, 9 February). Augmented Reality Helps German Automakers Drive Future Of Connected Vehicles. PYMNTS. https://www.pymnts.com/connectedeconomy/2023/augmented-reality-helps-german-automakers-drive-future-connected-vehicles/ (accessed 23 January 2024).

12. Taylor, M. (2021, 30 November). Holographic breakthrough in the Wayray Holograktor could disrupt car interior design. Forbes. https://www.forbes.com/sites/michaeltaylor/2021/11/30/holographic-breakthrough-in-the-wayray-holograktor-could-disrupt-car-interior-design/ (accessed 23 January 2024).

13. Saracco, R. (2023, 4 March). Using the metaverse for automonous driving. IEEE Future Directions. https://cmte.ieee.org/futuredirections/2023/03/04/using-the-metaverse-for-autonomous-driving/ (accessed 23 January 2024).

14. Feng, Y., Bao, S. and Liu, H. (2024). Connected and automated vehicle (CAV) testing scenario design and implementation using naturalistic driving data and augmented reality. University of Michigan Research. https://ccat.umtri.umich.edu/research/u-m/connected-and-automated-vehicle-cav-testing-scenario-design-and-implementation-using-naturalistic-driving-data-and-augmented-reality/(accessed 23 January 2024).

15. Fan. L., Tu, Z. and Chan, S.H. (2021). Recent development of hydrogen and fuel cell technologies: a review. *Energy Reports*, 7: 8421-8446. https://www.sciencedirect.com/science/article/pii/S2352484721006053 (accessed 23 January 2024).

16. Truby, J., Philip, P. and Lorentz, B. (2023, 19 June). Green hydrogen: energizing the path to net zero. Deloitte, Perspective. https://www.deloitte.com/global/en/issues/climate/green-hydrogen.html?id=us:2ps:3gl:4green_hydrogen:5GC1000229:6abt:20230802:GCP100058:us_gh2_google_ads&gclid=CjwKCAiA9dGqBhAqEiwAmRpTC8wESks5MqNkqwMim38YDESWSF8tzbWqi2Tlrm8qepVam01hhSh1XxoCDtsQAvD_BwE (accessed 23 January 2024).

17. Evans, S. (2020, 13 October). Solar is now 'cheapest electricity in history' confirms IEA. CarbonBrief. https://www.carbonbrief.org/solar-is-now-cheapest-electricity-in-history-confirms-iea/ (accessed 23 January 2024).

18. Solar Power Europe. (2023, 13 June). New report: Solar for the masses as global solar rooftops skyrocket by 50%. Press release. https://www.solarpowereurope.org/press-releases/new-report-solar-for-the-masses-as-global-solar-rooftops-skyrocket-by-50-2 (accessed 23 January 2024).

19. MIT Technology Review Insights (2022, 5 January). Digital twins improve real-life manufacturing. MIT Technology Review. https://www.technologyreview.com/2022/01/05/1042981/digital-twins-improve-real-life-manufacturing/ (accessed 23 January 2024).

20. PWC. (2024). Solving for skills training with virtual reality. PWC. https://www.pwc.com/m1/en/services/consulting/technology/emerging-technology/solving-for-skills-training-with-virtual-reality.html (accessed 23 January 2024).

21. GlobalNewswire. (2023, 26 January). Comstock awarded DOE grant for breakthrough cellulosic fuels process. GlobalNewswire. https://www.globenewswire.com/en/news-release/2023/01/26/2596415/0/en/Comstock-Awarded-DOE-Grant-for-Breakthrough-Cellulosic-Fuels-Process.html (accessed 23 January 2024).

22. Krisher, T. (2023, 15 May). Why Americans are holding on to their vehicles longer than ever. PBS News Hour. https://www.pbs.org/newshour/economy/why-americans-are-holding-on-to-their-vehicles-longer-than-ever#:~:text=And%20while%2012.5%20years%20is,would%20have%20in%20the%20past (accessed 23 January 2024).

23. Hardesty, C. (2023, 15 May). Average miles driven per year: why it is important. Kelley Blue Book. https://www.kbb.com/car-advice/average-miles-driven-per-year/#:~:text=The%20average%20miles%20driven%20per,to%20Department%20of%20Transportation%20statistics (accessed 23 January 2024).

24. Polygon is a 'layer two' or 'sidechain' scaling solution that runs alongside the Ethereum blockchain – allowing for speedy transactions and low fees.

25. TechCrunch (2022). Robo-taxis in the metaverse. TechCrunch. https://techcrunch.com/sponsor/polygon-technology/robo-taxis-in-the-metaverse/ (accessed 23 January 2024).

26. Burke, K, (2022, 8 December). '23 and AV: transportation industry to drive into metaverse, cloud technologies. NVIDIA blog. https://blogs.nvidia.com/blog/2022/12/08/2023-av-transportation-industry-metaverse-cloud/ (accessed 23 January 2024).

27. Landram, K. (2024). Driving autonomy into the metaverse. Carnegie Mellon University. https://engineering.cmu.edu/news-events/news/2022/12/19-driving-autonomy.html (accessed 23 January 2024).

28. Saracco, R. (2023, 4 March). Using the metaverse for autonomous driving. IEEE Future Directions. `https://cmte.ieee.org/futuredirections/2023/03/04/using-the-metaverse-for-autonomous-driving/` (accessed 23 January 2024).

29. IEEE Vehicular Technology. (2023). Call for papers: Special issue on metaverse for connected and autonomous vehicles and intelligent transportation systems. `http://www.ieeevtc.org/vtmagazine/specisu--Metaverse-CAVS.php` (accessed 23 January 2024).

30. Heineke, K., Khan, H., Möller, T. (2023, 4 January). The metaverse: driving value in the mobility sector. McKinsey & Company. `https://www.mckinsey.com/industries/automotive-and-assembly/our-insights/the-metaverse-driving-value-in-the-mobility-sector` (accessed 23 January 2024).

31. `https://www.usatoday.com/money/blueprint/auto-insurance/fatal-car-crash-statistics/` (accessed 10 March 2023).

32. Lammert, M. (n,d,). Truck platooning. NREL. `https://www.nrel.gov/transportation/fleettest-platooning.html` (accessed 23 January 2024).

33. Shaheen, S., Cohen, A. and Martin, E.W. (2016). Smartphone app evolution and early understanding from a multimodal app user survey. Escholarship.org.

34. National Academies of Sciences, Engineering and Medicine. (2021). *The Role of Transit, Shared Modes, and Public Policy in the New Mobility Landscape*. National Academies Press. doi: 10.17226/26053.

35. Mitropoulos, L., Kortsari, A., Mizaras, V. et al. (2023). Mobility as a service (MaaS) planning and implementation: challenges and lessons learned. *Future Transport*, 3(2); 498–518. doi: 10.3390/futuretransp3020029.

36. National Academies of Sciences, Engineering, and Medicine. (2021). *The Role of Transit, Shared Modes, and Public Policy in the New Mobility Landscape*. National Academies Press. doi: 10.17226/26053.

37. Kitchen, P. (2016). Editorial. *Journal of Marketing Communications*, 22(6): 561–562. doi: 10.1080/13527266.2016.1244960.

38. Pamintuan, C. F., Mallari, D. G., Garcia, N. T. et al. (2018). The use of WeChat application on CFL learners' vocabulary acquisition. *TESOL Journal*, 13(4): 288–38.

39. 68% of the world population projected to live in urban areas by 2050, says UN. United Nations Department of Economic and Social Affairs, (2018, 16 May). `https://www.un.org/development/desa/en/news/population/2018-revision-of-world-urbanization-prospects.html` (accessed 23 January 2024).

40. Yadav, P. (2022, 28 November). What is Dubai's metaverse strategy and will it boost its digital economy? *Indiana Times.* https://www.indiatimes.com/explainers/news/what-is-dubais-metaverse-strategy-and-how-it-will-boost-its-digital-economy-585908.html, Woetzel, J., Remes, J., Boland, B. et al. (2018, 5 June). Smart cities: digital solutions for a more liveable future. McKinsey Global Institute. https://www.mckinsey.com/capabilities/operations/our-insights/smart-cities-digital-solutions-for-a-more-livable-future (accessed 23 January 2023).

41. UN Habitat. (2022). *Envisaging the Future of Cities, World Cities Report 2022.* unhabitat.org.

42. Smart Nation Singapore. (2024). Transforming SG Through Tech, smartnation.gov. https://www.smartnation.gov.sg/about-smart-nation/transforming-singapore/ (accessed 23 January 2024).

43. Boeckenfeld, M. (2023, 1 September). Eyes to the future: where do you want to live? Linkedin article. https://www.linkedin.com/pulse/eyes-future-where-do-you-want-live-dr-martha-boeckenfeldEyes (accessed 23 January 2024).

44. World Economic Forum. (2023, August). Digital twin cities: Key insights and recommendations. WEF. https://www3.weforum.org/docs/WEF_Digital_Twin_Cities_2023.pdf (accessed 23 January 2024).

45. European Commission. (2023, 11 July). Towards the next technological transition: Commission presents EU strategy to lead on Web 4.0 and virtual worlds. EC. https://ec.europa.eu/commission/press-corner/detail/en/ip_23_3718 (accessed 23 January 2024).

46. FROST & SULLIVAN. (2020, 29 October). Smart cities to create business opportunities worth $2.46 trillion by 2025, says Frost & Sullivan. Press release. https://www.frost.com/news/press-releases/smart-cities-to-create-business-opportunities-worth-2-46-trillion-by-2025-says-frost-sullivan/ (accessed 23 January 2024).

47. PWC. (2022). How digital twins can make smart cities better. PWC. https://www.pwc.com/m1/en/publications/documents/how-digital-twins-can-make-smart-cities-better.pdf (accessed 23 January 2024).

48. Santa Monica , CA. (2024). Santa Monica, CA is partnering with FlickPay to launch a play-to-learn metaverse mobile app. https://govlaunch.com/projects/santa-monica-ca-is-partnering-with-flickplay-to-launch-a-play-to-earn-metaverse-mobile-app (accessed 23 January 2024).

49. PR Newsire, (2022, 20 September). Mesmerise opens its first U.S. office, deepening investment in North America as growth in the enterprise VR market accelerates. PR Newswire. https://www.prnewswire. com/news-releases/mesmerise-opens-its-first-us-office- deepening-investment-in-north-america-as-growth-in-the- enterprise-vr-market-accelerates-301627637.html (accessed 23 January 2024).

50. Zhang, C.Y., You, N., Kerimi, D et al. (2023). Tampere metaverse vision 2040. The Metaverse Institute

51. Ramos, A. (2023, 13 April). Seoul is the first city to join the metaverse (and this is what can already be done), *Tomorrow City*.

52. Hasan, S. (2022, 28 September). Dubai leads the way for metaverse econo- mies across all sectors at the Dubai Metaverse Assembly | WIRED Middle East. https://wired.me/technology/dubai-virtual-worlds- sectors-dubai-metaverse-assembly/ (accessed 23 January 2024).

53. Ford. (2019, 29 January). Ford collaborates with Gravity Sketch to explore new tool for designing vehicles to meet customer needs. Ford Media. https://media.ford.com/content/fordmedia/fna/us/ en/news/2019/01/29/ford-collaborates-with-gravity-sketch .html#:~:text=Gravity%20Sketch%20allows%20designers%20 to,scalable%20vehicle%20around%20their%20driver (accessed 23 January 2024).

54. Hyundai. (2022, 14 April). How Hyundai is using the latest VR tech- nology to transform car design and make it more sustainable. Hyundai Press release. https://www.hyundai.news/eu/articles/press- releases/how-hyundai-is-using-the-latest-vr-technology- to-transform-car-design.html (accessed 23 January 2024).

55. NVIDIA. (n.d.). NVIDIA DRIVE sim powered by omniverse. NVIDIA. https://www.nvidia.com/en-us/self-driving-cars/simula- tion/ (accessed 23 January 2024).

56. BMW Group. (2021, 13 April). BMW and NVIDIA take virtual fac- tory planning to the next level. BMMW Group. https://www.press .bmwgroup.com/global/article/detail/T0329569EN/bmw- group-and-nvidia-take-virtual-factory-planning-to-the- next-level?language=en (accessed 23 January 2024).

57. Ligouri, F. (2021, 4 February). DTNA tests augmented reality for future of aftermarket service. Daimler Trucks. https://northamerica.daim- lertruck.com/PressDetail/dtna-tests-augmented-reality- for-future-2021-02-04/ (accessed 23 January 2024).

58. PR News. (2022, 5 January). Hyundai Motor shares vision of new meta-mobility concept, 'expanding human reach' through robotics & metaverse at CES 2022. PR News.

59. Gooding, M. (2021, 15 October). Data from your connected car could be sold to the highest bidder. Tech Monitor. https://techmonitor.ai/policy/privacy-and-data-protection/connected-vehicle-data-apply-carplay (accessed 23 January 2024).

60. Minespider. (2023, 17 May). Minespider to disrupt the EV battery market with the first advanced open battery passport. Minespider press release. https://www.minespider.com/press/minespider-to-disrupt-the-ev-battery-market-with-the-first-advanced-open-battery-passport (accessed 23 January 2024).

Chapter 8 Conclusion: Living to Love the Fast Future Blurs

1. World Economic Forum. (2023). The WEF global risks report 2023. WEF. www.weforum.org/publications/global-risks-report-2023/digest/ (accessed 23 January 2024).

2. World Economic Forum. (2015). The global risks 2015 interconnections map: how are global risks interconnected? WEF. https://widgets.weforum.org/global-risks-2015-interactive/risk-explorer.html (accessed 23 January 2024).

3. World Economic Forum. (n,d,). The Global Future Council on the future of complex risks. WEF. www.weforum.org/communities/gfc-on-complex-risks/ (accessed 23 January 2024).

4. World Economic Forum. (2014). The WEF global risk report 2014. WEF. www.weforum.org/publications/global-risks-2014/ (accessed 23 January 2024).

5. Seelig, T. (2012). *inGenius: A Crash Course on Creativity*. HarperOne. An internationally bestselling book on enhancing creativity. Introduces her 'Innovation Engine' framework.

Index